There's nourishment to be found in the shad

- Explore the magickal potential of poisonous and maligned herbs

- Experiment with fasting and other forms of self-sacrifice as a spiritual act

- Navigate the danger and intensity of ritual invocation and godform assumption

- Study the significance of Da'ath, the "hidden sephira" on the Qabalistic Tree of Life

- Delve into cross-cultural forms of mysticism, including the Qabalah and Sufism

- Discover how the shadow is a platform for spiritual manifestation

- Analyze negative behavioral cycles that can impede spiritual development

- Find out how shamanism corresponds to shadow magick

- Practice soul retrieval, astral travel, sigilry, and obscure methods of divination

- Learn about dark animal helpers and spiritual guides

- Tap into the power of lunar and solar eclipses

- Explore the deeper meanings of autumn and the dying season

- Read an in-depth history of the European Witch hunts

- Learn about so-called "fantasy magick" and its potential danger to Neopagan spirituality

Praise for Shadow Magick Compendium

"*Shadow Magick Compendium* opens the way for us to reconcile our visible self with our shadow self...Once a lamp is lifted into the darkness, there is nothing left to fear."

—Leilah Wendell, author of *The Necromantic Ritual Book*

"Many mainstream spiritual texts limit themselves to working the 'light.' Raven's approach, however, is to embrace the shadow self so as to attain self-awareness and balance, rather than focusing on pure light or pure darkness. The meditations and rituals allow readers to experience Raven's approach in a very real, practical sense."

—Tony Mierzwicki, author of *Graeco-Egyptian Magick: Everyday Empowerment*

"Raven joins the writers and authors giving the world workable occult technologies—systems of understanding to prepare individuals for the dangerous journey to wisdom and fulfillment. *Shadow Magick Compendium* is a treasury of resources for just that."

—Robin Artisson, author of *The Witching Way of the Hollow Hill*

"Combining extensive research with clear instructions, Digitalis draws on sources ranging from E. A. Poe to Christopher Penczak, from Deepak Chopra to Dead Can Dance. Those seeking to explore their inner darkness will find an invaluable roadmap here."

—Kenaz Filan, managing editor of *newWitch magazine* and author of *The Haitian Vodou Handbook*

"This important book belongs in the library of any serious student of magic, self-evolution, and spirituality...Amid a wealth of fascinating information and inspiring exercises, Raven not only covers the psychology of magic—perhaps its foundation stone—but also the history of modern magical practice, in terms of the Shadow...It's truly refreshing to find a book on magic that has new things to say, as well as including thoughtful interpretations of existing beliefs and practices."

—Storm Constantine, editor/founder of Immanion Press and author of the *Wraeththu* novels

"To recognize the Shadow and embrace it is the first step in learning to harness its limitless potential....This book shows that the dark side of our inner nature can illuminate and liberate just as readily as it can curse."

—Donald Tyson, author of *Necronomicon*

"A guide to unearthing the darker aspects of our self as well as a guide to integrating them in both the beginning and advanced practitioner."

—David Allen Hulse, author of *The Western Mysteries* and *The Eastern Mysteries*

"By examining how magic works in various realms from the internal to the external and beyond, Raven shows how Shadow energy can be tapped as a positive force in bringing balance back into one's life . . . this book is a wellspring of information that competently transcends all religious and spiritual paths. Well done!"

—Ann Moura, author of the *Green Witchcraft* series

"According to Jung, children become adults through a process called individuation. . . . As the world of magick moves boldly into the twenty-first century, it is time that magick, too, individuates from its eighteenth- and nineteenth-century parents and its twentieth-century childhood. Part of this maturation is the realization that wherever there is light, there is also shadow . . . Jung pointed out that our most famous myths are variations of a universal "Hero's Journey." *Shadow Magick Compendium* doesn't merely share this mythic Journey, it gives you keys and guidance to follow it yourself."

—Donald Michael Kraig, author of *Modern Magick*

"Each of us responds to the darkness in our soul differently—some with fear, avoidance, and denial; others with courage, curiosity, and sorrow. For the courageous, this book provides strategies, ideas, and knowledge . . . Digitalis draws from the wisdom of older cultures and religions as well as from younger, radical cultures."

—Gail Wood, author of *Rituals of the Dark Moon* and *The Shamanic Witch*

"An exceptional guide to exploring the shadow side for a fully integrated path of magickal and spiritual enlightenment."

—Rosemary Ellen Guiley, author of *The Encyclopedia of Witches, Witchcraft & Wicca*

"One of the most basic tenets of Witchcraft is also its most challenging: *Know thyself*. Raven Digitalis, author of *Goth Craft*, gives us a new tool for this important task . . . a 'must have' for White Witches, Dark Witches, and everyone in between."

—Deborah Blake, author of *Everyday Witch A to Z* and *Circle, Coven & Grove*

"Embracing and exploring what society codes as 'dark' can lead us to discover the light that resides within. In this ambitious yet practical guide, Raven Digitalis gives readers an array of tools for doing just that and provides valuable insights into the shadow's role in everyone's spiritual evolution."

—Mark A. Michaels and Patricia Johnson, authors of *Tantra for Erotic Empowerment*

"Full of inventive rituals, meditations, exercises, and practices, this book can help guide readers into a fuller understanding of their own dark natures and provide them with grounding, balance, and healing."

—Timothy Roderick, author of *Wicca: A Year & A Day* and *Dark Moon Mysteries*

About the Author

Raven Digitalis (Missoula, Montana) is a Neopagan Priest and cofounder of the "disciplined eclectic" shadow magick tradition and training coven Opus Aima Obscuræ. He is also a radio and club DJ of Gothic, EBM, and industrial music. With his Priestess Estha, Raven holds community gatherings, Tarot readings, and a variety of ritual services. From their home, the two also operate the metaphysical business Twigs & Brews, specializing in holistic bath salts, herbal blends, essential oils, and incenses. Raven holds a degree in anthropology from the University of Montana and is also an animal rights activist and black-and-white photographic artist. He has appeared on the cover of *newWitch* magazine, is a regular contributor to *The Ninth Gate* magazine, and has been featured on MTV *News* and the 'X' Zone radio program. He can be found online at www.RavenDigitalis.com and www.myspace.com/oakraven.

Shadow

Raven Digitalis

Magick

Compendium

Exploring Darker Aspects of Magickal Spirituality

Llewellyn Publications
Woodbury, Minnesota

First Edition
First Printing, 2008

Book design and format by Donna Burch
Cover design by Kevin R. Brown
Interior illustrations by the Llewellyn Art Department
Llewellyn is a registered trademark of Llewellyn Worldwide, Ltd.

Library of Congress Cataloging-in-Publication Data

Digitalis, Raven.
  Shadow magick compendium : exploring darker aspects of magickal spirituality / by Raven Digitalis.—1st ed.
    p. cm.
  Includes bibliographical references and index.
  ISBN 978-0-7387-1318-2
  1. Spirituality—Miscellanea. 2. Magic. 3. Occultism. 4.
Witchcraft. I. Title.
  BF1999.D486 2008
  299'.93—dc22

2008019702

Some of the activities described in this book may be dangerous or illegal. None of its guidance should be considered a substitute for the advice of a health care practitioner. Please exercise responsibility, and remember that what works for some may not work for you. As you proceed, use care, caution, and common sense. Neither Llewellyn nor the author will be held responsible for personal actions taken in response to this book.

Llewellyn Worldwide does not participate in, endorse, or have any authority or responsibility concerning private business transactions between our authors and the public.
  All mail addressed to the author is forwarded but the publisher cannot, unless specifically instructed by the author, give out an address or phone number.
  Any Internet references contained in this work are current at publication time, but the publisher cannot guarantee that a specific location will continue to be maintained. Please refer to the publisher's website for links to authors' websites and other sources.

Llewellyn Publications
A Division of Llewellyn Worldwide, Ltd.
2143 Wooddale Drive, Dept. 978-0-7387-1318-2
Woodbury, Minnesota 55125-2989, U.S.A.
www.llewellyn.com

 Printed in the United States of America on recycled paper

Other Books by Raven Digitalis

Goth Craft: The Magickal Side of Dark Culture

Forthcoming

A Darkly Spellbook

Acknowledgments

All my love to both my blood family and my soul family. Words don't do justice to the gratitude I feel.

Estha, thank you for inspiring me as a person and as a Priest, and for having so much impact and influence on my writing. You continue to enable me to be the best person I can be, and greatly help me navigate my own shadow. There is no end to the appreciation I have for your invaluable teachings, arduous work, and constant love.

Special thanks to those who directly assisted with some of the information herein, including Esthamarelda McNevin (DaBunny Papyrus), Kala Trobe (Kate La Trobe), Christopher Penczak (Christophiel), John Michael Greer (Oldschool Space Cadet), Zanoni Silverknife (Queen Z), Lupa (LupaBitch), Taylor Ellwood (Tay), Madeline Keller (Lady Datura), Anjuli King (Skylet Moog), Lisa and Ray Allen (Calantirniel and Námovaryar), Erasmus (Erastaroth), Abel Gomez (Jablé Gonzales), Justin Whitaker (Little Buddha), and Paul A. Dietrich (Secret Mystic).

Acknowledgments to my friend and spiritual comrade Damien Echols. Once a victim of judicial injustice and social intolerance, now an example of diligence and peace, thank you for your sacrifices and forbearance. Your role in the consciousness of this world is grand.

Finally, I give much gratitude to Anna-Varney Cantodea of Sopor Aeternus and the Ensemble of Shadows. Your unique art and unconditional friendship continues to touch me on the deepest levels. Thank you, Queen of the Dark Underground, for helping bring the magick and beauty of shadow to this world.

Dedication

This book is dedicated to my dear training coven, Opus Aima Obscuræ: the magick we weave is like none other, and our individual paths are aflame. With love, progression, awareness, and evolution, may our Will be woven! We are bound in Love, and there is absolutely nothing we cannot do.

Additionally, though this book is not focused on Gothic culture, I would like to dedicate it to the memory of Sophie Lancaster (1986–2007), who, after attempting to protect her partner Robert Maltby, was beaten to death in Lancashire, England, as a result of simply expressing herself as a Goth. May your beautiful spirit be blessed in the world beyond the setting sun. Thank you for your sacrifice; you are a martyr to the cause of social acceptance and diversity. Blessings upon you both, and to all those who have ever suffered for daring to be themselves.

Blessèd Be all those who dare to face the shadow—that of the world, the universe, and the self—for means of bringing progressive change and evolution to this plane and beyond. Our time on earth is limited, and we must do our best to align with our greater purpose and reclaim the shadow in order to harness the light of consciousness.

Contents

com·pen·di·um

[kuhm-*pen*-dee-uhm]

1 a brief summary of a larger work or of a field of knowledge : abstract

2 a : a list of a number of items

   b : collection, compilation

—*Merriam-Webster's Dictionary*

The Tao Te Ching: Section 52
Lao Tzu

In the beginning was the Tao.
All things issue from it;
all things return to it.

To find the origin,
trace back the manifestations.
When you recognize the children
and find the mother,
you will be free of sorrow.

If you close your mind in judgments
and traffic with desires,
your heart will be troubled.
If you keep your mind from judging
and aren't led by the senses,
your heart will find peace.

Seeing into darkness is clarity.
Knowing how to yield is strength.
Use your own light
and return to the source of light.
This is called Practicing Eternity.

Alone

Edgar Allan Poe

From childhood's hour I have not been
As others were; I have not seen
As others saw; I could not bring
My passions from a common spring.
From the same source I have not taken
My sorrow; I could not awaken
My heart to joy at the same tone;
And all I loved, I loved alone.
Then—in my childhood, in the dawn
Of a most stormy life—was drawn
From every depth of good and ill
The mystery which binds me still:
From the torrent, or the fountain,
From the red cliff of the mountain,
From the sun that round me rolled
In its autumn tint of gold,
From the lightning in the sky
As it passed me flying by,
From the thunder and the storm,
And the cloud that took the form
(When the rest of Heaven was blue)
Of a demon in my view.

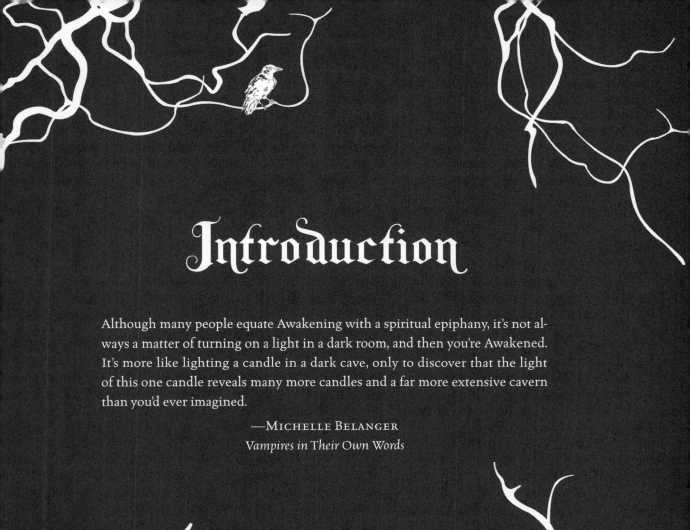

Introduction

Although many people equate Awakening with a spiritual epiphany, it's not always a matter of turning on a light in a dark room, and then you're Awakened. It's more like lighting a candle in a dark cave, only to discover that the light of this one candle reveals many more candles and a far more extensive cavern than you'd ever imagined.

—MICHELLE BELANGER
Vampires in Their Own Words

The very essence of the concept of "shadow" is ambiguous. Throughout the ages and around the world, various cultures, religions, and individual philosophies have approached this idea in various ways, often discovering deep wells of meaning in the divine polarity of "light" and "dark." A number of shamanic religions, including those indigenous to Asia, Europe, and the Americas, have long recognized the portion of the self deemed "the shadow" for its role in human spiritual development and understanding. The view of shadow as a spiritual force has also been carried into a number of modern religions. It is from the shadowed aspects of the psyche that our magickal reality is brought into vision.

But no single tradition, no single person or book, including this one, can fully capture the meaning of shadow, because its significance is so very personal. It is my hope that this book will inspire readers to explore and interpret esoteric darkness in their own ways, taking into consideration the suggested and proposed interpretations of shadow herein.

To begin this exploration, it's essential to make note of the Swiss psychiatrist Carl Gustav Jung. A student of Sigmund Freud, Jung recognized the *shadow self* as the often nonconscious aspect of the human psyche that contains repressed thoughts and impulses. It is the portion of our mind that usually goes unrecognized, harboring fear and other unpleasant emotions that we have consciously rejected for one reason or another.

In Jung's own words: "Everyone carries a shadow, and the less it is embodied in the individual's conscious life, the blacker and denser it is."[1] That is, the more repressed one's shadow self is, the darker—and more intense—it becomes. Jung also notes, "The shadow is a moral problem that challenges the whole ego-personality, for no one can become conscious of the shadow without considerable moral effort. To become conscious of it involves recognizing the dark aspects of the personality as present and real. This act is the essential condition for any kind of self-knowledge."[2] With this psychoanalytical concept of the shadow, Jung suggests that recognizing internal darkness leads to self-awareness. The more we ignore our darker aspects, the more burdened we actually become, even though it may seem quite the opposite in the immediate sense.

Modern industrialized humans have, generally speaking, come to fear the shadow, maligning and conflating it with concepts of evil. Jung's concept further recognizes that when the shadow self is ignored, people tend to project their own shadows onto others, shifting their own darker characteristics to anyone but themselves. It's no wonder that we in American culture—a society that fears and maligns the internal shadow—are masters of the blame game.

Shadow as the Holy Child

Both actually and metaphorically, the shadow is the essence from which all things come into manifestation. A few cross-cultural examples will show the shadow's profound significance in humankind's stories and mythologies through the ages.

One recent example is E. Elias Merhige's 1991 silent dark art film *Begotten*, whose opening scene depicts a robed, veiled figure killing itself with a blade. The figure is visually distressed as it welcomes a suicidal death out of what seems necessity. From the gruesome wreckage of the disemboweled figure—who is cited as "God Killing Himself" in the credits—a masked Venusian woman, Mother Earth, appears. Upon masturbating the fallen god, she impregnates herself with his seed.

The corpselike "child" the woman gives birth to appears as a quivering, helpless, and constantly convulsing humanoid, said to be the "Son of Earth: Flesh on Bone." A quote at the beginning of the film refers to this figure as representing humankind: "Like a flame burning away the darkness, life is flesh on bone convulsing above the ground."

✳ ✳ ✳

The characters in *Begotten* portray a particular archetypal pattern seen in many of the world's ancient spiritual systems. The representation of the divine Mother, Father, and Child is seen across the board, mythologically speaking. Also common in religious pantheons is the theme of death—or representational death—of the father figure. These archetypes are of particular importance to anyone living a spiritually progressive path, especially those who actively practice magick.

In truth, all deities are but psychological imprints representing aspects of the human psyche or the psyche's perception of the natural world. The gods exist within us as representatives of our experience. They also exist outside of us as egregores, or independent, energetic embodiments in the mental and astral planes. This spiritual dichotomy—this Hermetic "As Above, So Below," the Principle of Correspondence—both creates and maintains our very own existence.

The cycle of reproduction fuels all aspects of reality, from the microcosm of humans, animals, and plants to the macrocosm: the creative and destructive ebb and flow of the birth and death of planets and stars. Because this cycle reigns over all experience, it's of utmost importance to spiritualists.[3]

Just as a mother and father create a child, certain deities represent these forces in virtually all mythological systems. In this example, because motherhood, fatherhood, procreation, and birth occur on the physical plane, these forces are in turn mythologized and even anthropomorphized into recognizable forms. Whether the deities were actually humans who were later deified or whether they were created as thoughtforms, the archetypes live on.

Understandably, ancient pantheons deified natural forces in all their aspects. Across cultures, we see deital representations of the birth of plants, the birth of animals, and the birth of humans, as well as the corresponding equal-opposite of their deaths and appropriate harbingers of death. Virtually all aspects of reality have been deified in one theistic culture or another. For when a deity is said to represent or rule a force of nature, this ethereal vibration can be tapped and the deity's specific alignments worked with magickally. This old truth is now rebirthing itself in the minds of spiritual seekers much as a "begotten" child of the old ways appears in a new aeon.

The word "begotten" is a form of the verb "beget." To beget something means to bring it forth. More often than not, fatherly associations are drawn: this fathered that. In many mythological systems, and thus in many ancient and modern societies, the father or paternal deity passes his power—in whatever form it takes—on to his son. The father or paternal figure's death, whether it comes before or after this transfer, serves to solidify this passing down of energy.

Many ancient and modern societies, both patriarchal and matriarchal, tend to view the feminine as a constant force that never truly dies; this idea is also seen in their mythos. Thus, although power is distributed from mother to daughter, the two remain aspects of one another. The male, however, dies and is regenerated.

Wicca and many forms of Neopaganism tend to accept this view of the Goddess and God. The Goddess is viewed in her many aspects through the solar year cycle. But her two consort gods, the Oak King and the Holly King, actually die; the Holy Father's energy is mutable and regenerating while the Goddess's energy fluxes but never ceases.

To mirror the seasonal shifts, the Oak King is killed by his Holly King brother at Midsummer, and vice versa at Midwinter. Each aspect of the divine masculine rules half the year. Starting on the Sabbat following his death, each brother again begins the process of being reborn by the Goddess, or Mother Earth, so he can again rise to metaphorically slay the opposing *Doppelgänger*. These brothers depict the balancing forces of nature; the Oak King aligned to fertility, life, and the Upperworld, and the Holly King aligned to decay, death, and the Underworld. They are both simultaneously the Holy Father and Holy

Child, one always equally opposing the other. The Holy Mother stands as a consort. The mythos of the Holly King and the Oak King entered Wicca by way of Robert Graves's poetic work *The White Goddess*.

The myth of the slain-and-resurrecting God also permeates the ancient Greek pantheon—although, interestingly, that pantheon includes so much procreation that it's hard to discern the nifty triumvirates! Still, we find that a slew of individual Pagan deities, both Greek and otherwise, encompass these three-part archetypes in their own general energies.

✳ ✳ ✳

In another modern spiritual tradition, Jesus the Christ, a healer, shaman, and master of compassion, is deified as the "only begotten son of God." Like many deities, both God and Jesus in Christian mythology can represent many aspects of the human psyche, depending on the account in which the godform appears.

Archetypally, Jesus's mother Mary represents the virginal, untainted aspect of the Mother Goddess. Like other mythological Holy Mothers, she was blessed as the chosen individual to birth a highly spiritual being into the earth plane. Jesus, like his counterparts in many other myth traditions, was born as a pure beacon of merciful guiding light. He is also an avatar, a prophet in this case, much like Krishna and other deities. The Christian God, like many other divine father figures, conceived Jesus in a nontraditional or *occult*—that is, a "hidden" or "shrouded"—manner. Thus, the story of the Christ, including the tale of his resurrection, is nearly identical to the messianic tales of countless ancient mythic traditions. It is one of the more modern accounts of these particular ancient archetypes.

✳ ✳ ✳

Arguably, the religion of ancient Egypt served as the framework for all Western religions. Looking at its pantheon, we see Isis and Osiris as an aspect of the Great Mother and Great Father. Isis, the Goddess of Love, is consort to Osiris, a king of the earthly realm.

According to the mythos, Osiris's brother Set (Seth) manipulated him with a malevolent joke that ended in Osiris's live entombment in a coffin cast to the Nile. After a period of searching and mourning, Isis recovered her now-dead lover's coffin. But before Isis could perform the customary funerary rites and take the coffin to a proper burial ground, Set and his men tracked down and destroyed Osiris's corpse, distributing his body parts across the land in a fit of rage. With the help of her sister Nephthys and nephew Anubis (in some accounts), Isis eventually recovered all of her husband's body parts except for his penis.

In a solitary magick rite, Isis pieced together and mummified Osiris's body parts. She then thaumaturgically created a phallus, breathed life into the corpse, and made love to him in his momentary reanimation. (In some accounts of this myth, Isis made love to a reanimated Osiris directly after finding him dead in the Nile-cast coffin. After this sacred coitus, Set then scattered Osiris's body parts. After Isis gathered them together, she gave Osiris his eternal afterlife.)

The Holy Child conceived was the hawk-headed Horus (also called the baby Harpocrates or Hoor-pa-kraat), the ruler of the skies, whose eyes represent the sun and the moon. Some believe that Horus is the metaphorical reincarnation of Osiris and also carries multiple aspects of his mother Isis. Horus is now considered the Crowned and Conquering Child of the new aeon by many occult circles such as orders of Thelema. Therein he is often referred to as Ra-hoor-khuit, Horus's older and syncretized Ra-exalted aspect, or as Heru-ra-ha, his dualistic aspect (both the younger *and* older Horus). Ra-hoor-khuit is the child of the macrocosmic and infinitely expanded sky goddess Nuit and the microcosmic and infinitely contracted Hadit; the Isis-Osiris myth plays out one phase of this Holy Trinity.

In fact, Thelemites believe that the present and newly unfolding Age of Horus was preceded by the Age of Osiris (overseeing patriarchal ideology and masculine worship), which was preceded by the Age of Isis (overseeing matriarchal ideology and feminine worship). It is believed that the present Aeon of Horus is that of the great balancer, that which will merge the positive principles of the two preceding ages.

Taking a look at Hinduism, we see Krishna (Krsna) as an avatar, or human emanation, of the deity Vishnu the Preserver. Vishnu is an aspect of Hinduism's *Trimurti* of three great gods, the others being Brahma the Creator and Shiva (Siva) the Destroyer/Regenerator.

Though he is mythologized as having been born a deity, Krishna was the eighth child of the human parents King Vasudev and Princess Devaki. In the myth, Devaki's brother King Kamsa planned to put Devaki's eighth child to death because a prophecy said that this child would grow up to kill him. But luckily, with the god Vishnu's divine intervention, the child Krishna was saved. Krishna grew up to become a divine warrior, prince, and charioteer for his friend Arjuna, the King of India ... and he did indeed kill the evil King Kamsa. These stories and more are preserved in the Bhagavad-Gita, a story of Krishna from the later Vedic epic poem the Mahabharata.

In many ways, and certainly to Hindus who worship Krishna as the central deity, Krishna is seen as a Holy Child. A god in human form, he is seen as transcending the human predicament. His associations as a miracle worker and supreme godhead have earned him much adoration.

∗   ∗   ∗

The epicenters of Eastern spiritual thought, Hinduism and Buddhism are two of the world's largest religions. In Buddhism, the story of the Buddha's birth is a mythologized and fanciful tale, with imagery noticeably borrowed from the vibrant spiritual legends of Hinduism. According to the story, the child Siddhartha Gautama of the Shakya tribe was a god before birth, a god who chose to be born human. He descended from the Heaven of the Contented, a divine realm, and entered his mother Maya Devi's womb, which created an immeasurable light in even the darkest realms of consciousness.

It is said that the Buddha was of a "pure birth." Purity, if course, is entirely subjective. The Buddha was born "from his mother's right side," according to early Pali Buddhist canonical texts—the non-vaginal birth implying that he was delivered either from his mother's actual side, below the ribs and above the hip, or from her armpit. In common Indian thought, the armpit is seen as an area similar to the pubic region but rather less "impure." Siddhartha was dry at birth, clean of any "contaminating" blood or amniotic fluid. After his birth, his mother passed away and is said to have been reborn in the Heaven of the Contented.

Legend says that when the Buddha was born, a cool and warm stream of water poured from the heavens for Siddhartha and his mother to bathe in. The young Buddha then stood upright, took seven steps to the north, surveyed the land, and declared himself a king of the world. Some accounts tell of lotuses growing from the child Buddha's footprints.

Though the story tells of divine birth, most Buddhists understand it as *mythical* truth rather than *historical* truth, as one portrayal of the birth of the Holy Child. However, because the Buddha is recognized as entirely human, simply enlightened, there is no direct representation of the Holy Father and Holy Mother (unless one counts Maya Devi as a Holy Mother figure), a factor that separates Buddhism from common theistic religions.

✳   ✳   ✳

The spiritual tripartite of the Great Mother (life/nature), Great Father (death/destruction) and Holy Child (resurrection/redeemer) is expressed in many Western Mystery Traditions as the Greek Gnostic mantra of Iota-Alpha-Omega (IAΩ), each letter representing a phase in this infinite pattern. These letters also correspond to the three Hebrew Mother Letters of Shin, Mem, and Aleph. Many occultists attribute "I" to Isis, the Giver of Life; "A" to Apophis, the Destroyer; and "Ω" to Osiris, the Redeemer or the offspring of I and A. This is the sequential progression of light to darkness to the supremely transcendental balance of the two polarities. IAΩ is also another term for the *Demiurge* (the power of creation itself), or an archon thereof.

It may be worth noting that the Fool card of the traditional Tarot holds the position of zero in the deck. Being both the "highest" and the "lowest" card of the pack simultaneously, the Fool represents, amongst other things, naïvety and carefree-ness, which are characteristics of children (and frequently of the inexperienced or uninitiated). The rediscovery of the truly pure and innocent Self is often viewed as the ultimate goal of magicians of many varieties. It can be said that reconnecting to humility, egolessness, and spiritual surrender are true keys to enlightenment—a truth reflected in both the Tarot and the Holy Child mythologies. It also correlates with the common Qabalistic saying that "Kether is in Malkuth and Malkuth is in Kether."

In Qabalism, the Holy Trinity of the *supernal triad* also has deep creational significance; these are the Sephiroth above Da'ath on the Tree of Life. (We will discuss Da'ath further in chapter 1.) From Kether the Crown, Chokmah was born, followed by Binah. In terms of the Holy Mother-Father-Child association, the supernal Sephiroth on which these are aligned can be interpreted in various ways.

In all cross-cultural depictions, the Holy Child is the outcome of the Holy Mother and Father, and it is this offspring who perpetuates the cycle. It is this Child who is the redeemer of sins, the peaceful balancer, the radiant light-bearer, and the bringer of the new age—*this* age! His vast incarnations remind us of a very important fact: that images of the Holy Child represent humankind's potential.

Each and every one of us is a sacred being who was physically birthed from a man and woman. Likewise, the masculine and feminine currents rule the cycles of nature and ourselves. In all aspects, the yin and yang, the Holy Mother and Holy Father—the God and Goddess, if you will—mirror our human experience. Our physical bodies and the balancing energies of the earth plane have arisen from these forces.

Every single thing we do is significant. Every thought, every action, every reaction and interaction is of absolute importance. Every step of the way, we co-create our lives. Magick permeates every person's being and, through our thoughts and actions, we are constantly casting magick—manipulating reality—throughout the day, whether we are aware of it or not. The whole of our earth experience manifests from our own consciousness: a fact that confers the utmost responsibility, and the goal of self-awareness, on all those who dedicate themselves to a spiritual path.

The healing, conquering, compassionate, and venerably enlightened aspects the Holy Child represents are mirrors of who exactly we *can* be and ought to strive to be; for we are indeed the children of the gods and our influence echoes through the planes.

✷　✷　✷

This book is about shadow magick, examining the ways we can harness the shadow, in its various forms, for spiritual purposes. The myths and metaphors retold here can remind us of the importance of the self in this game we call "reality." Far too many people ignore the greatness, value, and mind-blowing mystery of life itself—many forget to *realize* that they're actually alive and conscious in the present moment, experiencing a paradigm like none other. In a modern world where it's all too easy to get trapped in the charade of everyday life and lose touch with the cycles that forge our evolution, it's equally easy to forget our own power—or what's worse, place our power entirely in temporary mundanity.

I believe that shadow magick, particularly internal shadow magick, is about embracing the Holy Child. It's about reaching into the womblike darkness and depths of our minds and our experiences to uncover an internal diamond in the rough. It's about examining the extremes and rediscovering balance. This is the work of the shaman. The archetype of the Holy Child suggests that the offspring is more balanced than its progenitors—the Mother and Father—and thus brings a balanced light of blessing, discernment, and wholeness to the world.

To embrace "O" we must not only realize "I" but dance with "A." To know the self we must understand the divine polarity in all its forms. We can't know the day unless we know the night; we can't perceive the glory of light until we examine the darkness; we can't go outside of ourselves until we go within.

Interpreting Shadow Magick

Those who describe themselves as dark Witches, dark (Neo)Pagans, or dark magicians tend to practice shadow magick in one form or another. The term "dark Pagan" was coined by magician Cliff H. Low in the early 1990s, and is used by many Pagans who are attracted to darker energies, philosophies, and methods of working magick.

Many magickal-spiritual individuals who do *not* identify themselves as "dark" also practice shadow magick, finding that an emphasis on light alone proves incomplete. Because interpretations are so personal, what one person might deem magick aligned with "shadow" another would not. Some people might interpret shadow magick as magick that works with the Jungian-defined shadow self, others see it as magick dealing with external occult forces, and others may simply view it as Witchcraft or magickal spirituality practiced at night. It would be silly to think that any one person or group understands every aspect of shadow magick; all of us have a different view, a different angle to share on the topic.

Shadow magick is not a tradition, nor is it a trend. I view shadow magick more as an *interpretation*, and herein I will present portions of my own.

Some topics that I would normally cover in a tome of this type are discussed in detail in my first book, *Goth Craft: The Magickal Side of Dark Culture*—topics such as ancient and modern necromancy, vampyrism, blood magick, shamanic body modification, entheogenic drug use, and working with sorrow. So I refer the reader interested in these subjects to that book. But in fact, any reader of *Shadow Magick Compendium*, whether they identify with Gothic subculture or not, will benefit from chapters 3, 4, and 5 of *Goth Craft*. These focus more generally on esoteric darkness, and their ideas and practices complement the material found here, in this non-Goth-specific book.

Shadow Magick Compendium is not "ur book of teh black majiks!!!1!" in that it doesn't emphasize the esoteric use of shadow for destructive or manipulative purposes. This is not a book of black Witchcraft, predatory sorcery, or self-aggrandizement. While self-service is necessary to an extent and should (in my belief) be balanced with honest altruism, the magick I proffer focuses more on knowing the mind and journeying the beautiful (yet sometimes dreadful) shadows than on dominating one's environment. Nor is this book simply glorified Wicca in a dark skin; the methods herein are all over the map in terms of Witchcraft and variations of shadow-work.

This is not a beginners' book, either. Readers with some familiarity with basic principles of Witchcraft, spirituality, and the magickal arts will be best prepared for the more obscured elements of magick covered here. The material is wide-ranging; some is introductory, some advanced, some historical, some academic, some psychological, and some practical. Some material is deep and heavy, and some is light and fun. It is a *compendium*, after all! As such, it is perhaps best called an intermediate-level book, considering its wide spectrum of material (for a wide spectrum of readers!).

I have also included a ritual meditation in each chapter (two in chapter 3). Meditation is invaluable for any spiritual seeker, and these are best done sequentially, as the reader progresses experientially through the book. A variety of simpler exercises, chants, and spell suggestions are also included. All of these practices are designed to be done at night, ideally by candlelight or outside in a safe, natural environment. The ideal time of night is midnight, the "witching hour," or around three AM, which is the peak of stillness and astral quietude.

All the possible topics and subtopics under the term "shadow magick" could fill encyclopedic volumes of text—an impossible prospect! Instead, I'll focus on the ones that are most relevant and have the most practical value. The material herein leans neither too far toward the Left Hand nor the Right: it stands solidly in the middle. Its focus is neither entirely negative nor entirely positive. It focuses mainly on one's personal connection to the divine darkness and the manner in which we dance hand in hand with life and death, light and darkness—the father and mother of us all.

It would be naive to think that spirituality and magick have ever been entirely about love and light. Love and light are incredibly powerful, transcendent, and ultimately illuminating forces, but fully partaking of those currents isn't always easy. True light is often buried beneath chaos and turmoil that can take years or lifetimes to come to terms with.

Contrary to popular belief—even in magickal circles—those who are drawn to and work predominantly with the "darkness" are not necessarily to be feared or shunned. Sure, there are those occasional pervs or power-mongers who are drawn to every religion or imaginable expression, but they certainly do not represent the whole range of shadow magicians. Indeed, those who work with the shadow, in its multitude of forms, are not so very different from their other magickal brothers and sisters. The only real difference is the *approach* to magickal and spiritual evolution.

Those who practice shadow magick do not *worship* the darkness but seek to *understand* it and actualize it for positive ends. Embracing the darkness is part of divine balance. While some would like to disregard the darker aspects of Deity and pretend they don't exist, that whole half of the spectrum is waiting to be understood. While it may be comfortable to believe that spirituality is pure blissful light, this is only half of the equation. Spirit is the paradox; it is both, it is neither. We would not have the light gods if it weren't for the dark ones, and vice versa. Nearly all occult paths, including Witchcraft, emphasize *balance* rather than pure light or pure darkness.

The Western world continues to see a stronger and steadier resurgence in ancient spirituality, occultism, and syncretized religious thought. Some would say that spirituality took an ascending path at the dawn of the commonly recognized Aeon of Horus (a Thelemic concept) in 1904, and has risen at an unprecedented rate ever since. The Hermetic Order of the Golden Dawn had been founded in 1888, and Witchcraft was revived in the twentieth century, confirming the trend. From Helena Petrovna Blavatsky's takes on (mostly Hindu) ideas of reincarnation and Karma in her system of Theosophy to the rising interest in Masonic and Hermetic occult systems, the New Age movement rapidly gained momentum. Later, it would be particularly embraced by the 1960s countercultural movements and psychedelic explorations. Meanwhile, orthodox and dogmatic forms of religion were losing their appeal—and their fear factor—on a mass scale.

Still, the force of darkness was never entirely negated. As Helena Blavatsky noted in her 1888 book *The Secret Doctrine*, "According to the tenets of Eastern occultism, darkness is the one true actuality, the basis and the root of light, without which the latter could never manifest itself, nor even exist. Light is matter, and darkness pure Spirit. Darkness, in its radical, metaphysical basis, is subjective and absolute light; while the latter in all its seeming effulgence and glory, is merely a mass of shadows, as it can never be eternal, and is simply an illusion."[4] It's unfortunate that such ideas about the positive attributes of darkness were never expounded upon as the New Age movement evolved.

Currently, "New Age" serves as an umbrella term for a number of spiritual paths, often loosely encompassing Paganism, Witchcraft, and occultism. Of course, many adherents to these paths abhor the association, but truth be told, we're all interconnected in terms of spiritual exploration.

Unfortunately, some so-called New Agers wish not to focus on personal and global darkness, instead emphasizing "light" as a mechanism—sometimes the *only* mechanism—for spiritual progress. But if darkness is suppressed or ignored, a dangerous and imbalanced lifestyle results. Many who focus solely on the lighter side of spirituality are just as imbalanced as those who give thought only to its darker aspects. Self-awareness includes acknowledging both the shadow and the light within ourselves and the world around us.

Beneath a candy coating of light often lies a rotten core. This fact *demands* to be addressed when one is engulfed in spiritual work and practice. No matter how much white light a person is surrounded with, if the darker portions are pushed back and not constructively released, no real balance can be had. Declaring pure love, light, and transcendental awareness without reclaiming inner and outer darkness can push a person to a delusional state of mind, forcing the darker currents to manifest in negative and often harmful ways. Perfectly natural feelings such as sorrow, discontent, anger, and dissatisfaction can snowball if ignored, often resulting in nervous breakdowns and extreme depressions as a counterbalance. And disorders such as manic depression, multiple personality disorder, bipolarity, pathological lying, and other emotional-psychological imbalances can manifest even more intensely if not recognized and controlled through proper means.

Shamans across the globe have long understood the necessary balance of the light and dark, both within and without. From these shamanic ways many of our own healing and magickal practices have been born, including aspects of Paganism and occult rites of initiation, divination methods, and views of the ethereal planes.

Balance is rare these days. Goddess knows only a handful of people have truly achieved it—the rest of us are still trying to find proper footing! Many forms of shadow magick, particularly those that emphasize the shadow self, are mechanisms for regaining balance. Certainly, one must practice both "light" and "dark" magicks to achieve this equilibrium.

A number of things that could be considered shadow magick fall in the negative realm. (In general, I use the term "negative" to refer to what is harmful—while noting that both positive and negative currents are necessary to sustain our existence. The term is shorthand.)

Qabalists and other magicians refer to harmful, destructive, or consuming energies as belonging to the Left Hand Path, or the Pillar of Severity on the Tree of Life. This pillar serves as a necessary balance for the Pillar of Mercy (the Right Hand Path), the two of which frame the Middle Pillar of Equilibrium. The Left Hand Path (LHP) encompasses religions like Satanism, Setianism, Demonolatry, and others. Without question, many people who claim to follow "light" paths are instead treading in negative darkness: just look at the religious extremists! Immoral and amoral people of all kinds, religious or not, can be viewed as living a Left Hand lifestyle; this we can easily see in statistics of violence, assault, and murder as well as in the ever-more-obvious instances of political and corporate crime. Still, other cultures might classify as a "Left Hand Pather" anyone who goes heavily against the norm—even the ascetic *saddhus* of India who practice extreme self-mortification. (These wandering holy men, often called renunciants or aspirants, are discussed in chapter 2.) Those who blatantly go against the grain can be perceived as threatening to the masses. To use the age-old saying, people fear what they don't understand. Undoubtedly, "freaks" of Western culture, such as us kooky magickal folk, are viewed by many as Left Hand Pathers, at least socially, even if that view may be inaccurate.

Shadow magick is not a negative practice. However, it does require coming to terms with the shadow self, and reaching into those crevices of the mind is sometimes perceived as a negative experience. Seeing reality and the self as objectively as possible is essential to the spiritual seeker and most definitely so to the Witch or magician.

Within the vibration we call shadow lie energies both beneficial and maleficent. The focus of this book is spiritual evolution; thus, we must analyze both the "negative" and "positive" aspects of shadow. Often, these polarities are defined by interpretation alone.

The aspects of shadow magick range widely. In many ways, those that deal with the *internal* darkness of the self can be considered positive in nature: practices such as magickal work on the emotional plane, mysticism, and types of deep meditation. Other arts, such as divination, astral projection, automatic writing, and dreamwalking, are clearly not negative in nature (and are in fact shared by nearly all Witches). But some shadow magick can be deemed more negative: demonic evocation, Qlippothic or Goetic work, uncontrolled psychic vampyrism, cursing, and some types of necromancy, for example. While I respect those who cautiously and compassionately practice some of these arts, many of which could be considered of the Left Hand Path, I do not delve too deeply into them here. They just "ain't my thang."

𝔄bout 𝔗his 𝔅ook: 𝔙ariations of 𝔖hadow

In its most obvious, physical guise, "shadow" is a phenomenon we see on the physical plane: the darkness cast by a lit object, the darkness of the night sky, the color black, and so on. Moving on from that initial guise, this book interprets shadow in five basic ways, which are reflected in its chapters: the internal, the external, the astral, the natural, and the social. Taking the initiative to face the shadow—in whatever form—allows a fuller view of self to emerge, and working magick with these elements of darkness can be invaluable. When doing so *ritualistically*, however, remember that a securely structured energetic circle is a must. It can protect a practitioner from external astral vibrations and entities, giving a space of clarity and discretion regarding which aspects of the shadow should be worked with and how.

In these five guises, the shadow can reveal its wisdom to us.

The Internal Shadow (chapter 1)

In Jungian psychology, this is the darker side of human nature. Portions of the self that have been repressed exist here, as does the "Dweller on the Threshold," "the critic," and Choronzon.[5] When denial occurs, thoughts are pushed to the back of the mind, into the unrecognized internal shadow. When darker emotions arise, such as sadness, anger, and apathy, it may be considered a conscious surfacing of the internal shadow. Awareness of these darker characteristics is the first step in working with one's inner shadow.

The External Shadow (chapter 2)

One's external shadow is simply a projection of the internal one. Gone unrecognized, the external shadow can manifest through projection. For example, we may believe that no one finds us attractive, when the truth is that we do not accept our own attractiveness ourselves. Such projection can happen in countless ways, arising from any repressed belief. The external shadow also includes the shadows of others. In other words, any aspect of "shadow" that is not your own can be considered external. This chapter explore types of magick that rely on external forces, yet connect with and influence one's internal reality.

The Astral Shadow (chapter 3)

The astral plane is a reflection of the physical world and carries energies that are generally invisible to the untrained eye. The astral is the realm of guides, guardians, and ancestors.

Thoughtforms, deities, dreams, and "everything possible to be believed …" exist on the astral plane.[6] Naturally, it carries currents of darkness that are directly linked to the shadow of the human psyche and the natural world.

The Shadow of Nature (chapter 4)

Nature has many shadow aspects: for example, the food chain in which one life form must feed on another to survive. Destructive acts that we call murder, rape, and theft are "natural" crimes of the animal kingdom, existing in the primitive aspect of the animal psyche. While animals cannot always choose to control these survival-driven instincts, humans have the unique gifts of morality and ethical discretion, allowing us to choose against these behaviors. Consider, too, the destructive aspect of nature herself, such as natural disasters and even poisonous plants. Nature also has other shadowed aspects such as eclipses, the dark seasons, the dark moon, and other mysteries to be explored in this chapter.

The Shadow of Society (chapter 5)

The unseen, hidden, suppressed, or overlooked aspects of our culture and society belong to this guise of shadow. In my own view, the shadow of society is predominantly *not* a positive one. Skewed cultural worldviews, underhanded corporate crime, religious fanaticism, and self-serving politics can be considered a part of society's shadow. The social shadow is greatly shaped by the internal shadow. For example, even the most devastating sociopolitical crime is often no more than horrid projections of certain people's inner fears and psychoses. This chapter explores the social shadow in connection to magickal spirituality.

A Word on Cursing and Black Magick

Because of this book's subject, the "black magick" stone will undoubtedly be cast by a handful of people. Whether the accusation is "This book is black magick!" or "Why is there no black magick in here?," I should at least clarify my stance on this subject!

Blatantly harmful magick is a pathetic display of powerlessness. "Black" magick, as some would term it, can be defined as magick that seeks to control another person's free will, gain dominance over them, or inflict unnecessary harm for personal fulfillment. Black magick can be seen as manipulation for personal gain. Such practices are almost always used for boosting the ego for the sake of personal validation. Intimidating and dominating other individuals is no more advanced than the behavior of the schoolyard bully.

Anything that violates another person's free will can be called black magick, though most Witches and magicians prefer to simply call it "negative" or "harmful" magick. This places less emphasis on the color (because, of course, no color is inherently bad) and encourages people to recognize that all magick is neither black nor white, but a very mutable shade of grey.

Deep psychoses underlie harmfully sadistic behavior, be it in the magickal realm or the physical realm. This harmful conduct, whether it's that of the playground bully or the adult using manipulative magick, is a form of psychological projection: the person inflicting such harm is hurting dreadfully within, and feels a type of comfort in making others suffer. This is, in other words, an external projection of an aspect of a person's internal shadow. Harming others can momentarily relieve loneliness, giving the attacker a sense of justification for the internal pain they so desperately wish to avoid. What's more unfortunate is that this behavioral mistreatment can perpetuate through generations of children, never really healing until someone chooses consciously and decisively to break the vicious cycle.

It is said that a Witch who doesn't know how to curse doesn't know how to heal. True 'dat. I'm certainly not one to say that cursing and the like never have their time and place. They do. I, like most Witches, have used manipulative and necessarily harmful magick—but never without objective and intelligent reason, and certainly never nonchalantly. The purpose of cursing should, at least in my eyes, always be progressive—for the spiritual benefit of all involved. Not for revenge, not for a display of power, but for the intention of helping another person see the light and find healing.

It seems to hold true that, for example, an abusive and apathetically self-serving individual will respond better to a Karmic magickal jolt of chaos rather than a visualization of healing white light. The need for performing harmful magick is exceedingly rare, and it should only be practiced after deep consideration and down-to-earth logical thinking. I once heard that, after the decision has been made to cast a spell, a person should wait twenty-four or forty-eight hours to perform the magick. This ensures that the mind is in a balanced and objective state. Any Witch or magician worth his or her salt knows that the misuse of magickal powers is a spiritual death wish. I'm not necessarily talking about Wicca's (commonly misunderstood and superstitious) "rule of three" here; I'm talking about universal Karma. What goes around comes around, and our behavior—magickal and otherwise—directly influences ourselves.

Humans, and all things in reality, are fractions of the Great Whole. The singular forms in which we perceive ourselves (bodies) and to which we affix an ego (identification) are but a grand illusion. No thing is apart from you, me, or our surroundings. Because all things are undeniably connected, if a person consciously harms a point on the fabric of reality, they in fact are harming themselves.

The Nature of Darkness and the Color Black

The shadow is darkness, and the darkest color of all is black. Simply said, the color black plays a role in shadow magick because of its embodiment of dark energies. It is primordial. Its very essence is ancient and mysterious, containing the entirety of the past and future, retaining memories in its cosmic space. But is it ultimately consuming; is there reason to fear it? Neither light nor darkness is inherently "evil." I don't believe anyone or anything is *completely* good or evil, completely this or that. Reality works through varying degrees: not in black or white, but instead in shades of grey. Nothing fully embodies one end of the spectrum or the other. Similarly, the light would not exist without the dark, and vice versa.

Black forms a polarity with light. But this should not be confused with the polarity of good and evil: they are two separate things entirely. Polarities exist to depend on one another. Hot and cold, active and passive, sweet and bitter, male and female: one is a positive pole, the other a negative. Obviously, this doesn't mean that one is inherently evil or equatable with any other polarity. Each has its own individual essence. The Taoist yin-yang symbol exemplifies the philosophy that nothing can exist without its equal but opposite balance; each extreme is dependent on the other, including light and dark in all its forms. The examples are limitless and are directly reflected in nature.

Pagans of all types celebrate Deity in a variety of forms, and this is reflected in the Wheel of the Year. Each major Sabbat is equally important. As the wheel turns to its darker tide, death and rebirth of the season is respected and celebrated. If death did not happen, there would be no life. If life did not happen, there would be no death. The light and the dark are not separate entities but very much one whole, holding the equal balance that is necessary to sustain it.

Those who work with the shadow understand the need for negativity but don't glorify it. At the same time, lightness is understood but we are not blinded by it. An abundance of light is just as consuming as an abundance of darkness; a balance between the two truly is the Middle Path. An important way to express the lightness is through our healing work and optimism. An important way to express the darkness, the other end of the spectrum, is through art and introspection. Both forces must operate to cultivate balance.

Most creation myths begin with darkness. Even the biblical "Let there be light" implies that, yes, *darkness* was prior ... gasp! From the darkness, the light of spirituality—the light of life—springs forth. Black is the color of the cosmos whence we came and whither we go again upon death. The sun and other stars act as beacons in a vast expanse of black nothingness.

In occultism, black is most often associated with two things in addition to creation: energetic protection and the destruction of negativity. When banishing harmful influences, Witches burn black candles to vanquish the energy into the Abyss, and magicians of all types use black as a general protective shield. Black is the combination of all colors *and* is the lack of color. The same is true for white. Qabalists and other ceremonial magicians also use the color black when working with Binah on the Tree of Life, which is ruled by Saturn.

When black is worn on the body, it surrounds the person with a rampart of protection, a cloak from surrounding energies. Just as light is drawn to dark colors, black also absorbs such energies. Instead of letting them pass further (such as into the wearer's sphere), it banishes them into its own darkness.

Nowadays, the color black is most often associated with death and dying, and it is the color of preference worn at wakes and funeral services. It is certainly a color of mourning, as it draws on energies shrouded and obscured. Black can represent the unfathomable and unknowable, the Great Beyond, the infinite dreamscape entered upon death. It can also be associated with "blacking out" or the loss of consciousness. After the death of a close friend or relative, some people are naturally inclined to wear black clothing for therapeutic reasons, trying to cope with the reality of death. Expressing one's mourning in blackness can provide a deep-seated comfort.[7]

People who are depressed are often subconsciously drawn to the color because it can contain their energy, whereas extending energy outward could open them to potential harm. In magick, items intended to keep a very specific energy pattern are covered in black cloth and stored in the dark. This cloaks the item, not allowing adverse vibrations to penetrate.

Black represents no thing, nothingness ... the Abyss or the void into which anything unwanted can be tossed (or drawn from). Black stones, candles, and fabric are best used in spells of banishment and releasing. Black is said to help remove hexes and also aid in binding or cursing when need be. Black is associated with the womb of the earth in some cultures; it may be used for grounding and reconnecting with humankind's roots by way of ancestral communication and past-life regression. Just like white, black is an all-purpose color. It is associated with the night, rebirth, divination, and the eternal journey of awakening to spiritual truth.

Black has different associations for every culture. For some, like most Western cultures, it's a color of mourning, sorrow, and despair. For others, it's the color of rebirth and coming back to the center of the soul. It is both a symbol of release and cultivation and may be seen as a neutral color. Black not only represents *nothing*, but also paradoxically represents *everything*—all colors and energies—and is ideal when used for boosting the conduction of energy in a magick circle. Most Witches I know weave their magick under the cloak of night because of its calm and mysterious implications. Certainly, daylight has its own distinct vibration that should also be used.

We have a good idea about how Westerners commonly view the color black. What about other nations? Many spiritualists associate black with the darkness of the dreamscape as well as the starry, infinite night sky (Nuit). One very interesting association is seen in the traditional Egyptian viewpoint. *Khem* means black in Coptic and refers to the fertile soil on the banks of the Nile River. *Khem* is also the root-word for *alchemy*. Egypt and its surrounding areas are often called Kemet, or "the black land." Because of this fertile soil's wide-ranging yield of crops, black gained sacred associations with sustenance and abundance—a far cry from the Western associations with adverse energies!

While the general New Age community commonly links the color white with purity and transcendence, other cultures associate it directly with death. White is the color of bones and the paleness of a body before decomposition. White is a color of purity and the release of mundane ties upon death.

Many of these associations are widely held in many parts of Asia, particularly. Some Asian cultures, such as Chinese and Hindu, see death itself as tainting, or polluting. Thus, the color white is worn in mourning to purge the individual of these associative impurities, creating a rampart of reflective protection around the individual so that death energy cannot enter their space. Because the color white is not bound by any color on the light spectrum, it can esoterically disallow perceived "impure" energies into the spirit of the individual in mourning. It may, along similar lines, prevent the soul of the departed from entering into another's physical vehicle as well.

Another example of white as a death color: male members of the Masai peoples of Kenya and Tanzania cover themselves in white chalk at the point in their lives when they transit between warrior and eligible husband status. In this rite of passage, white represents their status as "socially dead," in the liminal space between youth and man, being members of neither rank. In ritual, the men engage in ecstatic dance, heavy chant, trance, and spirit possession (invocation). Obviously, the group of men can still be seen by others but they are individually unidentifiable due to their ghostly appearance for the ceremony. In this case, white represents the realm between the death of old social status and the rebirth of a new role.

White also physically represents the semen of males and the maternal milk of females and has associations with fertility across many cultures, including Egypt. So, cross-culturally, both black and white are associated with death *and* birth! This is only appropriate because death is a form of life, as an entrance into the Otherworld, and life is a form of death, as we are all in a constant process of physically dying while incarnate. The processes of birth and death are really not as separate from one another as they may seem, and neither are the colors black and white.

---

1. Carl G. Jung, *Psychology and Religion*. London: Routledge, 1970, 93.

2. Carl G. Jung, *The Collected Works of C.G. Jung, vol. 9ii: Aion*. Princeton, NJ: Princeton University Press, 1959, 8–9.

3. I use the term "spiritualist" synonymously with "spiritual seeker," and occasionally use "spiritualism" synonymously with "spirituality," but neither refers to the nineteenth-century Spiritualism movement whose followers were called Spiritualists.

4. Blavatsky, Helena P. and Hillard, Katharine (editor), *Abridgment of H.P. Blavatsky's Secret Doctrine*. Whitefish, MT: Kessinger Publishing, 1996, 59.

5. Also called the Watcher on the Threshold, the Dweller on the Threshold represents the sum of the magician's delusions, fears, accumulated negative Karma, misunderstandings, limiting beliefs, and anything else that can possibly interfere with the magician's path to enlightenment and spiritual attainment. Many psychologists recognize "the critic" as part of everyone's unconscious mind; it is viewed as the portion of the psyche that concludes perceptions in favor of failure, acting as the absolute protagonist. The "Dweller in the Abyss" and the ultimate embodiment of antispiritual ego, Choronzon was originally recognized as a demonic figure by Edward Kelley and John Dee (Enochian magick), and later expounded on by Aleister Crowley. He (or "it") is said to be the last thing the magician faces in his or her path towards enlightenment, and is quite often recognized as being an aspect of the magician's own mind, much like "the critic," rather than being an entirely external force.

6. "Everything possible to be believed is an image of truth" comes from William Blake's *The Marriage of Heaven and Hell*.

7. This also tends to draw upon psychological associations commonly expressed in the Gothic subculture.

I

The Internal Shadow

Witches do not claim their power from darkness, as the dominant culture tells us. Witches claim their power *through* darkness. The word is an active one, and it implies that Witches actively pursue their power—it is not a manifestation of some external source. They honor their *power from within*.

—Timothy Roderick
Dark Moon Mysteries

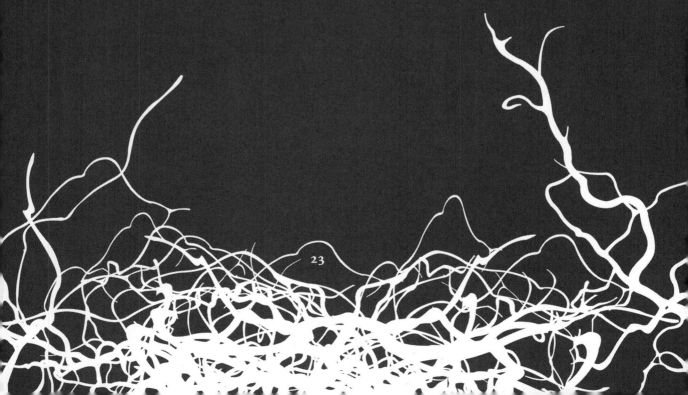

Understanding Negative Behavior Cycles

People attracted to both dark energies and the spiritual-magickal arts must, in some manner, work with the personal shadow daily (or nightly, as it were). Constantly monitoring the self and the mind is essential for magickal and spiritual progress. Spirituality of the shadow requires looking at behaviors, actions, and reactions regularly and objectively. One of the best ways to do this is by frequently practicing the self-evaluation exercise below. It appears here, in the first chapter, because this awareness must be honed before we move to other forms of shadow work.

Our perceptions, actions, and reactions *form our reality*. It's easy to get so swept up in the drama of life that we lose focus of the vital role we play in building our experience. Objectively examining our own behavioral patterns is, in my view, the most important aspect of shadow magick. From there, it's just a matter of "How deep do you want to go?" We can only change the external world by transforming the internal; both simultaneously co-create each other. Every single one of us has behavioral and perceptual patterns that somehow hinder our full spiritual development—or else we wouldn't be here!

Everything in existence is linked by an ethereal web. This is not fancy New Age ideology, but a strict observation of the nature of reality. Mystical religions have always recognized that no one thing is separate from the next; even modern science seamlessly backs this ancient notion. When one point on the multidimensional web of life changes, it naturally influences the rest of it, even ever so slightly. As we examine and positively change ourselves, we change our own reality cycles and influence all others' paradigms to shift. If we let ourselves see the nature of our own psyche, we permit ourselves to heal on deep levels. If we actively recognize and change harmful patterning (even if it's an incredibly painful task), progress occurs both on the level of the earth's general energetic vibration, and on the level of our own personal connections and daily experiences.

It's a good idea to analyze your actions and reactions regularly—constantly, even. If you find it difficult to step "into the moment" and observe your mind, try meditating in the evening, rewinding and reviewing your day, piece by piece. The most significant points of energy exchange in the day will enter your consciousness first, letting you immediately analyze your own behavior and that of others. Were there moments when you overreacted to something? Were there instances of stress and frustration? What happened in your day that made you upset, sad, apathetic, or resentful? How could these emotional imbalances have been avoided through your *own* behavior?

Internal Shadow Magick: A Self-Evaluation

I would like to propose a simple psychological self-evaluation, one that will deepen your self-knowledge—an invaluable asset on your path. This exercise helps expose our most ingrained and deep-rooted patterns, opening us to understanding and healing them. Please grab a piece of paper and a pen, or get to your computer and keyboard. No, seriously, do this right now. C'mon! Pretty please, *avec sucre*? This exercise is powerful, and the resulting material will be worthy of everyday reflection and expansion, if you wish. Over time, more observations will naturally come to you, especially if you do this self-reflection regularly. Then you can perform the magick you deem necessary to regain balance—even if it requires searching the deepest, most repressed portions of the mind.

Start by dimming your environment. Get some candles and incense going, turn off the phone, unplug the television … whatever you have to do to reach a comfortable and serene state of being that is at least somewhat different from the everyday. If it means getting some tea, turning on some music, and wrapping up in a warm blanket on your bed, go for it. If you do play music, make it light and instrumental—perhaps darkwave, ethereal, classical, ambient, or New Age, with few or no vocals. If you feel that this exercise would best be performed in a properly cast circle, have at it. The deeper you go within, and the more time and effort you devote to this exercise, the more meaningful the results.

Elemental Alignments

Even if you are already familiar with the common Neopagan and Hermetic concepts of elemental associations, first review them here, taking a few moments to center each element's qualities in your mind.

Earth concerns structure: Stability, security, sustenance, materials, and physical reality (plant, animal, and mineral).

Air concerns the mind: Perception, ideas, intellectuality, study, science, communication, society, and information.

Fire concerns activity: Motivation, invigoration, lust, sexuality, sensuality, passion, confidence, and transformation.

Water concerns intuition: Emotions, love, empathy, compassion, healing, psychic ability, astral travel, sleep, and dreaming.

Each of these lists could continue forever. Literally all aspects of reality are contained within these four elementals; this aspect of occultism is recognized across many traditions. One can attribute cardinal directions, planets, astrological signs, senses, seasons, emotions, colors, Tarot suits, deities, archangels, and countless other things to these four primaries—and I won't even touch on the Qabalistic associations!

Now consider what harmful cycles in the human psyche are suggested by these divisions, resulting from either an overabundance or a lack of the associated qualities. A person with hard-to-control anger issues could be seen as having too much Fire energy, whereas a person who has difficulty remembering things might lack Air energy.

The four lists to follow show some such possibilities, in statement form. Browse these lists now with yourself in mind, reading each item with an honest, analytical eye. On your paper, write the headings Earth, Air, Fire, and Water, and below copy any statement that you feel applies to you. If you think of others not listed here, simply write them under the element that seems most appropriate. Take it slow, and let yourself detach from your ego as you contemplate. If you're like most people, you'll probably have a relatively large list of harmful behavioral cycles. If you can't recognize yourself in *any* of these patterns, there's a problem. I bet even Gandhi could have picked out a couple!

Should you consider what other people have said about you? Remember that insults or critiques are *always* subjective, and therefore may or may not be accurate assessments of your character. At the same time, our own self-perceptions are subjective, too, and it often *takes* another person's perspective for us to finally see our cycles. Contemplate not only what others have said about you, but behaviors that you often beat yourself up about. You may be surprised by the list you create as you go deeper within. Also, there's no shame in patting yourself on the back if you discover things about your character that you hadn't recognized before, or had chosen to ignore in the past! The further you immerse yourself in the shadow of your mind, uncovering that which is repressed or ignored, the deeper you allow self-awareness and healing to enter.

Much of the material in this section is incorporated into Opus Aima Obscuræ, the shadow magick tradition founded by my Priestess Estha and me. I encourage readers who are also metaphysical teachers to use this or any parts of this book in their own teachings (as long as credit is given to the OAO spiritual system). Because magickal spirituality is largely based on promoting healing and personal growth, its teachers often incorporate potentially transformative material from various sources, and I would not expect the methods here to be an exception.

EARTH: SHADOW TRAITS

I am often unmotivated in life.

I often forget the borderline between fantasy and reality.

I often turn to certain vices, and I may be an escapist.

I tend to be neglectful of other people's needs.

I tend to give too much, being neglectful of my own needs.

I feel that everyone always hurts me in the end.

I may be addicted to role-playing games.

I stress about the order and structure of things.

I disallow anyone from getting too close to me, for fear of hurting or getting hurt.

I could say that I live a double life.

I only feel secure if I'm in a romantic relationship.

I am very resentful toward my family and friends when I feel wronged by them.

I sometimes think that people of a certain ethnicity, religion, orientation, age, class, gender, social identity, body type, culture, disability, and so on are inherently flawed.

Money is always the first thing in my mind.

I often imagine myself having supernatural powers.

I rarely follow through with plans I make.

I frequently hold grudges.

I stress about my obligations and requirements more than I should.

It's usually difficult for me to see other people's viewpoints.

I only feel secure when surrounded by material abundance.

I depend on others to carry me through life.

I tend to consider people's social labels more than their character.

I overwork myself.

I sometimes starve myself or purge what I've just eaten.

I'm never really satisfied with anything.

I am often apathetic and disinterested.

I am often quite fearful and have many phobias.

I almost never leave my home.

I become fanatical and extremist about new ideas.

I usually feel responsible for other people.

AIR: SHADOW TRAITS

I have the habit of lying, exaggerating, and creating tall tales.

I have a bad memory and am usually forgetful.

I am often spacey, flighty, and ungrounded.

I always need to have the last word.

It's difficult for me to embrace new beginnings.

I am obsessed with my image and public presentation.

I almost always see people's negative qualities first.

I feel unattractive without makeup or when naked.

I feel I'm more aware and knowledgeable than almost everyone I know.

I believe I never know enough and feel shame when others know more than I.

I present myself as having more knowledge than I really may.

I look down on others when I feel more informed.

My attitude changes at the drop of a hat.

I tend to manipulate other people.

I often perceive myself as being nonhuman.

I often get lost in my thoughts.

I always doubt myself or my ideas.

It's frequently difficult for me to communicate or to comprehend certain things.

I try to appear differently to other people.

I approach things from an extremely academic standpoint.

I tend to eavesdrop on other people.

I usually believe everything that people say.

I have a tendency to overanalyze.

I am easily distracted.

I place personal worth in what others say about me.

I believe that others should be like me.

I believe that I should be like others.

FIRE: SHADOW TRAITS

I am usually nervous and anxious.

I often regret being liberal with my sexual behavior.

I have insecurities about sex and sexuality.

I often violate other people's boundaries.

I tend to lack self-confidence.

I am fascinated by death and destruction.

I feel the need to dominate conversations and draw attention to myself.

I tend to cut myself or otherwise harm my body.

I often have uncontrollable outbursts of anger.

I have been known to destroy people's social identities.

I have an erratic and spontaneous personality.

I often steal things instead of paying for them.

My personality is frequently bitter and critical.

I often force people to see things my way.

I sometimes have traumatic panic attacks.

I get pleasure in seeing others suffer.

I have an addictive personality.

I often put others down to make myself feel better.

I constantly seek attention from others.

It would be very difficult for me to detach from technology.

I am almost always overexcited and extroverted.

I get overwhelmed and frustrated at even the smallest things.

I am extremely rebellious.

WATER: SHADOW TRAITS

I usually just don't want to wake up in the morning.

I have difficulty escaping from certain memories.

I find myself being unable to stop crying.

I find myself unable to cry.

I tend to overuse mind-altering substances.

I am almost always introverted.

I feel that I do not deserve to experience true love, joy, and happiness.

I usually just "go with the flow" and am passive in life.

I have a shy personality because I'm overly sensitive.

I always go with my feelings instead of logic.

I often make big deals over small occurrences.

I can usually sense other people's emotional states to an uncomfortable degree.

It's difficult for me to tell other people's emotions from my own.

I often misread others' emotions.

I always take any insult to heart.

I have a hard time being alone.

I have difficulty "letting go."

I often feel sorry for myself.

The past never really seems to heal.

I find myself reverting to childhood behavior frequently.

I may be emotionally codependent in my relationships.

I feel empty without others' sympathy.

I often feel a rush to change.

What Lies Behind Behavior?

This is where things get tricky, for it is not sufficient to simply list your observations and consider the process complete. Nearly all of these negative cycles, whether directly from this list or personal variations thereof, have underlying influences. Like the layers of an onion, imbalances have the tendency to be shrouded by other imbalances. For example, a person may recognize a pattern of manipulating other people, a trait linked with Air because it concerns the mental plane. This recognition is the first step in a progressive and positive shift of consciousness … but it is still just the springboard.

The next question is, why does this person manipulate others? It might be for the sake of fitting in and being accepted (Air), or to get some sort of attention (Fire), or to gain material objects or physical security (Earth), or to receive a sympathetic or emotional response from others (Water). Further, the underlying motivation *itself* can be traced to other influences more deeply embedded in the conscious mind, usually having come about from triggers in childhood or adolescence. For each of us, behavioral cycles come from different sources; everyone reacts differently due to their imprinted stimuli.

To use myself as an example, I realized only a few years ago that I had issues accepting the validity of my own opinions and perceptions, and tended to keep quiet rather than speaking up. This seems to relate to the element Air because it has to do with ideas and perception. Just beneath that layer, however, was a lack of self-confidence, which relates to the element Fire because it has to do with the strength of assurance. Upon deeper introspection, I remembered two incidents in my past that had undermined my self-confidence more directly than I had realized before. The more recent incident was during my freshman year in high school. After years of acting with a local theatre, I tried out for the first school play of the semester. Unbeknownst to me, it was a *musical* production. When it was my turn to audition at the tryouts, I said to the teacher, "Umm, I can't really sing …" whereupon she held up my application form and, in front of everyone, ripped it in two and threw the pieces in the air, saying, "Then you will not be considered." Because this incident involved a feeling of social rejection, it can be classified as an Air occurrence.

After digging deeper in my head, I discovered an earlier imprint affecting my lack of self-esteem. In middle school, I was involved in speech and debate. At this time, I was heavily interested in stage-performance illusory magic—go figure! After one presentation where the other kids gave their speeches and I did my tricks, I walked offstage in a silly way, showing off and being goofy the way kids do. Later, someone I knew (who was also a neighbor) asked me, "Why were you walking like that? You looked stupid."

Looking back, I see that this comment damaged my self-esteem more than I realized at the time. Elementally, I would call it an Earth occurrence because of my immediate feeling that I did not fit into a certain structure. It had more to do with social roles and norms (Earth) than social acceptance (Air), especially because the person was a neighbor and thus part of my *structural* reality. This initial Earth imbalance affected my other elements, leading to a lack of self-confidence. Had I not caught this early in my adulthood, some seriously detrimental issues could have developed out of these minor incidents. Naturally, I'm still working on this issue and will be for some time. Nothing heals instantly, but if a wound is dressed and cared for regularly, it will recover in due time. Similarly, if the wound is ignored, it grows, festers, and overtakes other areas—a perfect analogy for our psycho-spiritual ailments.

Because the subject of emotional triggers and psycho-spiritual deconstruction is so large, I'll leave the "root causes" description at that. I can only encourage readers to examine their own overarching behavioral patterns, underlying motivations, and embedded occurrences of spiritual damage. Even though many behavioral cycles can be easily deconstructed psychologically, everyone's case is different. We all must tread across the abyss of our own mind, journeying through the psychic depths where these cycles originate.

Magick for Cyclical Change

I strongly recommend meditating at length on each item on the list you've made. This will allow you to desconstruct and analyze all possible triggers for these behaviors. When personal issues arise and beg to be conquered, spirituality and magick are our tools of transformation. We can all change our harmful patterns. When these cycles are brought into awareness, we can choose to change our everyday behaviors. Magick, meditation, and prayer most definitely assist in the process of transforming negative patterns. When we send our intention for personal change into reality, the mind shifts its own mechanisms to allow for this change. You may find yourself becoming ultra-aware of your actions and reactions, or feel a renewed sense of balance in the area you choose to work on. Still, if a person is actually *unwilling* to create these life changes, all the magick in the world could be cast and no change would occur. One must become keenly aware of one's own behaviors and intend to change them every single day.

It is also worth noting that, physiologically, every cell in the body replaces itself every seven years. Thus, the body and mind basically regenerate in this period of time. We can recall that fact as we work on and heal the damaging occurrences of seven years ago or more: our self has entirely regenerated since then. (At the time of this book's printing, I realized that I graduated from high school just over seven years ago. I will thus begin working magick to fully come to terms with and release the imprints from that time in my life.) But just the same, incidents from the very near past can also be easily worked with because the wound is still fresh.

There are endless ways to work with harmful behavioral cycles through magick. Because we work with elemental classifications in this exercise, the most obvious way to balance oneself is to work directly with the imbalanced element. That means we consider our list of negative patterns, and regularly research, align with, and *get to know* the most imbalanced element or elements on it. There are a million ways to use spellcraft, meditation, and prayer to banish an overabundance of a certain element and cultivate an equal-opposite amount of another (although the most powerful spells are those we create ourselves). Again, this information would be another book in and of itself. And many books already on the market have some valuable pointers on spellcrafting and the magickal correspondences of various materials. A few of my favorites (also listed in this book's bibliography):

Spells and How They Work by Janet and Stewart Farrar

The Outer Temple of Witchcraft: Circles, Spells, and Rituals by Christopher Penczak

Cunningham's Encyclopedia of Magical Herbs by Scott Cunningham

If you regularly work with Greek deities and are comfortable with them, I recommend calling forth Mnemosyne, the goddess of memory and mother of the nine Muses. If you'd like to create an entire ritual wherein her aid is invoked, go for it. Or perhaps, for this sort of work, you fancy working with a primordial ancient god or goddess of time, such as Ishtar or Saturn.

Essentially, this exercise can be a form of regression into the past. Deeper forms of regression are not to be approached nonchalantly. It's not a bad idea to have someone very close to you assist in these deeper levels. If you have a trusted spiritual friend, partner, or family member, ask for their help; perhaps you could aid one another in your voyages of mind, trading roles as you wish.

Ideally, one person guides the other through a life timeline, listening and asking brief questions to help elicit stories. The other person, in meditation (lying down is okay), recalls various significant life occurrences and describes them aloud. They may seem trivial at the time, but speaking freely is essential; it will reveal what may have been previously hidden. As the person speaks, the other quickly writes those occurrences down. And of course, if the person revisits any seriously injuring moments in this meditation, the partner can help with calming the mind and grounding back to the present. If you don't have a magickal assistant, personal regressions can be done alone as long as you feel strong enough to endure potentially difficult moments on your own.

So, that's it: to uncover the deepest and darkest portions of the mind and to influence healing accordingly, you must think back, and back, and back. Replay your history, record your results, and do it all over again. Cultivate fearlessness, brutal honesty, and Actual Empowerment. Even if it hurts more than anything to revisit painful experiences, you must, to some extent, live the trauma all over again to really know it ... to really come to terms with it; to heal it. This is particularly important in cases of abuse and humiliation, and may additionally require assitance from a compassionate therapist or other third party. To recognize and actively work with the deepest and most imbalanced aspects of our consciousness is to constructively dance with the shadow. It lets us truly act on the ancient edict: "Know thyself."

Purging Negative Shadow: A Ritual Meditation

This meditation can easily be incorporated with the preceding section, or can stand on its own as a separate exercise. Much of the material herein intertwines with information within this book as a whole. Many thanks to Kate La Trobe (Kala Trobe) for assistance with creating this exercise.

It is best to perform this exercise at or just before the dark moon, ideally around midnight. If possible, abstain from food for at least three hours beforehand (nonalcoholic liquids are okay), or plan a fast for that day. I suggest a rice or juice fast (or both), breaking the fast after the ritual.

In many forms of shadow magick, the aim is to rid yourself of unwanted negative cycles and to use the dark aspects of your life as tools of empowerment. For example, if you have undergone abuse in the past, the idea would be to acknowledge and work with the experience rather than to suppress or ignore it. Shadow magick is all about navigating darkness, both internal and cosmic, assimilating its strengths and transforming it into something positive. Therefore, the apparently negative in your life may be used as fuel for advancement. In this exercise, only its harmful aspects will be offered up.

For this ritual, use a candle that is black throughout (rather than a white one with a black shell). First "magnetize" the candle by stroking it from the center both upward and downward, alternating strokes, whilst thinking of the emotional, spiritual, and physical habits you wish to shed. Imbue the candle with thoughts of the changes you wish to make. You might like to use some birch oil for this: it's incredibly evocative and smells like autumn in a bottle. This thick black unguent is ideal for imbuing your candle with the essence of creative decay and transformation. For an incense that also helps set the atmosphere, try a blend of rue and dragon's blood resin, which will bring focus and protection to your shadow magick. As you burn this, carve into your anointed candle a symbol or symbols of what you would like to shed or transform in your life.

As with all meditations in this book, the following may be read in a monotone style by a friend, or it may be prerecorded. It may also be memorized and put to application, or you can jot down short notes to refer to throughout if this doesn't hinder the meditation.

Alternatively, you could simply read the instructions step by step. After all, the act of reading itself stimulates the creative imagination. If prerecorded, allow plenty of time between steps, as there is no telling what events will take place moment to moment. Not to mention, time often ceases to exist in ritual. As with all rituals or meditations, read through it first before attempting it.

Nearly all of the meditations in this book begin with the same first step, for the sake of consistency. Some initial steps include additional special instructions, so be careful not to gloss over it every time, even if you already have a procedure for entering an altered state of ritual consciousness.

1. Construct sacred space around you by casting a circle and calling the quarters as you normally would. Sit comfortably to start the journey. Begin by clearing your mind. Take three deep breaths in through the nose, letting them out through the mouth. Let the thoughts of the day drift away like moving clouds. This is not the time to focus on what happened today or what you need to do tomorrow … let the common world dissipate as you enter the sacred terrain of the mind. For several minutes, sense the oxygen entering your nostrils and exiting your lips. Bring absolute focus to your breath.

2. Close your eyes and imagine yourself sitting in a black egg, the egg of your own nativity. Envision blackness all around you; you can sense the egg's shell containing you. Push away all daily concerns and thoughts of yourself; let your mind float in the nurturing darkness, losing all sense of your small life—as you would when looking up at a starry night sky. Sense this egg and solidify it around your body. Around you is nothing, just darkness; the same above and below you.

3. Your consciousness is germinal; your thoughts move in images now rather than words. Focus on this, allowing your mind to become more and more abstract. Visualize yourself freed of the negative cycles you no longer wish to participate in. Review these patterns in your mind, sending them out of your body and into the womblike atmosphere surrounding you. Eventually, as your anointed candle burns down and your senses are soothed by the incense and the candle's subtle smell of autumnal decay, the egg begins to slowly turn from black to dark purple, then to indigo.

4. Recite your own dark affirmation, or say these words: "By the Power of Night, by the Power of the Abyss, by the Power of Duality to create its equal and opposite reaction, I hereby shed my unwanted negative traits and replace them with knowledge, Gnosis, and compassion."

5. At this point, you might like to paint, write, chant, or sing something that affirms the termination of these patterns, but try to sense this transformation rather than being overly intellectual about it. If you do decide to create art of any kind, have any needed supplies at hand so you can remain in a trancelike state. Following that, slip back into the meditation and see the indigo-colored egg surrounding you.

6. Now visualize the Grim Reaper, as seen in your favorite Tarot deck or painting, riding toward you on horseback, scythe in hand. Sense his presence from far in the distance as he gets closer and closer to you. Hear the rhythmic percussion of the horse's trotting hooves, nearing you even more. Feel fear if that's what the image naturally evokes. Some may even feel a sense of comfort or relief.

7. The Reaper reaches you, swings his scythe at you, shatters the egg that surrounds you, and rides away from the scene as quickly as he came. An eerie illumination floods in from above, highlighting the shards. Look at these images in your mind and remember anything that occurs to you. Perhaps some of the broken shell looks like a symbol, a person, or an animal. Just gaze at it in your mind's eye and record what you see.

8. When you have gathered the information you were supposed to receive, emerge from your shattered past refreshed and reborn, and once the flame has burned past the symbols you have carved into the candle, burn a bit of your own hair in the flame to signify the transformation. Afterward, blow it out, saying "So mote it be."

9. When finished, smudge yourself with sage, frankincense, or a purifying incense blend. Deconstruct the circle and dismiss the quarters as you normally would. Relax, unwind, and take it easy for the rest of the evening.

Mystical Experience: The Paradox Behind the Veil

Mysticism is an invaluable part of spirituality and magick. I would go so far as to say that it lies at the *core* of legitimate spiritual practice. It would be incredibly progressive, I believe, if all spiritual traditions either retained or developed mystical practices, but that's not the reality of things. For modern spiritual seekers—particularly the magicians and Witches of our time—mysticism can serve as the mechanism for driving the spiritual journey home, solidifying our philosophies through personal experience.

I've heard a great number of Witches, magicians, and other spiritual people (of various paths) say that "something is missing" from their spiritual path. From my viewpoint, the missing element is the mystic experience; the transcendental connection—the oneness or Gnosis—with All Things. It's one thing to think and speak about oneness, another to actually experience it. Spiritual paths require that our worldview shift to a more expanded state of operation. The mystical experience accomplishes this, giving the practitioner (regardless of tradition) a connection to both the self and the surrounding world that simply *cannot* be captured in mere words.

I consider mystical experience an aspect of shadow magick because the practitioner emerges—internally, perceptually—into the subtle planes, that is, the dimensions of reality that ordinarily remain hidden to waking consciousness. Mysticism can be defined as the quest to attain *union with the divine.* The best-known and best-documented mystic traditions are the Kabbalism of the Jews and the Sufism of the Muslims, both of which I will review here. (The term is also spelled Cabbalism and Qabalism, among other ways.) A variety of Christian mystics through the ages have also had their experiences and philosophies well preserved.

Mysticism has always occurred within indigenous and Pagan cultures. Ancient and modern shamans can easily be called mystics because their practices reach into the Otherworlds for purposes of healing, divination, journeying, and magick.

Mystical thought often plays a key role in modern magickal practice, though many practitioners might not call it that. Unfortunately, a number of people drawn to the esoteric, occult, and magickal realms seek to alter the external world to their fancy rather than focus on the internal mechanisms that actually shape it.

In classical times, those who subscribed to Gnostic thought emphasized one's own transcendence into mystical states of awareness as a means of escaping the material world. Gnosticism is a classical religious movement and philosophy that holds that we, as humans, must escape our current mundane situation and return to a union with Spirit. Gnosis, meaning "saving wisdom," implies the reunification of man with God, so that we may understand our true nature and awaken from the dream that is common reality. Modern-day Gnostics also emphasize this ideology, as do some neo-mystical systems such as chaos magick and ceremonial orders. By the same token, many adherents of Eastern religions speak of experiences of oneness, enlightenment, and transcendence—though more often than not, these terms describe a perpetual state of being rather than an ephemeral one.

Judaism, Islam, and Christianity have long held strict religious standards. Thus, unsurprisingly, the pursuit of mystical experience hasn't always been viewed with empathetic kindness. Still, traditional doctrinaire religions have taken a variety of views of the place of the mystic. In Catholicism, mysticism is generally an honored practice (albeit, and in my opinion unfortunately, only pursued by the few), but one set clearly apart from everyday Catholicism; many of its mystics are actually regarded as saints and venerable figures. Of the branches in the Christian movement, Eastern Orthodoxy tends to have the most respect for mystical traditions, whereas the Protestant Reformation of the sixteenth century did much to suppress mystical thought by maligning it in the public eye. Again, every tradition's stance on the mystic is different.

In a mystical experience, a person perceives a personal unity with the divine. This is experiencing Spirit. For older, more animistic traditions, the divine is perceived as nature, or forces thereof. Of course monotheistic societies have perceived mystical union as being with God, while polytheistic societies have perceived it as being with either a number of gods or an individual deity depending on a person's spiritual alignments, such as with cults or tribes devoted to serving a specific godhead. Pantheistic and animistic societies seem to experience a unity with all things; a state of oneness with the All, due to their view of Spirit as permeating all things.

A number of the features of the mystical experience have been distinguished by religious scholars, such as the twentieth-century professor of mysticism W. T. Stace. For our purposes, I include these points to further compare our own theurgic[1] practices with those already documented. Many of the points made here have been influenced by the teachings of University of Montana professor Paul A. Dietrich.

A number of characteristics can define mysticism and accounts of mystical experiences.

- Ineffability: The sense that the experience is beyond the realm of words and impossible to accurately convey—it is purely experiential.

- Transcendence: The feeling that one has psychologically transcended space and time.

- Unity: The feeling of absolute oneness with the divine.

- Equanimity: Feelings of absolute peace, bliss, joy, and well-being.

- Passivity: The feeling that one is being acted upon rather than being an actor.

- Paradoxical experience: Feeling the governing forces of reality and understanding the polarity of existence, often realizing that "everything exists, yet simultaneously nothing all at exists."

- Persisting changes: The life-changing events provoked by the mystical experience; in many cases, this is conversion to a particular mystic tradition.

Jewish Mysticism and the Qabalah

Allow me to quickly review some aspects of traditional Judaism and how they intertwine with mystic branches of the religion, including the tradition of Kabbalism (Qabalism).

Judaism is focused on written tradition and, unlike many religions, relies heavily on ancient commentary and rabbinic interpretations of canonical texts. The Hebrew Bible, also called the *Tanakh*, includes the Torah, also known as the Law of Moses or the Five Books of Moses. This alludes to Genesis, Exodus, Leviticus, Numbers, and Deuteronomy. The Christian Old Testament includes these Hebrew-based scriptures, though the order in which they appear varies between the Hebrew Bible and the Old Testament.

Judaism emphasizes the practice of orthodoxy (called *orthopraxy*), and traditional Jews focus their lives on *mitzvoth*: pious deeds done with spiritually correct intention. In many ways, the Jewish tradition relies on *doing* the right thing over simply *believing* a certain way. Mitzvoth is said to have cosmic significance and is the act of aligning oneself with Holy Law.

Within Judaism, the first documented major mystical branch is called the Ma'aseh Merkabah ("Work of the Chariot"). This mystical system relies on the notion that a pious Jew may be carried through the heavenly spheres on a Holy Throne or Chariot (the Merkabah). This

Achieving the Mystical State

Twentieth-century philosopher Abraham Maslow pointed out that "peak" mystical experiences could occur at various times such as during prayer, whilst walking on the beach, whilst making love, and so on. Even if it's unexpected, one can have a true mystical experience that defies description in words. Certainly, the idea of peak experiences could be expanded to encompass other experiences directly aimed at unification with the divine, including deep meditation, ritual, dancing, playing music, sweatlodge practices, spiritual drug use, and ascetic practices—all of which have spiritually transcendental potential. Maslow also determined that people with non-hostile, self-actualized states of being, particularly those with humility and respect, those who are personable and have a sense of humor (all of which are *spiritual* qualities in my eyes), were more likely to experience and report mystical awareness.

Mystical experiences by way of mind-altering substances, if I may expand on this particular method, are commonplace in the modern day. Many would argue that drugs—particularly natural drugs such as marijuana, psychedelic mushrooms, peyote, *Salvia divinorum*, and so on—are divine gifts for attaining unification with the spiritual realms. I agree wholeheartedly, provided these experiences are approached with proper planning, research, and mindfulness of the substance consumed. Uses of certain drugs under certain circumstances can, do, and historically have induced intense mystical experiences and deep awareness of the interconnectedness of all things.

But with this "substance shortcut," some users associate the experience with the influence of the drug itself rather than the influence of the divine. It doesn't help that the vast majority of people who use drugs don't take them with the purpose of attaining mystical union with the divine. One's approach and one's environment, both externally and internally, greatly construct the phenomena one experiences.

Chariot is mentioned in the book of Ezekiel in the Hebrew Bible and was viewed by Jewish mystics as an analogy for God's eminence and his influence on the realm of humankind. The tradition examines this Holy Throne in detail, including its seven heavens and angelic inhabitants. Merkabah mystics focused on experiencing heaven from the earthly realm—why wait?!

A book called the *Sepher ha-Zohar* is particularly significant to Jewish mystics and of utmost importance to modern Kabbalah (discussed in a minute). Also called the Zohar, the Book of Splendor, the Book of Radiance, the Book of Lights, and the Book of Enlightenment, the Zohar is an exegetic and hermeneutic *midrash*, meaning that it is both a mystical interpretation of and commentary about a sacred text—in this case, the Torah. The Zohar's written style is esoteric, meditational, and novelistic. It is meant to comment on the Torah, but also contains a wide array of additional material including stories, narratives, and Kabbalistic treatises.

The Zohar was long accredited to a second-century Jew called Rabbi Shim'on (Simeon bar Yohai), who is said to have copied it from an even more ancient sacred book. According to Moses de León of Guadalajara, the Zohar was passed from teacher to student over many generations, eventually making its way to Moses de León in Spain in the late thirteenth century. However, the more recent discoveries of scholar Gershom Scholem (who passed away in 1982) suggest that the Zohar was almost undoubtedly written by Moses de León himself, a theory with which nineteenth-century Jewish historian Heinrich Graetz concurred. Regardless of authorship, the Zohar is considered a holy text of Jewish mysticism by traditional Kabbalists.

It was from a little-known branch of Jewish mysticism called the Ma'aseh Bershith ("Work of Creation") that one of the documents most influential to the development of the Kabbalah emerged.

In his book *Major Trends in Jewish Mysticism*, Gershom Scholem writes, "The existence of speculative Gnostic tendencies in the immediate neighborhood of Merkabah mysticism has its parallel in the writings grouped together under the name of *Maaseh Bereshith*. These include a document [the *Sepher Yetzirah*] ... which represents a theoretical approach to the problems of cosmology and cosmogony."[2]

The *Sepher Yetzirah* chronicles the development of reality. It is an early theosophical text, the first document known to mention the Tree of Life. Compact yet informative, the text was heavily influenced by Greek and Hellenistic thought, and is connected with early Jewish mysticism because of its emphasis on theurgic magickal practice. The book is often attributed to Rabbi Akiba Ben Joseph (Rebbi Akiva) around the year 100 CE. This authorship is possible, as modern scholars estimate its origins between 100 BCE and 900 CE. Earlier traditional sources attribute it to the prophet Abraham himself, though it is almost certainly *pseudepigraphical*, that is, a book falsely attributed to another author in order to establish its validity—either a single "ghostwriter" or a collection of individuals, as in most cases. Many books of both the Hebrew and Christian Bibles are pseudepigraphical, as is the Zohar of early Kabbalism. (The Greek *Odyssey* and *Iliad*, accredited to Homer, may also be pseudepigraphical.)

It is from *Sepher Yetzirah* that we receive the concepts of the Kabbalistic Tree of Life, including descriptions of the Sephiroth (the spheres on the tree, also called the "fruits," "emanations," and "lights") and the paths connecting them. The twenty-two letters of the Hebrew alphabet correspond to these paths, and planetary associations are aligned with the Sephiroth. A seemingly endless number of correspondences to these Sephiroth and paths, including Tarot cards, colors, scents, herbs, deities, stones, incenses, elements, materials, symbols, emotions, areas of the body, and many more, are currently recognized within the Qabalah of the Western Mystery Tradition, and much of this information was drawn from the Book of Formation.

Modern esoteric (Hermetic) Qabalism is the most significant to modern magicians, and is often spelled as such to distinguish it from traditional Jewish Kabbalism (or Cabalism) or any of its subsequent Christian interpretations. This esoteric, magickal Qabalah was greatly developed by Eliphas Lévi in the nineteenth century upon his studies of the traditional Kabbalah and his application of Hermeticism and comparative mythology. It was later significantly expounded upon by the Hermetic Order of the Golden Dawn, and it is from their teachings that many current views, practices, and metaphysical associations of the Tree of Life have entered modern esoteric circles.

Da'ath and Shadow Magick

Within the Western Mystery Tradition, the sephira Da'ath (Da'at) on the Tree of Life can be seen as resonating with the essence of shadow magick. Da'ath is called the eleventh, or hidden, sephira. This Hebrew word means "knowledge" and sounds surprisingly like the word "death" in English.

Though sometimes called "the non-sephira," this sphere, whose obscure origins are still debated, can be viewed as a shadowlike integration of the energies of the tree's upper fruits (the *supernal triad*), that is, Kether, Binah, and Chokmah. Da'ath is situated on the Tree of Life in this area, which is called the Abyss. The Abyss is the space between the supernal triad and the others, the area where the ego, or sense of self, is released when journeying the Tree. Some believe that Da'ath acts as a seed for the upper spheres or as an invisible emanation of their excess energy. Unlike the Tree's other spheres, the energy of Da'ath is so enigmatic in nature that many Qabalists do not recognize it in their practices. Because Da'ath is not definitive, it is often depicted with a dotted line on the Tree of Life, if it is depicted at all.

Though some amount of darkness exists in each sephira, some occultists believe Da'ath to be the area in which the soul travels during the sorrowful Dark Night of the Soul, while others equate that experience to Binah. Like a black hole, the energy of Da'ath confronts us with the truth of impermanence, reminding us that nothing is fixed. It can be seen as the Underworld sephira, representing not only the depths of personal internal darkness, but also religious myths such as the Pagan Descent of the Goddess (particularly in the Greek pantheon) and the scriptural fall from Eden. Of course, associations such as these depend entirely on the view of the Qabalist or Kabbalist, or of their specific tradition.

Da'ath embodies all that is mysterious and urges us to face both sides of our human nature. Author Rachel Pollock, in her book *The Kabbalah Tree: A Journey of Balance & Growth*, gives Da'ath psycho-sexual associations, assuming it to be the place of balance between the genders (and any two polarities) wherein males metaphorically become females and females males. This reinforces the idea of Da'ath as a place of paradoxical polarity; of both nothing and everything ... the ultimate spiritual dichotomy.

Da'ath is situated between two polarities, and access is most favorable around Samhain. As a further correspondence, Da'ath can be seen as the gateway between two worlds: that of the living and that of the dead. Perhaps this is the point on the map in which souls depart from the physical world and enter the light of the Afterworld. In accordance with the

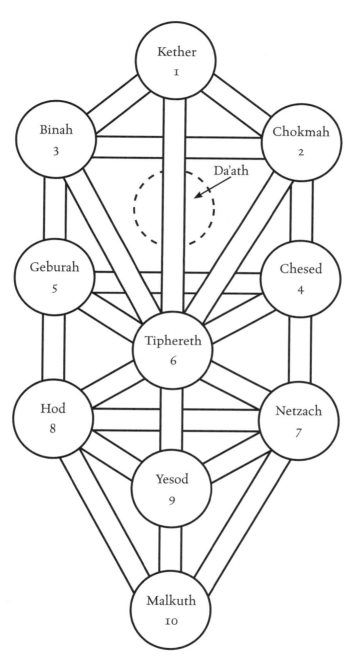

The Qabalistic Tree of Life, with an outline for Da'ath.

Judeo-Christian worldview, it may be seen as the invisible realm where God enters and exits from the earth planes to the others and can be seen as the seat of life or consciousness. Qabalists often believe that Da'ath is the Tree's dark portal, leading to Hell-like realms of demons on the dark side of the Tree, which is often called the Qlippothic realm.

Da'ath is situated in the Middle Pillar of the Tree and aligns with the throat chakra on the human body. Because Da'ath exists on the Middle Pillar, it would be foolish to think that it's all bad. Qabalists have reported mistaking Da'ath for Kether in their magickal or meditative work, proclaiming it to be dangerous territory. Others believe that Da'ath is actually a lesser emanation of Kether (absolute enlightenment), similar to Tiphareth. As you can see, there are many views of what Da'ath truly is. For this reason it is excluded from some depictions of the Tree, though it remains a part of it in essence nonetheless. In truth, everyone's experiences with the Sephiroth are quite different and each sphere holds a somewhat subjective meaning for every magician.

Each Qabalistic sephira embodies a different vibration or energy pattern that can be seen in immediate reality. Taking this idea further, each person vibrates with a particular sephira over another. For example, a highly intellectual person would vibrate with the sphere Hod, while a daydreamer might vibrate with Hod's equal-opposite, Netzach. Da'ath is relevant to shadow magick because it embodies the mysterious and the unknowable.

This does not mean that our attunement to a certain sephira is fixed. In fact, it's highly mutable. However, many people stay anchored to a particular vibratory state and branch out, always coming back to the base. Even though someone is almost always loving and compassionate (characteristic of Chesed), that doesn't mean the person cannot feel impassioned aggression (characteristic of Geburah). For people who often contemplate the darkness (in whatever form) or are introspective in a highly emotional way, Da'ath can be seen as that metaphorical base.

If you feel trapped within barriers of over-introspection and unhealthy depression, I would recommend researching the Qabalah as part of your magickal path. Both Qabalism and balanced Witchcraft identify and work with darkness as a tool for spiritual expansion. If you end up working with Da'ath ritualistically or meditatively, I recommend you not try to comprehend the sphere in its entirety. Simply know that it exists and that you may tend to gravitate toward its energy. Trying to fully understand Da'ath is like trying to fully understand the reality of death: it is impossible without actually experiencing death itself. Da'ath is seen by many as a black hole of trickery that can suck people in deeper and deeper as they feel their knowledge of it expanding. It's also for this reason that when we emerge from a place of absolute sadness and darkness, having refused to be swallowed by it, we come out stronger and more aware of the shadow—our own Da'ath—as a result.

The Mystical Valleys of Sufism

The Sufi tradition of Islamic mysticism originated as a response to traditional Arabian ideologies.[3] Sufis place ultimate confidence in the *Shahadah* (one of the five Pillars of Din), or the profession of faith that "there is no god but God." Similarly, they believe that "all things are God (Allah)." This animistic view is an aspect of *tawhid*, an Arabic term for the Unity of Being. Sufis also view the term *jihad* as referencing the spiritual seeker's challenge to align with God, and the struggles of acquiring virtues in place of vices, though the term is frequently used to refer to the Islamic view of a "holy war on behalf of God."

The word I*slam* means "surrendering to God's will." The word *Sufi* most likely comes from the Arabic word *suf*, referring to the coarse woolen garments that early Islamic mystics wore both to renounce materialism and to criticize the opulence throughout the Middle East.

Sufis interpret the Qur'an (Koran) in the manner that Kabbalists interpret the Zohar. Mohammad, the prophet of Islam, died in 632 CE, the Qur'an was edited around 650, and Sufism is commonly accepted as having begun in the ninth century.

Similarly to the birth of mystical commentaries from the Kabbalistic movement, a vast collection of poetry and literature arose from Sufism. The most famous Sufi poet is probably Rumi, an esoteric writer and the founder of the Mevlevi, the order of "whirling" Dervishes.

But an earlier Islamic mystic writer was Farid ud-Din Attar, who influenced many of Rumi's viewpoints and writings. One of Attar's most renowned works is the *Conference of the Birds*, an allegorical story featuring a variety of birds for characters. This metaphorical writing style has been used throughout history as a way to convey viewpoints. In this case, each bird represents a particular human vice, or sin as some would have it. Birds are a cross-culturally religious symbol of the soul, and their flight can represent a person's spiritual freedom and journey to higher consciousness. Here, Attar maps this journey in seven precise stages called "valleys." These stages encompass common mystical ideas found both within and outside of Sufism. These mystical valleys are said to be augmentative, in that the first leads to the second, which leads to the third, and so forth. Because of the strong identification that many mystics, both Sufi and otherwise, feel with these stages, let us review them here:

I. THE VALLEY OF THE QUEST

The first valley refers to the altruistic zeal or desire to embark on the path leading to the unity of Self and Spirit. Though hardships are a constant, a person's unquenchable desire to align with the divine serves as fuel to the fire of endurance and progression. When this solid motivation is held on to, the succeeding stages become available.

II. THE VALLEY OF LOVE

This valley refers to the state of absolute love for God and the spiritual journey. Affective rather than effective, this journey is more intimately connected to the emotional body than to the intellectual mind. Even if nothing else seems to remain, the limitless energy of transcendental love allows the spirit to hold on. This love is described as a consuming allegorical fire, within which all beings on the spiritual path must burn in the ecstasy of Spirit.

III. THE VALLEY OF KNOWLEDGE

This stage points to actual insight into the reality of mystical states of consciousness. Transformative rather than informative, this knowledge offers but a glimpse into the constant state of being available to spiritual seekers if they continue on the journey. There are various outlets of expression for this insight, an endless variety of individual perceptions from which this knowledge can arise.

IV. THE VALLEY OF DETACHMENT

A number of spiritual traditions also endorse this idea. A person must let go not only of "worldly" constraints, but of the very idea of enlightenment itself. Further, the seeker mush detach from the ego—the entire identity of "self"—to deconstruct the internal blockages that naturally hinder the journey. This concept affirms a person's extraordinary yet minute place in the cosmos.

V. THE VALLEY OF UNITY

Whereas the Valley of Knowledge is a reflection of the whole, the Valley of Unity is an unchanging integration of the Self and Spirit as one. This is the mystic's desired state of consciousness; a sustained experience of the interrelatedness of all things. From this platform, the greater picture comes into focus. Adherents of Eastern religion would call this oneness or enlightenment.

VI. THE VALLEY OF BEWILDERMENT

The path of the mystic doesn't simply stop at the stage of Unity. "Bewilderment" refers to a person's reintroduction into the world after having experienced full metaphysical awareness. This can be called a reintegration or rehumanization, in that the mystical state of consciousness must blend with the terrestrial. This is the valley of lamentation, of absolute sorrow and void. Here, one does not know whether one *is* or *is not*. The experience of the paradox of all things leads to this state of spiritual shock: a state of awe for the experience of existence itself.

VII. THE VALLEY OF POVERTY

A curious final step, the Valley of Poverty is a declaration of nothingness. This is "obscure oblivion," a final rejection of the self and its vices. Here, the notion of Self is permanently forgotten. It is the ultimate annihilation of the hallucinatory view of the life-charade. This perception is beyond rational comprehension and relies on experience alone. Here, self-consciousness is nonexistent, and two reunite as one.

---

1. Ritual magick practices aimed at self-transformation.

2. Gershom Scholem, *Major Trends in Jewish Mysticism*. New York: Schocken Books, 1946, 75.

3. This does not take into account the variants between Shia and Sunni Sufism, whose differences are too vast to cover here, and whose practices diverge in both ideology and association with orthodox Islam.

II
The External Shadow

One theory I favour is that the self-proclaimed "white Witches" tend to identify far too heavily with the "light" … This means that the darker sides of their nature, finding no honest expression, become suppressed into the subconscious. Since it is in these deeper realms of mind that the power of magick resides, this suppressed darkness tends to make itself known and give its force to their conjurations. Whilst such coveners are always harking on about "perfect love and perfect trust," they seem to me to spend an awful lot of time stabbing their athamé into each other's backs.

— NATHANIEL J. HARRIS
Witcha: A Book of Cunning

Invocation and Godform Assumption

Invocation refers to the act of drawing certain energies from outside oneself either into one's own body or, by some interpretations, into the magickal vicinity. This practice is also called "drawing down" in some traditions. I believe shadow magick is particularly relevant to this art: invocation is ultimately a mystical act of merging with the unseen, as one calls forth a deity not only from the astral plane, but into one's own person. The process of deital channeling is that of reaching through the veil of reality and tapping into the external energies of human archetypes, which all gods are.

Often, Witches simply use the term *invocation* to refer to the act of calling forth energies. This is just a matter of terminology. Technically, *invocation* only refers to inviting energies, such as a deity or ancestral spirit, into oneself. In contrast, the act of *calling forth* energies is also called *summoning*, such as asking a deity or spirit for assistance, or when calling the Watchtowers. Summoning an entity into manifestation is called *evocation*, as is the case with many forms of angelic and demonic magick.

The term *journeying*, on the other hand, refers to a person traveling astrally, in some manner, to a deity's terrain. The practitioner goes into a deeply meditative state and meets the deity on the astral plane. Once aligned, the journeyer relays messages from the spirit. These messages could take the form of entire streaming sentences, or they might be random phrases, sounds, and foreign speech including colors, names, and cryptic words that are seemingly nonsensical. A person who practices this frequently, especially with one particular deity, is a good candidate to advance to full godform assumption. If you wish to practice invocation but have no experience in the field, it's best to become comfortable and adept at journeying first.

For clarity's sake, I will use the terms *godform assumption*, *aspecting*, and *drawing down* synonymously with *invocation*, referring to the act of pulling an actual deity or spirit into your person. It is an act of oracular mediumship that is usually reserved for Priests and Priestesses in modern Witchcraft.

In my personal spiritual system, godform assumption is only practiced by Priests and Priestesses, and requires heavy training, research, and preparation. Invocation is not something to take lightly; it's both a tribal and an advanced Witchcraft practice—something I wouldn't hesitate to call high magick—and can be extremely jarring and dangerous if approached improperly.

A number of shamanic and indigenous cultures invoke deities regularly, incorporating such practices as drumming, yelling, and ecstatic dance into their ceremonies to strengthen the process. The results are profound. Successful deital invocations, pushing the channeler aside, allow the god or ancestral spirit to fully take the body over. This is seen frequently in Vodou, in which the Priests and Priestesses invoke the Lwa—the spirits of Haitian Vodou—the process of which is called *spirit possession*.

Many cultures still practice invocation as part of their common ritualistic observances. In Nepal, for example, animistic tribal Hindus, who are called the Newa, practice spirit possession. In this full-moon ritual a *Dhamini* invokes an ancestor, addresses the crowd, and performs shamanic healings individually. He or she also feeds or places cooked rice on ritual attendees in an act of bestowing blessings. In the invocation, the Dhamini crouches, so as to "carry" the deity on his or her back. A ritual assistant accepts offerings to give to the deity and helps the Dhamini during the possession.

Some Witches who practice godform assumption don't remember a thing afterward about what was said, having been a trance-channel the entire time, the waking self pushed completely aside by the deital or spiritual energy. Priest and Priestess are consciously removed from themselves. Their speech patterns, movements, and behavior noticeably change to fit the deity's or spirit's, which may be entirely separate from the invoker's typical behavior. When this happens, the invoker doesn't remember anything about the experience. This most extreme version occurs only when the person has practiced deital invocation for many years (or at least has a natural disposition for oracular powers). Most Witches and magicians remember portions of the experience but not the whole. Others remember every bit of it, though this is rare. I like to mark invocations by percentages; depending on the ritual, I often range from about 65 percent invoked and 35 percent conscious, to 85 percent invoked and 15 percent conscious. These ratio estimates are a good way to record and reflect on the experience.

When invoked, practitioners tend to take a backseat to the deity called in; it's much like watching a film, but from the actor's perspective. It can also be likened to dreaming. Most practitioners call this "stepping back," and it seems to be the most common experience when assuming a godform. It's also good to keep in mind that every experience is different, affecting each practitioner uniquely.

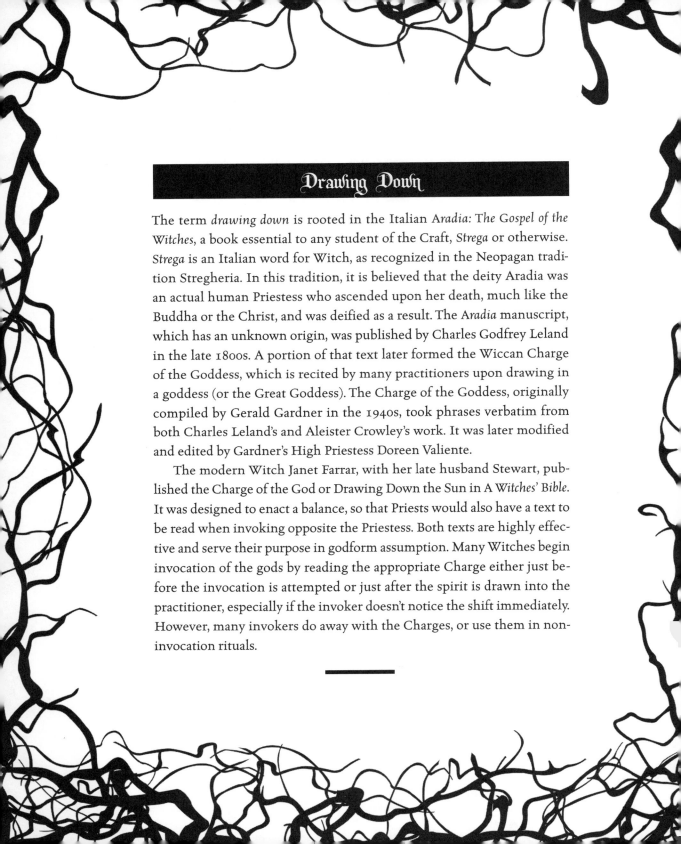

Drawing Down

The term *drawing down* is rooted in the Italian *Aradia: The Gospel of the Witches*, a book essential to any student of the Craft, *Strega* or otherwise. *Strega* is an Italian word for Witch, as recognized in the Neopagan tradition Stregheria. In this tradition, it is believed that the deity Aradia was an actual human Priestess who ascended upon her death, much like the Buddha or the Christ, and was deified as a result. The *Aradia* manuscript, which has an unknown origin, was published by Charles Godfrey Leland in the late 1800s. A portion of that text later formed the Wiccan Charge of the Goddess, which is recited by many practitioners upon drawing in a goddess (or the Great Goddess). The Charge of the Goddess, originally compiled by Gerald Gardner in the 1940s, took phrases verbatim from both Charles Leland's and Aleister Crowley's work. It was later modified and edited by Gardner's High Priestess Doreen Valiente.

The modern Witch Janet Farrar, with her late husband Stewart, published the Charge of the God or Drawing Down the Sun in *A Witches' Bible*. It was designed to enact a balance, so that Priests would also have a text to be read when invoking opposite the Priestess. Both texts are highly effective and serve their purpose in godform assumption. Many Witches begin invocation of the gods by reading the appropriate Charge either just before the invocation is attempted or just after the spirit is drawn into the practitioner, especially if the invoker doesn't notice the shift immediately. However, many invokers do away with the Charges, or use them in non-invocation rituals.

I recall one of my first experiences with deital invocation when I was acting as High Priest for a Beltane ritual. It was a circle of thirteen practitioners out in the woods at a friend's cabin, and I was to invoke Cernnunos. I was wearing the appropriate robes, veils, crowns, and makeup to align with his essence, and holding the adorned skull of a deer. The ritual assistant recited the Words of Power to help with the invocation while the rest of the group marched around the circle deosil chanting "Cernnunos, Cernnunos, Cernnunos..." My eyes began to close and I saw my friend's dog Herkie trotting along with the rest of the group as if he was just another practitioner. It was as if he was invoking Cernnunos along with the rest of them, and the surreality of it helped me enter a trancelike state. From there, I began to perceive faeries and astral beings circling the space. My eyes closed and a surge of power rushed through me as I surrendered to the energy with perfect trust. Upon closing my eyes, every part of my body began to tingle. My ego-thoughts ceased to be, and all that existed was sensation. I could feel the souls of the beings walking around me while I transcended normal time. Cernnunos was there—inside me, taking over my normal self and shining through like a beacon of pure sunlight. "My" eyes opened and with an enormous grin, the Horned One began to address the crowd, following that with individual consultations. I don't remember too much about what was said, but I was told afterward that it was profound and meaningful. For me, each invocation since then has become easier and more comfortable.

Personally, after practicing deital invocation, I cannot function for the rest of the night as I normally would. I need a series of grounding exercises and meditations, food, a bath, and a ridiculously long night's sleep. This is true for many practitioners, but over time, coming back from a trance state to waking life becomes less difficult. It becomes easier to separate the self from the deity if proper chakra exercises are done beforehand and energy is worked to secure a separation between the practitioner and the entity.

During the rite, each member of the Coven or group of practitioners should address questions and responses to the present deity, not to the Priest or Priestess who is acting as a conduit. In this setting, the one who aspects the deity is transformed *into* that being. During the experience, the person often delivers important messages to the group or the Coven, communicates symbolically (depending on the deity), and gives insight and prophecy to individual seekers. I've learned from my experiences that preparing proper offerings beforehand is a *must*.

When a deity is invoked, the actual Priest or Priestess who called the deity in mustn't be held responsible for what happens next. Usually, that person has little to no say in how the deity is channeled. Still, this is not an excuse for the Priest or Priestess to exaggerate the level of invocation, do inappropriate things, and put it all off as the deity's doing. Not only is that incredibly disrespectful to the deity, but those with a discerning eye can see what belongs to the invoker, and what belongs to the invoked. At the same time, the practitioner shouldn't hold back if he or she is legitimately invoked, especially if a ritual assistant is there to guide the process.

Some Covens and Pagan training systems require the third-degree initiate to undergo a drawing down of a deity of a different gender. Over time, it's spiritually rewarding to invoke deities who are both like and unlike you. While it may be easier to invoke a god, goddess, or spirit who you personally resonate with or feel is your patron, it's essential to mix this up and, eventually, come to invoke entities who oppose your general personality.

In his book *Magick in Theory and Practice*, Aleister Crowley says this about godform assumption: "The danger of ceremonial magick—the subtlest and deepest danger—is this: that the magician will naturally tend to invoke that partial being which most strongly appeals to him, so that his natural excess in that direction will be still further exaggerated."[1]

Aspects of Aspecting

Invoking—also called aspecting—does have plenty of dangers, and I don't recommend trying it unless you have a firm understanding of the workings of magick, ideally based on years of study in the Craft or another magickal system. The biggest danger is that if the deity is not properly channeled, the invoker will have trouble coming back to his or her own body and may suffer for days trying to realign. The best way to prepare for invocation is, of course, to study and fully investigate the deity who will be drawn in. All who will be present should do this study, not only the invoker—*or* the Priest or Priestess should inform them of the deity's mythos if they're unfamiliar with it. It's reckless to draw a deity into your person without knowing who or what it is. Especially at first, it's best to work with a deity of your own gender whose characteristics somewhat match your own: the experience will be less shocking, with less potential for trauma.

It takes time to work through the stages of light- to heavy-deital invocation. If you are attempting this magick, begin by working in small doses with a deity you have already familiarized yourself with for years, perhaps through *journeying*, as discussed above, or through personal devotion and ritualistic work. The invoker *must* be familiar with the deity's energy pattern, as it will be merged with his or her own.

In a more immediate sense, before the drawing down is attempted, the chakras must be opened in sacred space, so that the person is entirely receptive to the chosen deity. This is particularly true for Muladhara and Sahasrara, the Sanskrit terms for the base and crown chakras. When the chakras are opened, the invoker becomes an open channel of energy, allowing the deity to secure him- or herself in the body. After the process is completed and the deity has either up and left or has been thanked and dismissed, the invoker's chakras must be closed so that their own energy doesn't "leak" for any amount of time.

Godform assumption is usually done with the help of a Craft-experienced assistant. This person may read, chant, or otherwise raise energy to better call the deity forth. The assistant also closely monitors the magickal partner who is invoking, and can dismiss the deity if for some reason the deity refuses to let go or things get a bit too intense. In most cases, this isn't a worry, but is certainly a possibility.

Either specific deities or "greater deities" can be invoked. It's a good idea to begin the practice by working with a deity who is an embodiment of nature—a generalized form of the God or Goddess. (This practice is actually traditional in Gardnerian and Alexandrian Witchcraft.) Of course, the deity should be properly attuned to the season: for example, the Holly King would not be drawn down at the height of summer! Nature deities often embody properties of the seasonal tide; they may not have the well-defined characteristics that many more individualistic deities do. Therefore, working with them can be easier and more comprehensible, especially for those beginning the practice.

There are many ways to connect to a deity successfully. Aside from the necessary precautions and dedication, attendees can help draw the deital essence forth by chanting, drumming, and music-making, for example. The invoker may wish to dress up as the deity of choice, using masks, veils, jewelry, and garb. This is called *guising*, and it offers the deity an environment closer to his or her own natural or mythologized structure, attuning the invoker more deeply at the same time. The surrounding décor can also be attuned to the deity's mythology to better conduct him or her into the ritual space and make it a more comfortable setting for the high magickal act.

Pagan author Christopher Penczak, in a blog entry, has noted some further possibilities for invocations:

One of the things I like most about Pagan magick is the circle, and how all have an important place in the circle, not just the High Priest or Priestess. I'd like to see ritual possibilities where more than one person is aspected or invoked, and having rituals where multiple people are blended with divinity to perform the ritual in a highly inspired state. I think that might be part of our evolution, making the ritual training ground for everybody who desires to learn more about invoking divinity, from the traditional gods of myth to their own higher starry selves. Though I would say most groups I've worked with probably aren't ready for it, I think that this might be where the Pagan community, or at least an aspect of it, is heading. Interesting times, no?[2]

Fasting and Self-Sacrifice

As cross-cultural spiritual practices of endurance and cleansing, fasting and other forms of self-sacrifice can benefit any person practicing magickal spirituality.

With the act of abstinence comes a recognizable sense of emptiness; a cycle of fulfillment is replaced by a void. For the spiritualist, this space can be filled with divine light, thus replacing the ordinary with the sacred. Disciplining oneself through fasting or something similar can easily be a practice of spiritual devotion; self-sacrifice in any form is a dedication to the higher planes by a willful denial of desires. What material dependencies do we put ahead of our spiritual focuses? Fasting can illuminate many important issues.

Fasting is indeed a form of shadow magick: by restricting external stimuli, it forces practitioners to face themselves and their habits. Mental states and issues that were once unseen tend to tumble into focus during a fast. Portions of the self are questioned, and meanwhile the surrounding world seems to take on a new hue. Perspectives on the external world change drastically as the self is alchemized through the experience. As with taking a drug, one's perceptions change permanently, even if only to a small degree. Fasting brings a person out of the ordinary state of consciousness by restricting or altering usual habits. It's no wonder that fasting and other forms of self-sacrifice have long been practiced for cultivating self-awareness.

A Look at Fasting

Fasting is a form of abstinence that has been practiced in spiritual cultures for many centuries. Though each culture has used fasting for a variety of purposes, the most common ones are to gain self-awareness and communion with Spirit. This mystical connection is often gained through psychic vision during a fast. Any type of fasting practice forces a person to abstain from a regular cycle in order to let go of attachments. Fasting affirms one's placement in the Game of Reality by reassuring the practitioner that this plane and its comforts are but temporary stimuli.

Physically, the body is attached to a number of things necessary to function, such as air, water, food, shelter, and sexual release. In Western culture, excess is often socially encouraged, if not demanded! Limiting and rationing our physical necessities can be extremely trying in a society of overabundant hedonism. Spiritually, challenging one's own dependence on such things is one of the most beneficial things a person can do.

The body, or I should say the *mind*, is also attached to sensory experience beyond physical necessity. We may find ourselves addicted to certain modes of behavior, mindsets, or substances that may not exactly be beneficial in the long run. Fasting regularly from such dependencies shocks the mind and body out of habitual patterns that could gain unhealthy momentum over time. It is essential that we examine and bring to light our attachments, and anything on this plane that we may cling to, so we can see whatever is inhibiting our spiritual potential.

Personally, I dedicated a year and a day to learning the art of fasting and self-sacrifice, one of the conditions of the second year of Priesthood or Priesthood in the shadow magick tradition Opus Aima Obscuræ. (Much of the information and material in this section comes from that tradition, and the teachings of Priestess Estha McNevin.) Each full moon during that year heralded a different type of fast for me to learn. I think it's essential for anyone pursuing higher realms of spirituality to test the limits of the mind and body, pushing the spirit through initiatory levels of experiential knowledge.

One of the most important lessons was to simply *endure* and remain steadfast. Constantly complaining about the difficulty of a fast takes energy away from the sacrifice. When an overabundance of negativity arises during fasting, much of it is subconscious darkness reemerging, just aching to be released. Anger and sadness are easy filters—or covers—for energy that wishes to depart, and these emotions must both be recognized and analyzed. What are their roots? How are they connected to the fast itself? How can you constructively release these energies without letting them spiral out of control?

Each type of fast produces a different effect; for example, abstaining from food may produce lightheadedness, while abstaining from sexual release may produce frustration. One may feel anything from agitation and upset to increased energy and optimism—it entirely depends on what is being sacrificed and the practitioner's approach, both of which influence the intensity of the fast. In my experience, common effects are cravings (obviously), mood swings, spiritual visions, sensations of disconnectedness from the physical body (a "lightness of being"), sorrow, ecstasy, mental flight, awareness of the energetic body and the etheric planes, lethargy and weakness, increased dream activity, headaches, borderline emotional breakdowns, heightened senses, awareness of mental clutter, and mental clarity.

In some of the longer and more tedious fasts, the line may blur between the feeling of temporary "insanity" and the feeling of Gnosis or union with Spirit. The contrast between "pleasants" and "unpleasants" is less apparent. After experiencing the fast, a sense of holistic renewal and spiritual accomplishment occurs.

Cross-Cultural Fasting

Fasting is a worldwide religious practice. It is perhaps best known in association with Hinduism, as it is interwoven heavily into India's rich spiritual tradition.

Traditional Hindus observe a number of food fasts throughout the year. The Hindu year has twelve lunar months, each with additional solar correspondences; there are many variations on the traditional Indian calendar. Hindu fasts are frequently associated with various deities and serve to honor them. Often, the decision to observe a deity's holy day depends on personal preference or on the customs of each individual Hindu sect. There seem to be many fasts and *vratas* (vows) associated with deital celebrations in the four lunar months called Chaturmasya, during which Vishnu is said to sleep. This correlates with the rainy season in India, also called the monsoon season. The last of these four months is Kartika, which occurs either on the seventh or eighth month of the year, depending on the Indian calendar utilized. Many Hindus restrict themselves to one meal a day during Kartika, and practice various specific fasts during the whole period of Chaturmasya.

Fasting is incorporated in the stories of many deities and is reenacted as a form of celebration to align with each god and goddess. Many of the stories carry social and political messages in addition to spiritual ones, helping to perpetuate certain beliefs and modes of behavior within the Hindu religion.

Because many aspects of Buddhism were born of Hinduism, most Buddhist disciplines also include various fastings and vows in their regimes. Probably the most noticeable Buddhist self-sacrifice is the *tonsure*, or shaving of the head, which many monks and nuns undergo as a rite of passage and a declaration of sacrificing the ego for spiritual union.

Another religion heavily associated with fasting and self-sacrifice is Islam. In traditional Islamic religious practices, adherents observe full food fasting during the month of Ramadan. Ramadan occurs in the ninth month of the Islamic lunar calendar; as a result, its date in the (skewed?) Western Gregorian calendar shifts each year.

During Ramadan, Muslims practice various strict forms of fasting and purification as devotional practices to Allah. For the entire month, all Muslims are required to fast and purify from sunrise to sunset, traditionally abstaining from both food and sexual intercourse. Fasts are broken at sundown each day of Ramadan.

Many Muslims fast on other holy days, though these disciplines vary from group to group. Additionally, all orthodox Muslims vow to abstain from alcohol throughout their lives. Many take this a step further by vowing to abstain from any sort of harmful behavior including anger, jealousy, lust, and greed during daylight hours.

Various schools of Christianity also practice fasting: not only abstinence from food on some occasions, but also extended vows of celibacy for monks and nuns.

The Bible tells of Moses fasting for forty days and forty nights; Jesus, too, underwent such a fast. In other verses, such as Luke 6:12 and Matthew 14:23, Jesus engages in solitary prayer and meditation, refusing sleep and devoting himself to Spirit. Fasting is also discussed in Matthew 6:16–18, wherein Jesus explains that abstaining from food is a personal act between oneself and the divine rather than an attempt to win the approval of others. The many references to self-denial in the scriptures of Matthew suggest that its importance was well understood.

Many followers of the Christ also engage in lateral self-sacrifices as acts of dedication. Abstaining from sleep for religious purposes is often called "watching."

In Catholicism and Protestantism, Lent is observed during the forty-day period between Ash Wednesday and Holy Saturday (which follows Good Friday and precedes Easter Sunday). Traditionally, meat, wine, and festivities were abnegated during this holy time. But most modern observers choose to abstain from specific pleasurable activities to show penance before God; today, there is also a focus on acts of charity. A number of churches additionally require the faithful to adhere to a strict vegetarian diet, though this is not a worldwide Catholic or Protestant phenomenon. (The word *Lent* is Old English for "spring." Less food was eaten at this time because the rations of autumn were running short. It was necessary to consume less, so a virtue was born of necessity.)

Many other religions have codified fasting in various ways. Traditional adherents to Judaism observe a number of days of sunrise-to-sundown fasting in the year (with water also proscribed). Judaism and other religions also make use of fasting when in mourning, or to mark particular rites of passage.

Many schools of Taoism also recognize fasting, and some translate verses in the *Tao Te Ching* as referring to it. The practice is mentioned in the *Book of Mencius*, a text that greatly propelled the influence of Confucianism in China. Over time, Confucianism, Taoism, and Buddhism came to influence one another in many forms of Chinese philosophy.

Tribal religions have always made use of fasting. Tribal concepts of self-sacrifice are still present in virtually all religions, to varying degrees, depending on each tradition's evolution. Among the most visible preservers of indigenous religious practice are Hindu ascetics, *saddhus* or wandering holy men. These ascetics have always been out-castes in India, and their extreme lifestyles tend to keep them in such a social category. (Indian social systems are less strict than they used to be, but more legal equality in theory does not necessarily translate to practice.) These ascetics have renounced worldly pleasures in trade for a life of self-sacrifice, with the aim of growing closer to godhead. Buddhism and Sikhism also have their ascetic followers. Many, like the Buddha, were born in "higher" castes and renounced their former social status for asceticism.

Restricting one's food intake, sleep cycles, or speech; depriving oneself of sexual release or other sensations—these are all aspects of ascetic practice. Self-mortification, or torturing one's own physical body, is also common. All acts of self-sacrifice are undertaken with the goal of achieving spiritual illumination; it is thought that restricting and tormenting the physical body will push the soul to higher levels of awareness and union with Spirit. Asceticism is a lifelong path for many and as such it certainly dwarfs the small bursts of self-sacrificial devotions and fasts that non-ascetic spiritual seekers may attempt. However, no act of self-sacrifice should be underrated. It takes great determination, especially for those who are new to it. Though I imagine that nearly everyone reading these words is *not* an ascetic (myself included), integrating a bit of self-sacrifice can be a tremendously beneficial spiritual practice. For us, the goal is to step out of our normal modes of operation and allow new spiritual vibrations to enter our sphere. Restricting food and other forms of denial are not a punishment, but an opportunity to tap into that which may otherwise remain hidden.

In her Christianity-centered book *Fasting: Spiritual Freedom Beyond Our Appetites*, Lynne Baab notes: "Fasting as self-punishment denies the freedom God gives us in Christ. Fasting as self-punishment does not create space for prayer, give us energy to our prayers, or enable us to listen to God."[3] Regardless of one's religion—Christian, Pagan, Buddhist, Hindu, Jewish, Muslim, or *anything* else—fasting is one of the most spiritually beneficial disciplines a person can undertake when it is done not in the spirit of self-punishment, but as a door opening to spiritual revelation.

Planning Fasts

Fasting can be reasonably healthy if approached with awareness of the body and mind. Careful planning is necessary for a healthy and successful experience.

Before attempting any sort of food fast, think sensibly about what you will be doing to your body. Fasting must be approached with caution and awareness of the individuality of body chemistry—everyone is different and has different limits.

Just as our biological needs and limits differ, the same holds true for the mind. If a person has never before experienced any sort of fast, immediately attempting hardcore self-denial would be like jumping into the deep end before learning to swim. It's always best to start with a "small" fast and work your way up gradually.

A three-day fast is great for one's first experience. Three and seven are auspicious numbers in magick, as three represents the phases of the Great Goddess or God (and is the number of the Holy Child), and seven is the number of primary planets and the days of the week. If you decide to abstain from food, it's a good idea to start with a gradual fast or rice-and-juice fast, rather than completely halting your nutritional intake (this is discussed further on).

If you allow yourself some experimentation and remain devoted to observing the body's reactions, you can gain a greater wisdom of the limits of your own body and mind. Discomfort is a natural reaction to fasting, and it isn't always an invitation to give up partway through. During a fast, if you feel you should "quit while you're ahead," analyze the feeling and look for its origins. Is it the mind expressing discomfort or is it actually a matter of health? You be the judge, and take care of yourself while you push your limits.

If you are fasting from food and realize that you're growing too weak to continue, and that your health might be at risk, do not immediately cease the fast and reenter your normal mode of operation. Food fasts *must* be eased out of, as the digestive system (in particular) can be shocked and thus injured if, after processing nothing or next to nothing, it is suddenly digesting regular meals again.

You may have concerns as to the health risks of fasting; perhaps you take certain medicines that may not interact well with a decrease in food intake (for example). If your concerns are legitimate and medically based (rather than exclusively psychologically based), don't hesitate to discuss the risks and benefits with your health care practitioner.

When planning for fasts, pay strict attention to your work and/or school schedule. It's best to fast on days when it won't interfere and distract you from your other tasks at hand. (It's also best to avoid driving a car on those days, as the mind is almost always in an altered state.) For a three-day fast, I've found it beneficial to start on a Friday, still going about daily obligations. Of course, this option depends entirely on the nature of the fast and the practitioner's reaction to it. For example, a vow of silence while at work or school may be possible for some people, though it would unfeasible for others.

Fasting causes one to pause for a brief moment, suspended from normal habits. As a result, it's ideal to plan only small tasks that can either be easily done another time, or that necessarily challenge the purpose of the fast. As fasts become more intense, the focus should be on the self as much as possible. Any type of fasting brings focus to the spiritual body and mind, and physical-plane operation must often take a back seat.

If a person decides to undertake a fast, it must be carefully planned. The goal of the fast must be crystal clear; this will both strengthen the devotion and provide fuel to the fire of motivation that keeps a person going in the sacrifice. Doubt and frustration *most definitely* arise in the fasting process. Depending on the fast, that can be a bitch of a thing to overcome … but is absolutely necessary.

Members of my circle find it beneficial to do some sort of Halloween fast—usually a rice fast—for three days before and the day of Samhain, breaking the fast with a light feast after ritual. This process purges and purifies the body, preparing it for the final releasing and banishing ritual of Halloween. I also like to fast, in some manner, before taking an initiation or other Rite of Passage.

If you feel so inclined, you can fast from a number of things simultaneously. For example, one could fast from speaking, using technology, and using caffeine, all at the same time. I would term fasting from two things a "doublefast," three things a "trifast," four things a "quadfast," five things a "pentafast," and so on. For suggestions on various types, see the list on pages 66–78.

When enduring any type of fast, I like to keep a journal to monitor my mind and body's reactions. One of my journal entries during a seven-day pentafast is as follows:

5/13/06 ~ On this fifth day of fasting, I realize that this whole process seems to make the air outside come alive, filled with splendor, healing, and magick ... perhaps a greater attunement to nature ... I'm also gaining deep admiration for *all* weather patterns and feel considerably more connected to the vibrations of this world.

This may be a "chaos magician" thing to say, but during the fast, do whatever works for you. Set your own boundaries and limits, determine your current comfort-versus-discomfort threshold, then push that level accordingly. How you conduct a fast is entirely your call. If a full food fast is too difficult, consider eating only white rice during that period instead. If fully fasting from technology isn't feasible, consider allowing yourself to operate a car but nothing else. If fasting from tobacco is extremely difficult, consider using an herbal smoking blend as a tobacco-free substitute. At the same time, be very careful how much leeway you allow yourself—too much leeway and the purpose of the fast diminishes. Pushing yourself to your limits—and a little beyond them—and allowing yourself to be reborn from the experience is what it's all about.

Further, I recommend doing whatever works for you ritualistically. Meditation is a great asset during any type of fast. Sitting in silence and stilling the mind for an extended period brings greater focus and peace. Using visualization techniques, whether recommended by others or self-created, sharpens particular vibrations and makes waking life a bit smoother. Taking a bath also aids in calming the mind and body. Bathing can itself be an amazing ritualistic experience. I also recommend a healthy amount of reading; spiritual and occult studies can be great points of grounding and reassurance when fasting. Undertaking a metaphysical project during this time can also be a constructive way to ground spacey energies that can lead to discouragement. For example, during one of my seven-day fasts, I created "materia magicka" and "materia medica" reference cards for all the herbs I own. During others, I made it a point to learn as much as I could about one particular occult subject or another. Fasting is also one of the most ideal times to create art of any sort. The possibilities are endless!

During a fast, dedicatory actions are of immense benefit. If you are familiar with your spirit guide(s) or animal spirit(s), work with them. Meditate with them, invoke their energies into your being, and align yourself to their wisdom. If a certain deity is your patron, dedicate the fast to that deity from the outset and continue to ritualistically commune with that energy. If you have a penchant for working with elemental energies, surround yourself with nature as much as possible and perform personally meaningful elemental magick. In other words, take advantage of your own spiritual findings, leanings, and curiosities to make your fast a strictly personal spiritual experience!

A common metaphysical exercise that is profoundly effective for letting go of emotional attachment is that of "stepping back." During a fast, this exercise can increase dedicatory determination. It takes practice, but many of its effects can be felt immediately. If preferred, this may be performed within a ritualistic environment. I strongly believe that such exercises in awareness should be practiced regularly, both during fasting and in regular non-fasting life. The goal is to simply step back from yourself to see a greater picture.

To try it right now, first become aware of yourself at this very moment. You might first observe your present activity: reading. Simply *know* that you are reading. From there, take a step back: where are you sitting, how are you positioned, and what is the surrounding environment like? From here, you may take another step back: *you* are reading these words, but who does this "you" refer to? Become aware of the body as a simple vessel for the soul (or "spirit" if you prefer). This soul is perceiving and absorbing its current experience through the six sensory faculties of the physical (mortal) body. The body—and all of its sensory faculties—will perish, given time. It will change, it will die, it will return to the earth. Now become aware that all things around you, from the book you are holding, to the clothes you are wearing, to the seat you are positioned on, are only temporary forms that will eventually cease to be. Nothing is without change. From here, contemplate the division between the soul and physical reality. Come to think of your perception as an emanation of the soul: you are observing your body experiencing stimuli. *You* are not your body, but have chosen to inhabit this shell temporarily. Allow yourself to detach from the idea that the mind is subject to the body, realizing that the body is in fact subject to the mind.

This is one example of "stepping back," and can be performed at any time that circumstances permit. As we are incarnated in these bodies, it's easy to forget that the soul and the physical frame are separate paradigms, only working together for a brief period of time.

Should this type of work become overwhelming—and it should, as undeniable questions of existence naturally arise and seek resolution—proper grounding techniques should be performed to center the Higher Self and Lower Self as one. This dance of two bodies is the dance of life.

Food Fasting

Food is linked to creation. It not only allows survival, it is a link in the chain of life, death, and rebirth: a concept illustrated in the classical Hindu view that food itself is a direct reincarnation of human essence. Cremation is an ordinary procedure in India, and many believe that a person "becomes" smoke when cremated. The smoke is then integrated with the atmosphere and sky, and is partially brought back to the earth through rain. The rain nourishes plants, which are eaten as food, and thus reabsorbed into the living.

Many assume that fasting must involve denial of all food, and possibly water. This is undoubtedly the most jarring type of fast, and can also be the most dangerous. I would never advise a person to go without water—such asceticism can be more damaging than rewarding. I also have a difficult time advising people to go for more than a day or two entirely without food. Full fasts are noble but must be approached with extreme caution. For a person who has never fasted, I would recommend numerous partial fasts over time before jumping into what may be treacherous waters. Additionally, whatever you do, don't just drink a bunch of alcohol and take vitamin pills when you stop eating. That's called self-abuse, not fasting.

In his book *New Aeon Magick: Thelema Without Tears*, author Gerald del Campo recommends an *every-other-day* form of fast: eat normally on alternate days, allowing juice and herbal tea only on the fast days. I agree; playing with this method can be a balanced way to introduce oneself to this spiritual art. To keep natural vitamins and minerals flowing, keep various fruit juices on hand. I would advise against too much juice that is acidic in nature, such as orange, lemon, and grapefruit. I prefer apple, cranberry, and pear. Organic juice not made from concentrate is undoubtedly the best. There are tons of options!

One can also try a juice-only fast for a few days. These generally include both fruit and vegetable juice, and are extremely detoxifying. Juice fasts allow nutrients to still enter the body even when nothing is actually being eaten. With vegetable juice, ensure that it's not full of sodium and is, ideally, organic and not from concentrate.

Additionally, should one choose to permit it, fennel seeds are great to eat when enduring any type of food fast, especially a full fast. Fennel seeds were eaten during church fasting days in the Middle Ages both to curb the appetite and to freshen the breath.

Also, I've found that bentonite clay is an incredible asset to the process. This type of clay is sold in herb and health food stores in powder form, and is also known as calcium bentonite. It is also sold under the name Pascalite clay. It has extreme cleansing properties and is surprisingly versatile. It can be used to relieve a wide array of digestive ailments, and consuming this during a food fast of any sort will help cleanse and purify the body internally, not to mention energetically. I've had astounding success with this clay both within and outside of fasting. The Native American nations of the Wyoming Big Horn Mountains called it *ee-wah-kee,* "the mud that heals." Not only does it leach toxic materials from the digestive system (especially the colon), but it can be caked on wounds to prevent infection, and on scars or external marks as a topical healing ointment. Some accounts even speak of the clay healing more long-term skin ailments such as Candida, psoriasis, and even acne. If you're a Witch or herbal healer, this healing clay is a *must* for your cabinet!

THE RICE FAST

My circle performs this type of fast most often, consuming only rice (and water) for a period of days. Many people allow themselves only white rice, while others use brown. Some permit the addition of soy sauce, chili sauce, sesame seeds, seaweed, and/or olive oil, in which the rice is fried. These ingredients can add flavor to the "empty" quality of white rice in particular, as it is relatively flavorless and has little nutritional value beyond its calories. As an "empty filler," cooked rice is ideal to our purpose. It lets the digestive system keep operating, while at the same time denying the body most nutrients.

It's a good idea to thoroughly rinse rice before cooking it, to remove excess starch and any synthetic vitamins and minerals sprayed on it before packaging. Rice can also be consumed in a variety of other forms, including rice noodles, rice puff cereal, rice cakes, rice crackers, and rice milk. Read ingredients lists closely to avoid consuming more than is desired. Water is essential during a rice fast, and many people like to consume non-acidic juice as well. Either way, I recommend eating frequently—at least once every hour, even if just a small amount—to keep the digestive system working. Although the system is processing food of almost no nutritional value, the hunger pains are greatly eased.

Rice is the perfect fasting food; it doesn't shock the system too much, but it takes a person out of the ordinary eating cycle just enough to alter consciousness and bring certain issues to light.

THE GRADUAL FOOD FAST

Here the practitioner tapers off certain foods down to a certain fasting minimum, then tapers back up again. A seven-day gradual fast is ideal, as it allows one to go through the full week both spiritually and mundanely, experiencing the sacrifice. The ordinary grind of work, school, and so on, is experienced during the fast, and the planetary rulership of each day is encountered simultaneously. Each day of the week is ruled by one of the primary planets of classical Hermetic astrology. So devoting each day of the fast to a planet is ideal for a Witch or magician, following this pattern:

Sunday – Sun
Monday – Moon
Tuesday – Mars
Wednesday – Mercury
Thursday – Jupiter
Friday – Venus
Saturday – Saturn

Three seven-day gradual fast plans are outlined below, geared to meat and dairy eaters, vegetarians, and vegans. Depending on one's dietary habits, these variations help disperse protein and other vital nutrients and help prevent wear and distress on the body.

Nuts and seeds carry a particular vibration (and protein content) that are permitted on some days and not on others. All three plans include fruits and "surface" vegetables, those that grow above ground. ("Buried" vegetables that grow underground, such as carrots and potatoes, are dense and carry a certain heavy earth vibration, so they are not incorporated in these fasts.) Remember to *drink non-acidic juice every day of any fast* outlined below, so as to keep the vitamins flowing. Juice is essential as an everyday beverage, although it is mentioned only once in each plan, as a reminder to drink it on the rice-only days. Remember, too, to eat the permitted foods often, at least a small amount every hour during each fast day.

Note: I am not a nutritionist, so please consult a health care professional before attempting fasts of any sort, and always use your common sense.

IF YOU CURRENTLY EAT MEAT AND DAIRY:

- Day 1: Allow fruits, surface vegetables, rice, and dairy. No meat, nuts, or seeds.
- Day 2: Allow fruits, surface vegetables, and rice. No meat, dairy, nuts, or seeds.
- Day 3: Allow only nuts, seeds, and rice.
- Day 4: Rice (and juice) only.

- Day 5: Allow only nuts, seeds, and rice.
- Day 6: Allow fruits, surface vegetables, and rice. No meat, dairy, nuts, or seeds.
- Day 7: Allow fruits, surface vegetables, rice, and dairy. No meat, nuts, or seeds.

IF YOU ARE VEGETARIAN:

- Day 1: Allow fruits, surface vegetables, and rice. No dairy, nuts, or seeds.
- Day 2: Allow fruits and rice. No dairy, nuts, seeds, or vegetables.
- Day 3: Allow only nuts, seeds, and rice.
- Day 4: Rice (and juice) only.
- Day 5: Allow only nuts, seeds, and rice.
- Day 6: Allow fruits and rice. No dairy, nuts, seeds, or vegetables.
- Day 7: Allow fruits, surface vegetables, and rice. No dairy, nuts, or seeds.

IF YOU ARE VEGAN:

- Day 1: Allow fruits, surface vegetables, nuts, seeds, and rice. No cooked food besides rice.
- Day 2: Allow fruits, nuts, seeds, and rice. No cooked food besides rice, and no vegetables.
- Day 3: Rice and (uncooked) fruits only.
- Day 4: Rice (and juice) only.
- Day 5: Rice and (uncooked) fruits only.
- Day 6: Allow fruits, nuts, seeds, and rice. No cooked food besides rice, and no vegetables.
- Day 7: Allow fruits, surface vegetables, nuts, seeds, and rice. No cooked food besides rice.

In the latter half of a gradual food fast, when reintegrating each previously subtracted food, "celebrate" that item. And at any time we can deepen our appreciation for rice by honoring and contemplating the grain that has for centuries sustained people across the globe.

A less intense dietary variation is to simply abstain from unnatural foods for a period of time. With all the "food" products available on the market that are genetically modified or include disgusting, toxic ingredients like partially hydrogenated oil and high-fructose corn syrup, most spiritual seekers habitually tend to select all-natural or organic foods— even if finding them can be difficult at times. If you are not in the habit of eating only natural and organic foods, this type of fast may be a good introduction to fasting—or a dedication for life!

VEGETARIANISM AND VEGANISM

Another type of food fast is to immerse oneself in a vegetarian or vegan diet for a period of time. For non-vegetarians, the effects of subtracting meat from the diet often include feelings of "lightness," a greater sense of mental and physical purity, and expanded spiritual awareness.

Indeed, metaphysically, the death energy latent in factory-farmed animal corpses is heavy with misery. Perpetuating cycles of animal abuse and the absorption of such energies into the body is, I believe, antispiritual. Personally, I think that everyone who is physically able should be either vegetarian or vegan for life, or *at least* eat only ethically raised meat and hunted game. The horrors and tortures of factory farming are absolutely unspeakable; it is indeed hell on earth for literally billions upon billions of animals who deserve to be treated as sentient beings rather than financial "product." Our generation is blessed with *choice*, and consuming flesh is not, quite honestly, necessary for our health and well-being. Additionally, *we* are not our ancestors; rarely do we hunt and gather.

To those unfamiliar with factory farming, this point of view may sound overly compassionate or idealistic, but in truth, no being should be treated in the ways that countless animals are constantly treated, unseen and unregulated. Every time we take a bite of factory-farmed meat, we both contribute to and endorse a brutal and inhumane cycle of anguish for other beings in our immediate reality. The gruesome truth of this genocide mustn't be brushed aside or conveniently ignored or justified by spiritual seekers.

Not to mention that most meat and dairy products are full of harmful, DNA-altering chemical hormones, and that animal flesh itself clogs up the digestive system—over time, meat actually begins to decompose, rotting inside the body. Simple research into the reality of factory farming and the health risks of meat and dairy should back my case; we need not go into great detail here.[4] Trust me, I could go on about this for ages! But to sum it up, in the words of Mahatma Gandhi, "The greatness of a nation and its moral progress can be judged by the way its animals are treated."

Other Types of Fasts and Self-Sacrifices

VOWS OF SILENCE

As a teenager, I once had a dream about refraining from speech for a period of three days. Perhaps it was a result of seeing the film version of Marion Zimmer Bradley's *The Mists of Avalon*, in which a character (also called Raven!) has taken a lifelong vow of silence. The dream was a spiritual message nonetheless and, for me, the results were awesome. Since then, I've performed other vows of silence and have discovered the same spiritual success.

Vows of silence are beneficial in numerous ways. As humans, we are very used to communicating verbally. Removing that element from our lives for a period of time helps us become more aware of our methods of, and motivations for, verbal communication. A vow of silence allows us to catch instinctual vocal reactions, many of which accompany hand or body gestures. We also see exactly how often we inadvertently mumble or mutter to ourselves—and we're forced to bite our tongue!

The extent of the vow is up to the practitioner. Will you let yourself write notes or do visual charades whilst remaining silent? Will you let yourself respond to email and other written messages? Will you cease all forms of communication altogether? Whatever the case, I recommend carrying a notecard reading "I am undergoing a vow of silence for [however many] days, as a devotion to [Spirit, the gods, or your patron deity]," or something similar.

Vows of silence bring us a greater awareness of nonverbal communication and let us see how normal communications are conveyed through a combination of action, facial expression, motion, and voice. Simply observing other people's ordinary behavior during this fast brings many aspects of the realm of communication into clarity. When we are forced to become the observer, we truly observe. (And undertaking a vow of silence is often much more entertaining than it is stressful, making it a fast that's both fun and enlightening.)

A number of occult systems require that a person undertake a vow of silence *or* simply remain silent in regard to idle words, gossip, or negative speech, all of which are a variation of the vow of silence. Occultist and chaos magician Robert Anton Wilson was a fan of removing the word "I" from one's vocabulary. In the early twentieth century, Indian-born Bahman Pestonji Wadia endorsed various forms of silence and helped to integrate the teachings into

Theosophy. The mystic, scientist, and mathematician Pythagoras is also documented as having endured a five-year vow of silence in the sixth century BCE.

As Ayurvedic medical doctor and metaphysician Deepak Chopra writes in his book *The Seven Spiritual Laws of Success:*

> Initially your internal dialogue becomes even more turbulent. You feel an intense need to say things. I've known people who go absolutely crazy the first day or two when they commit themselves to an extended period of silence. A sense of urgency and anxiety suddenly comes over them. But as they stay with the experience, their internal dialogue begins to quieten. And soon the silence becomes profound.[5]

Indeed, vows of silence can help the modern magickal practitioner to better actualize the four Laws of the Magus, which are "To Know, To Dare, To Will, To Keep Silent." This is also called the Witch's Pyramid or Magician's Ladder.

VOWS OF CELIBACY

Particularly prevalent in Christianity, Buddhism, and Hinduism, vows of celibacy call for a person to refrain from sexual intercourse. Some people and traditions also disallow non-intercourse sexual pleasure and masturbation, while others permit either or both. Like the concept of chastity, celibacy is linked to notions of sexual purity, but it does not imply virginity as the term chastity does.

Some people take lifelong vows of celibacy in accordance with religious requirements. Many sects of monastic Buddhism practice celibacy, as do monks and nuns of many schools, the goal being to eliminate desire and the attachment to worldly pleasure that can easily arise. Some Christians, especially Catholics, and in particular Catholic clergy, take lifelong vows of celibacy as an act of dedication before God.

Sex and masturbation are often demonized in Western culture, mostly as a result of the Christian movement and the anti-pleasure mentality so prevalent in many of its sects. Christian chastity is often a result of shame. Many schools of Christianity disallow sex before marriage, and many condemn both homosexuality and masturbation. Many Catholics and Mormons expect homosexual members to be chaste, or even to endure severe sexual "reparative" treatment such as genital shock therapy, isolation, or hypnosis, depending on the sect.

For the average Westerner, voluntarily abstaining from any sort of sexual activity for a period of time can be quite a trial, since most people release sexually on a regular basis. For the most challenge and the most benefit, disallowing both sex and masturbation is particularly effective. Refraining from orgasm forces us to examine our own sexual tendencies and observe which thoughts induce arousal. This can allow us to reflect on our sexual motivations, think about sexual experiences of the past, contemplate sexual energy and orientation, and come to a more balanced state of mind regarding sex and sexuality.

FASTING FROM DEPENDENCIES

So … what's your crutch? Alcohol? Tobacco? Caffeine? Marijuana? Food? Television? Pills? Other drugs? Admittedly, most of us have one type of crutch or another. This isn't to say that every substance or habit is harmful, or that it's wrong to use recreational substances now and then. But we do often tend to develop psychological dependencies on that which has mood-altering effects on us. (My use of the terms "substance" or "drug" includes excessive eating, television, video games, and other habits.) While one person may use a drug recreationally, another may develop a dependency. While one person may experience no ill effects from the use, others may injure their bodies and cause harm in the long run. Either way, it's wise to examine addictions and potential addictions, and learn to operate with or without one's substance of choice.

Witches and magicians are pretty liberal about substance use. If using a drug causes no harm to oneself or others, it's generally considered okay to use. The desire to use substances to alter one's consciousness, whether to a small or significant degree, is quite natural. I would even argue that most people live a more productive and holistically healthy life if they have something to take the edge off now and then—so long as it's used sparingly and doesn't cause excessive harm to the body.

What about fasting from pharmaceuticals? Western prescription drugs can have positive or negative effects, or there may be tradeoffs of pros and cons. Some medicines are prescribed for physiological reasons, others for psychological reasons. If you are considering a fast from a prescription medicine—whether for physical or psychological health—first consult the doctor who prescribed it. Taking a break from it without understanding the implications can be damaging. Is the prescription something you feel you can do without at this point, or is it absolutely necessary? If you feel that you may simply be *psychologically* dependent on a certain medication, it may be beneficial to try easing off it, under a doctor's supervision, and see how you operate.

Many people *self*-medicate with substances, which can have either positive or negative effects, depending on the person's reactions in the short and long term. Depending on your physiological *need* for "self-medicating" or recreational substances, fasting from them can be beneficial. If a person self-medicates with caffeine, nicotine, alcohol, marijuana, or something similar, it can be spiritually rewarding to take a break from the substance of choice, allowing the body to cleanse and return to a more natural state. Do you feel that you can't start the day without drinking coffee or smoking a cigarette, or you can't relax in the evening without drinking alcohol or smoking a bowl? What, for you, would be safe to cut out of your system for a period of time? What is the degree of your dependency, if you have one, and how can you safely and healthily subtract the drug from your routine? Is your drug of choice relatively harmless, or is it something you should cease using altogether? Would you, and are you able to, take a break from a substance for a week? A month? A year? The rest of your life? The choice is personal, but the decision should be made intelligently, and with others' advice.

It's easy to become accustomed to using substances, which is why taking a break from them can be so helpful. We must be the ones in control, not the substance. Fasting from dependencies allows us to take a step back and realize that we *can* function without a crutch, even if it's difficult at first.

If attempting this sort of fast, it's a good idea to slowly ease off a substance, eliminate it from your system entirely, and then ease back into it if you so desire. A cold-turkey approach isn't always the best option, especially in the case of pharmaceuticals, but it may work best for recreational substance users, depending on one's body chemistry.

TECHNOLOGY FASTS

As I sit at the computer writing these words, I realize how dependent I am on technology. The computer is the most obvious form of technology I'm using at the moment, but as I look around I notice more. A sixty-watt light bulb is shining above me, the stereo is playing a Dead Can Dance album, my roommates are watching the BBC on another computer, the fan is rotating, the kettle is boiling water for tea, and soup is being heated on the stove. That's a lot of electricity!

Living in a modern world, we are *constantly* using technology for our daily needs. What if, one day, technology failed? Could we survive? This is something to consider when enduring a fast from technology. How truly independent from technology—particularly electronic technology—are we?

If you decide to undergo a technology fast, consider how strict you wish it to be. What is the scope of the term *technology*? Obviously, things like phones, computers, microwaves, and televisions are out of the question. Would you decide to stop driving or using public transportation? Would you use the stove? The oven? Lights? Electronic timepieces? The refrigerator? Would you allow others to operate electrical devices *for* you? Will you perform this in conjunction with another fast or two? It's up to you; just don't be too lenient on yourself! Imagine all the ways this sacrifice could be rewarding . . . books and baths by candlelight never sounded so good!

However you structure your technology fast, odd situations may result. This I know from experience: if a roommate on the way out the door sticks a CD in the player for you during a technology fast (since you cannot touch the stereo) and the disk starts repeatedly skipping a little while later, it *really* sucks, trust me!

Eliminating technology from one's daily operation is, like all sacrifices, both difficult and rewarding. Such an endeavor illuminates our modern lifestyle, and reminds us that humans operated without electronic technology for aeons.

SLEEP FASTS

Before I attempted fasting from sleep, I had never pulled an all-nighter. For the longest time, I held on to the belief that I could not function without at least eight hours of sleep—the recommended average. Now I realize that if the need arises, I can function on less sleep and catch up at a later time. Though I still get loopier than the average Joe, confronting the long-held fear by undergoing a sleep fast proved to lessen its intensity for me. People vary in the amount of sleep they need to operate well. Some people manage fine on only four hours a night, while others function best on ten. Any type of fasting is a highly personal devotion, as everyone's constitution is different, and this may be especially true with sleep.

Sleep fasts must be carefully planned, as should all self-restrictions. It's a good idea to start by staying awake for one night. If you hold up all right, try for two the next time. As a general rule, sleep deprivation produces effects of irritability, grogginess, forgetfulness, and weakness. It can make a person feel—or realize—that life is a dream. I tend to become more apathetic with sleep loss, feeling a sort of "pleasant frustration." One's memory, sense of time, and communication abilities alter with sleep deprivation. Two or three days of sleep fasting can produce minor auditory and visual hallucinations. One's reaction time and attention span can both be reduced, which makes meditation a much wiser choice than driving a car. If you are planning a fast from sleep, please be careful. Prolonged sleep deprivation can cause a state called oneirophrenia, in which a person not only perceives life as a dream, but has strong delusions and hallucinations. Don't push yourself too hard; fasting of any sort requires utmost self-awareness.

One option is to let yourself take a set number of forty-minute naps throughout the fast. This way we can brush up against the astral plane for but a moment, rejuvenating ourselves slightly before we return to this plane. A person usually enters the REM state (rapid eye movement, indicating deeper sleep) about thirty or forty minutes after falling asleep, so shorter naps will spare much of the waking disorientation caused by interrupting REM.

You may also wish to permit yourself stimulants such as caffeine, ginseng, and coca tea. I would, however, strongly recommend against using synthetic "uppers" such as energy drinks and drugs. The experience should be as pure as possible.

FASTING FROM SOCIETY

Also called isolation fasts, abstaining from contact with anybody but yourself is most definitely a form of self-sacrifice. Most of us interact with people regularly, if not constantly. When a person is undistracted by others, one's mental processes become more easily visible, allowing a better view of the mind and its workings.

If you live a highly social lifestyle, taking some time for yourself, and *only* yourself, can be an amazing, much-needed antidote. We so often integrate our lives with the lives of others. This is a natural part of human living, but forgetting to balance sociality with solitude (and vice versa) can be spiritually detrimental. For people who are highly empathic or simply energy-sensitive, restricting oneself socially can permit time for energy work, artistic expression, meditation, ritual, and healthy self-analysis. Foreign energies naturally attach themselves to our auras throughout the day, so one must always take proper time to cleanse and come to center. Setting aside time for solitude creates an opportunity for this grounding and centering to happen without distraction.

Many people undergoing a social fast prefer to isolate themselves somewhere other than at home. Some go camping, which sets a very natural, shamanic atmosphere. What a glorious opportunity to get in touch with true nature … and your own true nature!

If you perform the fast from home, it's essential to turn off your phone and email systems, and probably the radio and television. Alert friends and family of your self-isolation and stick a note on the door. If you live with a partner or roommates, obviously tell them beforehand what you're doing, but don't let their proximity distract you from your fast. Certainly, in the case of an honest emergency, the fast should be broken.

One much simpler modification of this fast from society is to simply refrain from purchasing anything. By not exchanging money with anyone, we temporarily remove ourselves from the extremes of our society's commercial sphere.

If you're planning a full isolation fast, how long would you like it to continue? Depending on your lifestyle, a few days or a week may be the ideal time frame. Perhaps refraining from purchasing anything could last a longer period of time, such as a month. It's your intuition and your choice.

APPEARANCE FASTING

We live in a culture that's unhealthily fixated on physical appearance. As individuals, we present ourselves to the world, and we are often judged by what we wear or don't wear, and other aspects of our looks. Our culture far too often equates a person's appearance with his or her worth. Many people spend their lives worrying about their appearance, constantly modifying themselves to impress other people and, unfortunately, depending on others' perceptions for their own sense of personal validity. Empowerment comes from separating oneself from others' expectations and judgments enough to find security in one's own expression and appearance.

Most Pagans and magickal folk understand that appearance is secondary to spiritual living. At the same time, our appearance can be a wonderful opportunity for artistic expression. For readers whose fashions often reflect either their subcultural interests or "alternative" mentality, I recommend wearing completely different clothing for this fast. Perhaps wearing ordinary pants, a T-shirt, a baseball cap, and no makeup would be a strong enough antithesis to your usual style that this fast would have strong effects. What would it be like to visually fit into the mainstream, instead of standing out?

For readers whose wardrobe is more "ordinary," perhaps just the opposite would be a noble change. I would recommend examining a subculture's common visual expression and dressing to the nines. To take it a step further, you may choose to immerse yourself even deeper in a subculture by going to a Goth club, punk rock concert, reggae show, electronic dance event, polka party, or what have you.

If choosing to fast from your typical appearance, it's a *must* to go out in public at least once a day in order to fully feel the effects of the sacrifice, and it's best to continue the fast for at least a week. Altering our visual appearance also alters the way people respond to us, both noticeably and energetically. Changing our appearance makes us look at things a bit differently; our perceptions can expand as we see what it's like to walk in different shoes.

Ritual Sacrifice: A Ceremony of Silence

Simply sacrificing one element of a ritual—in this case, speech—can do wonders in terms of changing the vibration, experience, and outcome of the ceremony. This is a ritual of silence. No words are to be spoken in the process.

So many rituals and spells place their emphasis on speech. We may have been told that the *words* create the magick, and Hollywoodization certainly doesn't help. Vocalization holds very intense power, but when an abundance of idle words are spoken in circle, the words become just as fleeting as the surrounding air.

On the other hand, when ritual is enacted with *intention*, words become secondary; they are but a guide for conscious will. (Of course, purely celebratory circles are a bit different because they are often fun and revelry-oriented!) In the following circle-casting meditation, we will see ritualism in a different light and work purely from the energetic plane, immersing ourselves in enigmatic silence. This ritual should get you comfortable with the idea of a silent circle for when the need arises in the future. (I don't recommend silence for *all* personal rituals; only for those in which it feels appropriate.)

Our intention with this ritual is pure *experience*, so it does not include any spellwork, but instead includes moments of communion and one strong apex of potential Gnosis. *Gnosis* can translate as "saving wisdom," referring to a feeling of union with Spirit, a profound experience of heightened spiritual awareness.

This ritual may be the perfect conclusion to a period of fasting, particularly a vow of silence. If so, no word should be spoken until the very end, to break the fast. Otherwise, if it's your practice, perform a Lesser Banishing Ritual of the Pentagram (LBRP) beforehand, or any other protective exercises you deem appropriate. In the case of the LBRP, no words should be spoken after the final "le-olahm, Amen" in the included Qabalistic Cross.[6]

For this ritual, have neither music playing nor any ruckus in the background. Prepare yourself, your altar, your tools, and your environment. Fire the candles and incense, turn off the lights, get naked or robed, and make sure your tools are properly placed, statues anointed, and dust swept. Taking a ritual bath beforehand will also serve to cleanse the astral bodies and prepare one for the rite.

1. Sit comfortably to start the journey, and begin by clearing your mind. (Please wait until step 4 to begin casting the circle and calling the quarters.) Take three deep breaths in through the nose and out through the mouth. Let the thoughts of the day drift away like moving clouds. This is not the time to focus on what happened today or what you need to do tomorrow … allow the common world to dissipate as you enter the sacred terrain of the mind. For several minutes, sense the oxygen entering your nostrils and exiting your lips. Bring absolute focus to your breath.

2. Kneel or sit before your altar to begin the ritual, simply gazing at your tools. Look at each one for at least twenty seconds. As you do this, form an awareness in your mind of each purpose. Is it frequently used or simply decorative? Rarely acknowledged or looked at every day? Physically, what materials is it made of? Energetically, is it highly charged or relatively empty? Consider these questions, taking as long as you need.

3. Reflecting on the tools, continue to meditate as long as you'd like, but for *at least five minutes.* This is important; as your focus slips to the mental plane, certain obdurate images or sounds are given the opportunity to flee. Simply bring your focus back to your breath if you get lost in thought.

4. Raise your hands to the East (where most traditional circles begin) and, instead of "thinking" words in your mind, simply feel the essence of the East, that of Air. Visualize all things that represent Air to you: rushing breezes, the breath of life, billowing smoke, clouds, or birds, for example. Envision any metaphysical associations the element has for you, too, such as **intellectuality, study, knowledge**, and so on, as well as any symbols you may associate with the direction. Mentally summon the element into the ritual space, slowly and with much intent.

5. Move deosil to face the South, the quadrant of Fire, and repeat as above, using the elemental properties of this direction. Visualization suggestions: brushfire, candlelight, the sun, the desert, and volcanoes, for example. Metaphysical visualizations can include **motivation, invigoration, sexuality**, and so on, as well as any sym-

bols you may associate with the direction. Again, summon the quadrant into the space.

6. Move deosil to face the West, the quadrant of Water. Suggestions: rivers, streams, lakes, oceans, dewdrops, fog … **emotions, change, psychic insight**, and so on, as well as any symbols you may associate with the direction.

7. Complete the circle with the North, the element of Earth. Suggestions: grass, trees, plants, ancient stone, fossils, minerals … **grounding, stability, the material world**, and so on, as well as any symbols you may associate with the direction.

8. Once the elements have entered the circle, a relatively brief communion will take place with the fifth "element," Spirit: that which is All Things. Rather than communicating with an individual god or goddess (or even *the* God and Goddess), the emphasis here is on Spirit: that which is both, that which is neither. Though Spirit is strongly in the circle already, it will be invited as an individual force as well.

9. Sit comfortably at your altar and give yourself time to soak up the presence of the various elements. When you feel centered and aware, raise your hands to invite Spirit unto you. Close your eyes and envision a single point about four feet above your head. This point is spinning and spiraling deosil, becoming a larger and larger spiral. Its color is white. Lower your projective arm (the one you write with), keeping your receptive arm raised. With that raised hand, form a pointing finger and invite the spiral's tail to touch the fingertip. Keep this brief: when you feel an intense pulse through your hand and body, drop the hand and envision the spiral's tail returning to the area above you. Let yourself bathe in this whiteness as it fills your aura and alters your consciousness. Pay no attention to the physical plane, only to the energy about you. Give yourself time to soak this up before closing the spiral.

10. When ready, envision the spiral spinning back widdershins and into itself, back to a point, and finally vanishing. Open your eyes and take a deep breath, blowing upward to dismiss it with a finale. Clasp your hands in prayer position and bow, wordlessly thanking the universe for this communion.

11. Dismiss the elements one by one. As you approach each direction, beginning with the North and ending in the East, see the energy you summoned (including the images, feelings, and symbols) being sucked in a widdershins direction, back into itself, and finally closing. Move your arms widdershins to gather the energy, spinning around a bit if necessary to help push it back. The doorway of each quadrant should be closed in the same way in which it opened on first appearance. At each quadrant, end the visualization with a forceful exhalation and a deep bow in *honest gratitude* for the energy's presence.

12. Once you feel the elements have been properly dismissed, take a moment to ground and center if need be, concluding by deconstructing the circle as you normally would (minus any voice, of course). Use your circle-casting tool for this, just as you did when building it.

13. End by tapping thrice, either by tapping the end of a ritual tool three times, or knocking three times against a solid surface. This will diffuse the energy and declare the rite completed. Before closing the circle, break the silence by bellowing a resounding "So Mote It Be!"

𝔗𝔥𝔢 𝔄𝔯𝔱 𝔬𝔣 𝔖𝔦𝔤𝔦𝔩𝔯𝔶

Austin Osman Spare is credited as the master of chaos sigil magick. He theorized that compacting a spell into a small, arcane form would trap the intention's energy into a singular symbol. From this idea grew the art of sigilry, in which the internal is drawn upon and channeled into the form of an external symbol based on letters or numbers. Spare saw the validity of sigilry in complex ceremonial magick but also felt that successful magick is possible in a variety of ways, unlimited to ritualism alone. Variations of his sigil-making theories became popularized with the rise of chaos magick in the late twentieth century.

I feel that sigilry is invaluable in any magickal practice, hence the description here. As an example, we will construct a sample letter-based sigil, followed by a few number sigils.

Begin by formulating an intention and writing it out in a single line, spacing the letters as evenly and compactly as possible. Any statements of intent can be written and transformed into a sigil, such as "Peacefully awaken my psychic sight," "Heal my perpetual migraines," "Manifest the perfect car for me," or "Make the cat stop harassing the hamster." The example here is simply the title of this book.

Begin by crossing out any vowels (A, E, I, O, or U), like this:

S H A D O W M A G I C K C O M P E N D I U M

Leaving us with:

S H D W M G C K C M P N D M

Next, cross out all instances of any letters that repeat:

S H D W M G E K E M P N D M

Leaving us with:

S H W G K P N

From here, the sigil can be made. If, for some reason, only one or no letters remain from your original statement, choose a different wording for your intention and give it another shot. If you only end up with two or three letters with which to create the sigil, no worries! That is enough.

The laying of symbols atop one another is called *superimposition*. Any string of letters can be superimposed and condensed in a variety of ways. A virtually infinite number of sigils can be made from these letters. Look at your own string of letters, decide which one you'd like to begin with, and work from there by layering the other letters atop the base letter. Lines can overlap and the letters can be backward, reversed, upside-down, written in a magickal alphabet, whatever you wish—as long as they're included somehow. If any lines stick out of the figure, they can be ended with an arrow or circle. I like to add circles onto protruding lines for spells designed for internal transformation, and arrows for those crafted for external manifestation. Three examples follow.

In the example opposite, I begin with the W, and the shapes of the letters have not been changed. In the second example (page 86), starting with the S, I've made the letters "masculine" in shape: straight lines, no curves. Some of the symbols have actually become runic letters, imbuing the sigil with additional meanings. The third example (page 87), starting with H, shows a combination of the methods used in the previous two, plus more alterations I made intuitively, the first symbol being a variation of the letter H, for example. Because no two sigils are alike, there is no code for onlookers to try to crack. Sigils remain cryptic and arcane, attuned only to the maker and its purpose.

If you practice numerology or gematria, you can do the same with significant numbers. You can keep the numerals' exact shape when binding them into one symbol, or you can play with the lines by straightening or looping them. Three simple number sigils are shown on page 88: for 13 (the number of moons in a sun cycle; the "Witches' number"), for 93 (the numerological value of numerous holy phrases in Thelema), and for the Qabalistic holy number 777.

Keep in mind that a finalized sigil is most powerful if it is only drawn once. It can be drawn on paper, etched on wood, metal, on the body, and so on. These can be carried on a person, burned, or kept in a sacred place. The options are endless!

Charging the Sigil

Sigils are activated when the magician's consciousness is heightened or altered and the energy of the experience is channeled into the symbol. Conducting sexual energy is one way to imbue it with power. This should be practiced in a magick circle or sacred space. When having sex or masturbating, focus on the symbol during orgasm and anoint it with sexual fluids afterward. Or simply enchant the sigil in circle using your own methods, such as elemental consecration, vocal vibration, emotional outburst, or reflective meditation. Personalize the

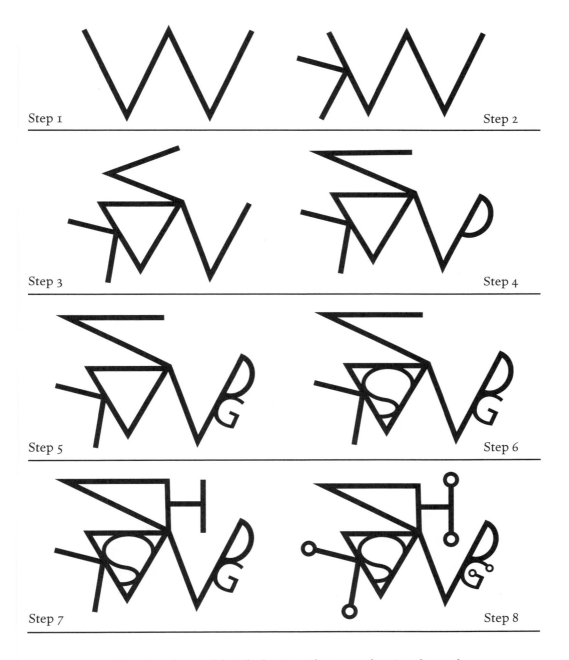

Step 1

Step 2

Step 3

Step 4

Step 5

Step 6

Step 7

Step 8

Form 1 of the three forms of the "Shadow Magick Compendium" sigil, in eight steps.

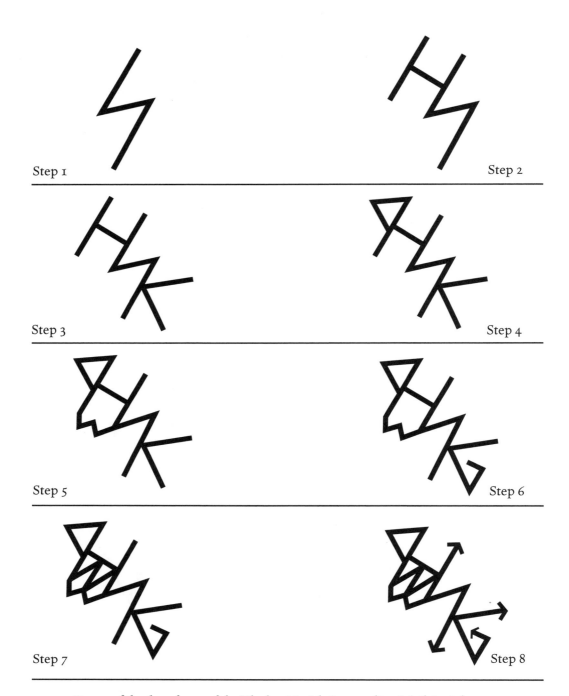

Step 1

Step 2

Step 3

Step 4

Step 5

Step 6

Step 7

Step 8

Form 2 of the three forms of the "Shadow Magick Compendium" sigil, in eight steps.

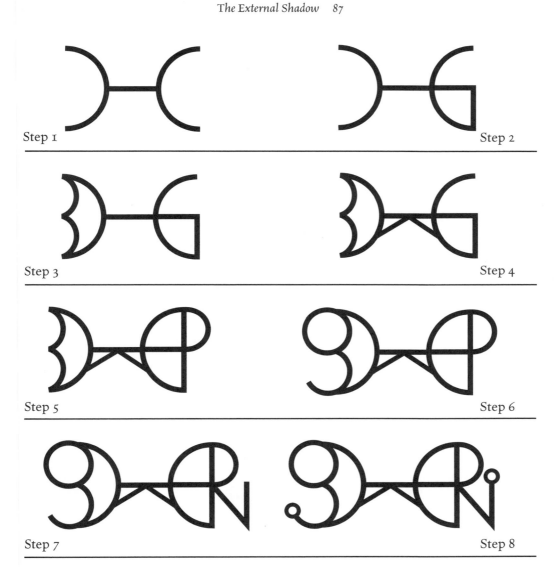

Step 1

Step 2

Step 3

Step 4

Step 5

Step 6

Step 7

Step 8

Form 3 of the three forms of the "Shadow Magick Compendium" sigil, in eight steps.

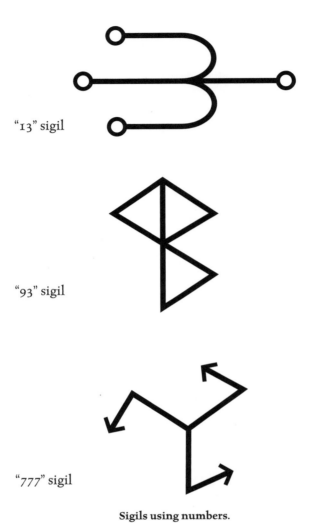

"13" sigil

"93" sigil

"777" sigil

Sigils using numbers.

experience so as to best fuse the symbol to your person; the only requirement is that you enter a heightened or altered state of consciousness and direct that high to the sigil to enchant it. One can also charge the sigil with a bit of one's own blood. (When the same symbol is drawn again, it retains the energetic imprint from the previous charging.)

After imbuing a sigil, it's a good idea to keep it in a secret place—ideally carrying it with you in a hidden spot—until you feel its energy is no longer needed. Otherwise, it may be hung above the altar or in the car, or even be tattooed on the body if the desired effects are to be irreversible and life-spanning. The symbol may be drawn anywhere appropriate, and it is best to keep reserved for "your eyes only" so as not to dissipate the magick.

Divination: Reading the Signs

The object of divination is to gain metaphysical prophecy and insight through the act of scrying or analyzing certain physical objects or occurrences. Throughout history, some sort of divination has been practiced by most cultures and virtually all religions. This is understandable particularly for animistic cultures, as the manifest plane is so often revered as a reflection of the spiritual plane or as a construction of spiritual forces. It only makes sense that the divine would deliver messages to us through the medium of our immediately perceived reality. As a magickal art, divination is external or "receptive" (rather than "active"); one observes signs outside of the self, relying on one's own perception of the external environment rather than strictly one's mind alone.

Literally thousands of books are available that discuss the divinatory arts, and many more focus specifically on one type of divination, the most popular methods being Tarot cards, astrological prediction, and dream interpretation, closely followed by runes, palmistry, crystal ball scrying, geomancy, tea leaf reading, the use of spirit boards such as Ouija, and the pendulum. So instead of repeating information that most readers have already encountered, I present a list of divinatory methods that are now considered archaic, and encourage readers to discover their own methods of embracing this most ancient art form.

Obscure Methods of Divination

Listed here are some more archaic methods of divination. I include them mostly for curiosity's sake, since few of them are practiced nowadays, but this list can also serve as a reference for those wishing to expand and experiment with their divinatory practices. Because we can use virtually *any* medium that is remotely open to interpretation, I hope this list inspires readers to reach creatively into the subtle planes for answers and insight. I must warn you: some of the historical methods of divination are absolutely hysterical in a modern context!

Aeromancy: Gazing at the clouds and interpreting the shapes

Alectryomancy: Having a rooster strategically peck grains of food placed on letters of the alphabet

Aleuromancy: Divining messages through flour or baked goods, as in fortune cookies!

Alomancy: Throwing salt

Amniomancy: Scrying in the caul around a child at birth (happens rarely and is said to be a magickal omen)

Anthropomancy: Examining a person's intestines; also called hepatoscopy

Apantomancy: Paying attention to random signs from the universe

Arithmancy: Reading the significance of numbers; also called numerology

Armomancy: Observing a person's shoulders to determine sacrificial worth

Aspidomancy: Trance-like oracular divination performed in a magick circle

Astragalomancy: Examining the knucklebones; can accompany palmistry

Belomancy: Observing the placement of (fallen?) arrows

Bibliomancy: Divination using a book, such as pricking it with a needle and reading the punctured words for prophecy

Capnomancy: Gazing at the smoke of a fire

Cartomancy: Divining with cards, such as the Tarot

Cartopedy: Reading patterns on the feet; similar to palmistry

Catoptromancy: Gazing in a mirror (such as a black scrying mirror)

Causimomancy: Throwing an object into a fire and answering a yes-or-no question based on whether it burns

Cephalomancy: Divination by means of a donkey's head

Ceraunoscopy: Observing weather phenomena

Ceromancy: Analyzing patterns in melted wax dripped on a flat surface

Chiromancy: Examining the lines and shapes of the hands; also called palmistry

Cledonomancy: Observing the significance of random things people say

Cleidomancy: Observing a string-suspended key, similar to the pendulum

Cleromancy: Throwing runes, dice, or similar items

Cromniomancy: Divination in onions

Dactylomancy: Divination with finger rings

Daphnomancy: Divination with twigs from the laurel tree, especially burning in a fire

Empyromancy: Interpreting the char marks on an object that has been burned in a fire

Geloscopy: Observing the pattern of a person's laughter

Gyromancy: Blindly walking in a chalk-drawn circle and noting the location at which you have stopped

Hippomancy: Observing the pace of horses

Horoscopy: Divination by means of the stars and planetary configurations; also called astrology

Hydromancy: Gazing in a body of water

Ichthyomancy: Examining the intestines of a dead fish

Lampadomancy: Observing an oil lamp (common in Egypt and Greece)

Lecanomancy: Throwing stones into water and observing the effects

Libanomancy: Gazing at the smoke of incense

Lithomancy: Reflecting on stones, especially precious minerals

Lychnomancy: Gazing at the flame of a candle or lamp

Margaritomancy: Divination in a pearl, most likely Asian in origin

Metoposcopy: Examining a person's line on the forehead; similar to palmistry

Molybdomancy: Dropping melted metal into water, particularly lead

Myomancy: Divination by means of rats and mice

Necyomancy: Examining the nervous system in a dead person or animal

Oinomancy: Divination in wine

Ololygmancy: Paying attention to the howling of dogs and wolves

Omphalomancy: Divination by the navel or belly-button

Oneiromancy: Interpreting the symbolism of dreams

Onomancy: Interpreting the letters in a person's name; similar to forms of numerology

Onychomancy: Interpreting the pattern of reflection of the sun's rays on a person's fingernails; can accompany palmistry

Oöscopy: Observing the pattern of eggs that have been burst in a fire

Ophiomancy: Observing the movement or pattern of snakes

Ornithomancy: Observing the pattern of birds' flight

Ovomancy: Divination in eggs

Pessomancy: Divination using beans

Phrenology: Reading the bumps on or shape of the skull; was considered a science in the Victorian era but is now obsolete

Phyllorhodomancy: Divination by using rose petals and leaves; Greek in origin

Physiognomy: Interpreting features of the face

Psychomancy: Conjuring departed spirits; similar to necromancy

Pyromancy: Gazing into fire

Rhabdomancy: Divination with sticks or rods to discover hidden objects or caches of precious substances; also called dowsing

Rhapsodomancy: Opening a poet's work at random and interpreting meaning from the words

Sangomancy: Divination and magick by using blood in a ritualistic setting; these methods are often associated with vampyrism and chaos magick

Sideromancy: Throwing straws on a hot iron

Sphondulomancy: Divination in spindles

Stolisomancy: Observing a person's manner of dress

Tasseomancy: Interpreting the shape of tea leaves left in a cup

Tephromancy: Divination in ashes

Tiromancy: Divination in cheese

Xylomancy: Observing the pattern of thrown sticks or staves

---

1. Aleister Crowley, *Magick, Book Four: Parts I–IV.* Boston: Weiser, 2004, 145.

2. Christopher Penczak, "Pagan Oracles: The Next Step?" September 2007 blog entry at www.amazon.com/gp/blog/A1XG6W2NOQ5YU5/ref=cm_blog_dp_artist_blog.

3. Lynne M. Baab, *Fasting: Spiritual Freedom Beyond Our Appetites.* Downers Grove, IL: IVP Books, 2006, 13.

4. I recommend first watching the video "Meet Your Meat," available for free from many sources online, such as YouTube.com. Numerous websites, such as Action for Animals and GoVeg.com, also offer free vegetarian starter kits and informative pamphlets to those interested in learning more about the meat and dairy industries.

5. Deepak Chopra, *The Seven Spiritual Laws of Success: A Practical Guide to the Fulfillment of Your Dreams.* Hertfordshire, UK: Motilal Books, 2003, 14–15.

6. These Hebrew words translate as "Forever, Amen."

III
The Astral Shadow

The Horned God, so often associated with shamanism, not only illuminates nature for us but also opens our eyes to the shamanic realms. Even Hades can be said to illuminate the world of the dead …

—Michael Alexandra Davida (Magdalena Merovingia)
Dominus Satánas, the Other Son of God

Astral Projection and the Etheric Planes

The web of life is very mysterious indeed. Every intention, thought, prayer, and act of magick travels at will along this web. It connects every astral plane, physical location, thought, emotion, and, well, *everything*—period. All things are linked, and intention creates our reality through this perceivable web. It is nonphysical, of course, existing outside the boundaries of normal human perception. The appearance of separateness between people, objects, items, and thoughtforms is the veil of illusion, known in Buddhism as *maya*. The great web exists beyond this illusion. This astral web, both infinite and etheric, is the true shadow of the dimension in which we find ourselves incarnate.

In ritual, we enter a sacred space between the physical plane and the Otherworld. This Otherworld is very much connected with the ordinary waking realm, yet it remains separate in everyday life because of the separation of ego and the Higher Self. Though interconnectedness is so often veiled, spiritual paths rooted in shamanic practices—such as Neopagan paths—understand that no portion of life is isolated from the next. Think of a place and your energy is immediately transported there. Visualize someone and you've aligned with their energy pattern. The web interconnects "this" to "that," and it's through this web that astral travel is possible.

Among Pagans, it's often accepted that the astral plane and physical plane were much closer together at one time, but grew farther apart as ignorance and intolerance began infecting the masses. Many of the realities seen in times past became buried and avoided as the vibration of fear overtook the common minds of subsequent generations.

Quantum physics recognizes the fact that all atoms making up physical reality are in a constant state of vibration. They are constantly moving—slow or fast—showing that nothing is truly solid; all matter is made of atoms condensed at different vibratory rates. It has been discovered that the entire atom, from the electrons to the nucleus, is constantly jumping in and out of reality. The particles exist, disappear, and return to the physical plane *constantly*. Where do they go?

Though I'm not an expert in quantum mechanics, my supposition is that the particles enter the astral plane—parallel with our reality, yet invisible to our physical eyes. If this is to be believed, an *exact* imprint of our physical reality exists on the astral, alongside exclusively astral matter. Many astral travelers note the visibility of the physical plane when seeing with "astral sight." The objects exist as real (or unreal) figures on the astral, just as they do on the physical. Because the astral is formed through thought and intention, these physical imprints are also mutable. The mind shapes the astral and determines the astral experience. The plane itself is a collection of thoughts and is constantly changing form. Physical laws don't necessarily apply to the subtle realms, and the traveler is unrestricted as with mortal existence. Both physics and metaphysics confirm the existence of additional dimensions, which adds to the validity of the astral plane.

The astral is the plane on which emotion, imagination, and thought exist. The astral is the realm of pure unconsciousness. Dreaming exists on the astral as co-created by the mind. Visionary experiences and the effects of many drugs tap into the astral realm as well.

The occult philosopher Eliphas Lévi theorized that all magickal energy is composed of "astral light," and this ethereal matter is the essence of the subtle realms. Writer and magician John Michael Greer describes the astral realm as existing between the time-space restricted physical/etheric planes and the timeless and spaceless mental/spiritual planes. This is one of the most concise descriptions I have found. It must still be kept in mind that many branches of occultism characterize the etheric, physical, mental, and spiritual planes as all interwoven, so the divisions between them may go only so far as one's own perception of them.

The astral plane has various levels and layers; some say the levels are infinite, which makes perfect sense considering the infinite nature of the mind and cosmos. With proper focus, planes that have been previously created may be accessed, or new ones can be formed. Many magicians and Witches actually create personal lodges—temple spaces—in the astral plane, which they access to perform astral magick. Many have found it just as effective as performing magick on the physical plane, if not more so. At the same time, however, when magick is performed on the physical plane it is identically performed on the astral. When energy is worked within ritual, its essence is drawn from the astral. This idea holds true for anyone who casts spells with actual *intention*, not simply going through the motions of blending herbs, stones, candles, and the like.

The astral plane contains a variety of beings, including departed spirits, thoughtforms, larvæ, spirit guides, animal guides, astral "floaters," scavengers, faeries, elementals, dragons, shapeshifters, and a wide array of other ethereal residents, including creatures mythologized in many cultures. These beings may be contacted on the astral journey. Some are vibrationally restricted to a single form, though most can shapeshift at will. The form in which they choose to appear to the astral voyager is up to the being itself, which usually knows the best guise under which to approach the seeker.

Friends and magickal partners can meet in the astral plane if the appropriate time and place are secured. The two people must energetically link beforehand. They can talk on the phone or in person just before the projection to exchange vibrations, then reconnect moments later on the astral. If the two are very close, it will be easier to connect. If either is new to astral projection, the experience will take time and practice to become more real. When they project simultaneously, the two can shapeshift together, travel side by side, and journey to distant astral territories. If the two are also next to each other physically, short sentences can be spoken if telepathy isn't a viable option, so long as brief speaking doesn't break the trance or bring one back to the body.

Various teas, spells, sigils, and focal exercises can help achieve astral projection if the ability doesn't come naturally. Experiment with various methods and find what works best for you. The first plane you perceive is sure to be the mental plane, where thoughts run rampant. Though it's tough at first to distinguish between the thought plane and the astral, know that one builds on the next and that they're closer together than they may seem.

Before attempting astral projection, ensure that proper protection is in place. Evils exist just as much on the astral plane as they do on this one. The only difference is, instead of hurting you physically, they can sap your energy—and this can be just as devastating!

Many people fear leaving the body. This unconscious fear is rooted in losing control of the physical body and possibly opening it up to harm if left behind. If astral projection is approached as similar to sleeping, it will be understood that the body is in no greater danger than it is every night.

For detailed information on achieving astral projection, I highly recommend the following books (also listed in the bibliography):

Initiation into Hermetics by Franz Bardon

Soul Flight: Astral Projection & the Magical Universe by Donald Tyson

Mastering Astral Projection: 90-Day Guide to Out-of-Body Experience by Robert Bruce & Brian Mercer

Shamanic Soul Retrieval: A Ritual Meditation

The levels and layers beyond our immediate reality hold a special place for Witches and magicians, especially those of a darker flavor. Connecting to alternate levels of reality is a form of shadow magick. Those who use magick in their spiritual path regularly work with what is hidden from our usual view, that which is obscured in darkness.

As we know, the shadow manifests in a multitude of forms. The subtle planes lie beyond our usual sensory experience, yet they make up our very existence. We interact constantly with the subtle—the astral or ethereal—but may not recognize we're doing so. It can even be said that our minds and emotions exist on other layers of reality (mostly because they are nonphysical) and, in many ways, these are what make up the astral. Magick that deals directly with these layers and levels of reality is itself shadow magick.

Its practitioners tend to concur that one manifestation of shadow magick is the act of journeying into the darkness, much as the shaman travels to the Underworld (or Lowerworld) to return with a pure diamond of light that manifests as knowledge and healing. Shamans across the globe have numerous similarities; the role is found in virtually all tribal cultures. Unsurprisingly, their methodologies are often quite similar.

Shamanic soul retrieval is one of these common tribal practices. It is simply one of the duties of the shaman, a type of ritual community service that has been venerated for ages. In the following meditation, we can draw on this practice ourselves. Witches and magicians with tribal or shamanic inclinations can practice it, whether or not they fully identify as walking the path of the shaman. In our eclectic culture, it only makes sense that we experience the rites and rituals of others. Not to mention that Witchcraft is heavily rooted in tribalism and shamanic practice, so rituals of this type can be easily blended with modern magick.

When we experience trauma, a portion of the soul (or "a soul" as it's often called) flees from our psyche with the fear that the self cannot continue to function properly if its presence remains. We thus become spiritually fractured ... damaged. "Fight or flight" are two psychological responses to extreme experience, and the "flight" response is both the easiest and most comforting way to deal with a situation. However, avoiding something for an extended period of time can slowly and subtly cause harm, feeding on the vital energy of the "healthy" soul body, aching for some sort of acknowledgement or resolution.

When a piece of us is fractured, our perception is altered. We may feel a sense of emptiness or uncertainty about life in general. There seems to be a void … but we can't put our finger on it. We may be physically ill, or at a loss mentally, but don't know its origin. We may feel that life is dull, or that we are stuck in the pointless monotony of living with little chance of escape. We may be chronically depressed, fatigued, confused, or forgetful, or perhaps we have nightmares or inexplicable mood swings.

In some cases, the reasons may be at least partly clear, such as in cases of post-traumatic stress after events such as combat, abuse, or natural disaster. But often they are not so obvious. The painful and traumatic events in our past, perhaps in our childhood, become buried. Unconsciously, we long to return to them—to deal with and heal them. But our conscious minds instinctively strive to avoid pain and painful experience, which is why so many issues become buried. We isolate portions of our minds, freezing them in time.

Daring to experience ritualistic soul retrieval is one way we can come to terms with aspects of self that have been shattered and are now buried, suspended in time. Seriously setting time aside to practice this intense pathworking can assist a person in regaining a sense of wholeness and self-awareness.

This meditation can be repeated multiple times if need be, but I recommend a maximum of twice a month. It can be difficult to encounter some of our fractured spirits, so please journey at your own rate; revisit the meditation if it's too painful initially. You may be shocked at what you discover; simply remember that these are portions of *yourself* and are nothing to fear. We all suppress aspects of ourselves for various reasons. Remember to trust your intuition, expand your senses, and be open to the experience. Wait until afterward to review it with a rational or analytical outlook.

1. After constructing sacred space around you by casting a circle and calling the quarters as you normally do, sit comfortably to start the journey. Begin by clearing your

mind. Take three deep breaths in through the nose and out through the mouth. Let the thoughts of the day drift away like moving clouds. This is not the time to focus on what happened today or what you need to do tomorrow … allow the common world to dissipate as you enter the sacred terrain of the mind. For several minutes, sense the oxygen entering your nostrils and exiting your lips. Bring absolute focus to your breath.

2. If you know your spirit animal(s) or spirit guide(s), call on them now to assist you on the journey. If you are unfamiliar with your guides, ask that they—whoever they are—be present, and that they lend clarity, protection, and success to the endeavor.

3. After meditating some more and further expanding your consciousness, lie flat on your back to begin the descent. Imagine your astral or conscious soul body sinking deeper and deeper into the earth. Feel, with your psychic senses, the cold and comforting soil around you. Go deeper, feeling the stones, the bugs, the worms, and the life inside the earth. Continue descending, feeling the solid layers of stone, compressed and fossilized deep within the earth. Allow yourself plenty of time to journey into the earth. (If you have another, more familiar way of entering the Underworld, feel free to use it instead.) At this point, you should find yourself miles beneath the earth's crust. Stop here.

4. Sensing the deep, dark earth embracing you, open your mind's eye. You have entered the Underworld and must now find your way. Expand your psychic perception in all directions, intuitively feeling which direction is pulling you. You are sensing your soul.

5. Continue journeying in the direction you're pulled. You may descend further into the earth, or travel elsewhere within. Allow plenty of time for the journey to continue. When you feel particularly close to your destination, you will begin to perceive a tunnel. Follow this tunnel, for it is leading you to yourself.

6. Once at the end of the earthen tunnel, you will find yourself in a cave. Sense the cave: is it damp or dry? Are there stalactites and stalagmites? Crystals and gems? Sense the environment.

7. As you walk further within, you begin to sense the location of your fractured soul. Continue until you discover this portion of yourself, and approach it with curiosity and compassion. What does it look like? How old are you in this vision? Does this fractured soul interact with you, or does it not notice your presence? Observe and sense this spirit. Why has it left your conscious mind? What trauma or incident caused this aspect of yourself to flee?

8. Spend some time getting to know this soul. With love and kindness, tell it that you would like to know it once again, and ask it to merge with your present-day self. Hear any messages it has to give, and respectfully interact in return. Reassure the soul that you will continue to perform healing work with it. If the soul is willing to reintegrate, invite it to step into your astral body and become one with you again. If not, accept this for now, but plan to return in the future.

9. After this experience, monitor the area to see if any other souls—aspects of yourself—are present in the cavern. If so, communicate as you did with the first soul and see what results. When you are finished, bow to the cavern, thanking the astral space for its hospitality.

10. Turn around and depart, taking your time to travel out of the cave, out of the tunnel, and eventually out of the earth, back into your physical body. Once you have reached your physical body, move your fingers and toes, take deep breaths, and very slowly open your eyes. Take plenty of time to return to your physical frame.

11. When you have fully returned, meditate on the experience and write in your journal about your discoveries. How do you feel different? Did you experience the unexpected? Did you have an inkling that the soul(s) would be there? Do you need to return soon? Record your experience so you may continue to reflect on it. Finish by closing the circles and dismissing the quadrants as you normally would.

12. Following this exercise, if the fractured soul(s) told you their reason for leaving you at one point in time, devote yourself to working with the internal resolution of this energy for a long time thereafter. How has its fleeing damaged you in the present, and what can you do now to heal this aspect of yourself?

Dark Animal Guides and Helpers

The world of animals is enigmatic, fascinating, and magickal. The beauty, the adaptable behavior, and the inherent wisdom of animals give us reason enough to admire them. Animals are everywhere around us, constantly adjusting to humans' invasions into nature. Their subtle presence is always felt but rarely acknowledged; they are the hidden seers of humanity. Our pets are our loyal companions. They are with us when no human seems to care about us, and their nonjudgmental attitudes are priceless gifts from the gods.

The human species is, of course, part of the animal realm, but animal consciousness belongs to a vibration different from ours. Animals do have distinct personalities and character traits, though less defined than our own. They also have astral doubles, as humans do. Animal energies accompany us throughout the day, usually remaining unseen. Connecting to their energies connects us to nature; animals are living and breathing emanations of nature's beauty and must be wholly respected as such. Our respect solidifies the ties that bind humanity to the natural world and lead us to the mysteries of the earth.

Animals are telepathic, communicating on a vibratory level. This is natural and instinctive to all animal species, including humans, although most of us have forgotten about this inherent ability. As a species within their realm, we are connected to animals biologically and spiritually and have numerous similar traits, hence our ability to connect with them psychically. Human fear, and preoccupation with the material planes, have damaged our telepathic links with animals. As we have turned from an earth-focused society to a monetary, industrial, and corporate society, we have grown more distant from the animal realm, even to the point of mercilessly destroying their natural habitats and painfully exploiting and enslaving them for monetary gain. Connecting to the medicine of our spirit animals and other astral helpers lets us rekindle the once-revered relationship between human and animal, reminding us that we are very much a part of their world.

In ritual, we can summon the energies of various animals and access their astral substance for good use. Many Witches and Pagans access and work with their animal guides regularly, especially in solitary ritualism. Not only does connecting with our animal helpers fine-tune our ability to perceive the astral, it adds to the energy of the animals' consciousness at the same time, so that human and nonhuman species are in a state of kinship and mutual development.

Some Pagans and earth-based spiritualists use the term *totem animal* interchangeably with *spirit, medicine,* or *power animal* and sometimes equate the word *familiar* with them as well. This is only a matter of terminology, and the choice of words may vary by tribe and culture as well. But there is a difference between personal spirit guides, energetic embodiments, and projections of group consciousness. The terms below explain the interpretations I have discovered in my own journey.

The Spirit Animal

One's personal animal guide is called one's spirit animal (or medicine animal). It is the embodiment of the collective animal consciousness of a particular species, the essence of an earthly animal, as opposed to a mythological beast or exclusively astral creature. It is typically an animal local to the place a person is born, for example, bison in North America, koalas in Australia, and dolphins in Jamaica. A spirit animal walks alongside someone from birth, though it may leave the person or drop into the background later in life. In shamanism, the spirit animal is also the psychopomp: the escort of souls to the spirit world.

Most people experience one to four animal guides in one lifetime. Some animals accompany a person throughout a whole lifetime, while others make themselves present only on occasion. Some people experience a plethora of animal guides, perhaps working regularly with many of them at any given time. The number of guides varies as a person's need for each animal helper changes. If a person changes little throughout life, multiple animals may not be necessary. Animals change as a person's energy dramatically shifts. In many native and shamanic tribes, multiple animals are ascribed to the cardinal directions as personal guardians and watchers—lenders of medicine. It is believed that each animal comes into our lives, physically or metaphysically, to teach us something about ourselves and reality. The animal simply *comes* to the practitioner rather than manifesting as a result of intention: that is reserved for the power animal, described below. Personally, my spirit animal is the raven, and I have also just recently "gained"—been given—the cricket.

Animal guides are protectors, remaining invisible to mundane eyes but lending their energy in every situation. They can guard a house, ritual space, or property. They can also be ritualistically sent to other planes to gather and report information, assuming the request is meaningful and correct thanks are given. Spirit animals assist in meditation and dreaming. Many practitioners meet their spirit animals in dreams or meditative trances—like the meditation at the end of this section—and align with their energy for astral travel and journeys to the hidden planes. (This draws on ancient shamanic associations of animals and humans; the idea of metaphysical animal helpers is not a recent revelation.)

Some people identify with their spirit animal to the point where they feel themselves to *be* that animal. Still knowing their humanness, they observe that their actions, responses, and perceptions reflect the energy of their animal guide. Many who feel this way don't feel comfortable saying "I am a bat" or "I am a wolf" to people who don't understand the concept, at the risk of such a proclamation sounding like fantasy. Regardless, people who work heavily with their spirit animal, to whatever extent it manifests and wishes to be worked with, often use astral shapeshifting to further attune their own energy to the animal's. People do not physically (biologically or genetically) shapeshift, but one's astral energy field can shift and mutate to certain forms if intention is properly focused. This can be most easily achieved in meditation or ecstatic shamanic trance-dancing, but it certainly also happens while dreaming.

Everybody has at least one animal guide. Its presence may be felt when alone in a room or ritual setting, as though something unseen is watching. Members of a particular animal's species may insist on following a person for long periods of time—a sure sign that the animal's spirit has something to teach (even if it is not a primary spirit animal). A person may feel an inexplicable affinity for one species or another and wonder why. Conversely, someone may be appalled or repulsed by a particular animal or insect. This is a sure sign that the medicine of that animal has something grand to teach.

I can sometimes tell people's spirit animal simply by looking at face and body features. Both face and body often exhibit minor details pointing to the animal's presence in the person's energy field, as does a person's idiosyncratic behavior. This signifies the merging of the person's energy with the animal's and shows that the animal is being brought forth, almost always more than the person realizes (myself included).

But facial features aren't the only giveaway. For example, my longtime friend Erasmus asked me to figure out his spirit animal, but after many moons, I still couldn't tell by scrying his facial features. I researched the influence of animals who were potential candidates, but nothing seemed to fit. It was then that I and a few other people began to notice things about him that made his spirit animal quite apparent.

When we were in ritual (nocturnal, obviously), Erasmus blended in with the darkness and people would forget he was in the circle—his presence wouldn't register! Not only that, he was energetically indistinguishable at a party or in a room full of people, ritualized or not. Erasmus preferred nighttime, had solitary tendencies, and the gift of acute psychic and energetic observation. He also tended to remain quiet and observant unless directly engaged in conversation. Finally, he exhibited some traits characteristic of a cat, such as "feminine" demeanor and cautiousness, though other feline medicine traits didn't fit him at all.

When the realization finally tumbled into view, it was apparent that he had a fox spirit animal. As it turns out, Erasmus had even had a face-to-face encounter with a wild fox as a child—bingo! It's funny how we often tend to look for the hidden without first examining the obvious!

I see humans as creatures capable of embodying vibrations of the animal kingdom as a whole. The potential medicine of any creature, great or small, mustn't be dismissed—from osprey to muskrat to anything in between. Reality itself is a living, vibrant pattern of immaculate synchronicity. Closely observing the signs, symbols, and omens around us helps us rend the veil between illusory reality (separation) and actual reality (oneness). When animals and creatures make themselves known to our conscious mind, we can choose to pay attention to the divinity expressed therein.

The Power Animal

While a spirit animal is more or less a "given" in a person's life, a power animal is conferred by another person, such as a tribal or Craft Elder, or invoked by practitioners themselves for their medicine. Like spirit animals, power animals are also astral helpers whose energy becomes attached to the person for one reason or another. Also like spirit animals, they are a piece of the fullness of the animal's group consciousness. By that, I mean that they are an embodiment of the specific animal's singular essence: a falcon is a splinter of the collective Great Falcon energy; the badger is an embodiment of the Great Badger energy and so forth.

Power animals are "gained" through intention. If the seeker honestly wants the help of a particular animal's medicine for a specific reason, that animal's essence can be petitioned for help by means of prayer, meditation, and appropriate offerings. Like the spirit animal, the power animal also goes by the name medicine animal, as it lends its sacred medicine from the astral plane to the human experience, including magickal workings. Certainly, the choice of animal summoned should depend on your circumstances. If you need grace and eloquence when speaking, perhaps Swan is the ideal invite. If you need more humor in your life, Hyena can help. For courage, Bear will lend a helping hand—er, paw.

Power animals have an infinite amount of energy to lend. With appropriate research and attention to detail, you can find an ethereal life partner and ally in magick. Power animals and spirit animals are also friends in astral travel. During astral projection, the animal may meet and escort the seeker through the astral landscape. Riding the back of your animal helper through astral lands can be fun and educational. Some who practice astral projection like to energetically shapeshift into the form of the animal helper before embarking on journeys or vision quests. This can allow for easier navigation and a deeper blending of the animal's energy with that of the seeker's.

The Totem Animal

Unlike the previous two, totem animals are often seen as guardians of a particular tribe, clan, family, or area of land.

Land-based totem animals, also called Land Spirits or *Genus Loci*, are similar to the Devas that East Indians speak about. It is imperative for the magickal person to connect with the Land Spirits of the area they reside in, visit, or move to. These animal spirits remain part of an area regardless of physical changes on the property. They will also influence any magick the Witch performs, patterning the energy in part to their own vibrational essence. Land Spirits may be created by human intention, or they may simply appear as manifestations of the energy of a particular area. Either way, they are very real, sending and receiving similar energy while remaining in one spot.

Totem animals are projected manifestations of personal intention and in that sense are *created*, not unlike a gollum (golem) or thoughtform elemental in high magickal traditions. They represent the collective consciousness of a group mind. Totem animals are often incorporated in a tribe's mythology and cosmology, and are ascribed specific traits. Several cultures do use amalgamated animal forms. For example, Persian and Scythian tribes created new mythological species that combine a number of animals: the gryphon is one of these.

Along similar lines there exist animal spirit guardians who embody an animal species' consciousness. For example, the Great Elk Spirit is the unification of all aspects (including personalities) of Elk consciousness put to a singular form. The Great Elk Spirit acts as the *oversoul*: the entirety of that animal's consciousness put into one body as an emanation thereof. These are the guides most often called forth in ritual when working with foreign animal medicine. The power animal, similarly, is a *piece* of the great oversoul.

Totem poles are effigies of the unification of animal spirits between, for example, people of two families. Some native tribal customs suggest that if someone of the Bear clan were to marry someone of the Eagle clan, the totem pole given to them would include both a bear and eagle in it along with images of guardians and other associated animals significant to the tribe. Totem poles exhibit highly symbolic animal figures custom-made for the family it was carved for. In the Gelede sect of the Boni peoples of West Africa, people craft large masks to forge a connection with local forest spirits—a practice similar to making totem poles.

The word *totem* also sometimes refers to a physical representation of an animal helper, such as feathers, fur, claws, and bones, which are used as physical links to it. Such an item can be carried in a medicine bag, placed on an altar, or constructed into a *fetich* (or fetish). A fetich is simply a representation of a particular animal's medicine. It is a physical object linked to the animal's essence, like a sculpture, painting, or other effigy. It can act as a makeshift totem pole, serving the purpose of imbuing an area with specific animal energy. Each must be charged and dedicated appropriately.

A Darkly Bestiary

The animals listed in the following pages are a few of nature's "darker" creations. By this I mean that they are naturally in sync with nocturnal and mysterious energies and particularly appeal to people attuned to darker energies. Many shadow-workers have one of these as a spirit or power animal, though it would be folly to assume that all do.

I do believe it beneficial for dark Witches to call upon these animals' power when needed, when a feeling suggests a mutual attraction between the practitioner's energy and the animal's. If you know your animal guide or wish to invite the essence of a certain creature into your life, it's very beneficial to call its energy forth in personal rituals. Its presence will be amplified, and it will actively listen when you communicate with it directly.

In this bestiary, I discuss the characteristics of each animal, physically and metaphysically. I review the many benefits of working with each animal's medicine, and also mention the possible dangers of using their energy when the work becomes consuming.

Not included here are mythological creatures such as dragons, phoenixes, werewolves, satyrs, and so on. This is not to say that these creatures don't exist, because I've certainly had my fair share of astral encounters with them. But indeed, many of these beings are strictly mythological, existing only as archetypal astral thoughtforms (even though my own encounters have sometimes seemed to filter into the physical). For information on these beings, and their connection with the human realm, I wholeheartedly recommend *A Field Guide to Otherkin* by Lupa, also listed in this book's bibliography.

The Familiar

Originating from the Latin *famulus* ("servant"), the term *familiar* gained currency with the European Witch hunts. Magick-workers have owned cats, dogs, birds, frogs, snakes, rats, toads, and other animals throughout the ages. But during the persecutions, Witch hunters deemed these pets devils and demons that supposedly carried out their owner's biddings—or they claimed that the pets *were* Witches who shapeshifted into an alternate form. Sadly, these harmless house pets were brutally tortured and killed in horrific ways, alongside their owners in many cases.

A familiar is a physical animal connected to a Witch or magician, and typically has little to do with the spirit animal. For most Witches today, familiars are their pets who attend circles and meditations, helping in magickal endeavors by simply being present. They deliver spiritual signs through their behavior, acting as conduits of divine energy. A familiar warns the Witch of strange shifts in energy, and the Witch in turn works magick for the animal's health and protection. The two are psychically linked and often communicate telepathically, at least in a broad sense.

A person's familiar need not be a pet. It may be a wild or feral animal that visits the home often, or an animal encountered in the past. Familiar energy can embody more than one individual animal: familiars may be wild animals whose presence is frequently noticed, perhaps several times a day. If your spirit animal is a squirrel or you have squirrel medicine, you may notice squirrels everywhere you go. If you find them nesting in your backyard tree, you understand that they were drawn there on an energetic level.

Some Witches call their spirit animals their familiars, in a twist on the usual terminology. Others believe their spirit animal is incarnated in their pet, or that its spirit enters and leaves at will. This is possible (though less likely) even if the spirit animal and the pet have contrary natures.

✳   ✳   ✳

A reminder: Always leave offerings to your animal guides. The ideal offering is a food that the animal enjoys on the physical plane. It can be left inside on your altar or outside in a special place where the guide's animal brothers and sisters will come and consume it. I also believe that non-synthetic incense, fresh fruit, and flowers make ideal offerings to any spiritual being. Whichever you choose, the guide consumes the food's essence; thanks are given and received.

Let us continue now to this darkly bestiary of sorts.

BAT

A symbol of intelligence, the bat journeys the night and sees things other creatures cannot spot. In various cultures, bats represent anything from happiness, rebirth, and initiation to vampyrism and the death cycle. Seeing a bat signifies that you must lay to rest a certain part of yourself that you are holding on to, such as a bad habit or maladjusted mind frame. It signifies that you have been avoiding looking at unhealthy aspects of yourself, aspects you now must face and overcome. Bats also evoke the energy of awe and fear, pronouncing that deep-seated fears must first be understood in order to become healed. The bat is a teacher of transcendence, reaching to the darkest crevices of the mind to discover and heal the energies at hand.

People with the medicine of these "miniature dragons" undoubtedly see the world through slightly different eyes and pay attention to details. They can see past the immediate and discover hidden things, like people's true intentions. For those with bat medicine, discernment is the key and intuition is the guide. They may also be able to discover pertinent information about an area based on its energy pattern alone. People with bat medicine naturally prefer a nocturnal schedule and mingle with mundane types only when necessary. Bats are the *only* mammal able to fly like a bird, so people with this medicine are therefore multitalented and unique themselves.

Because bats live in clusters, they symbolize unity among the like-minded. The bat will push its human companion to seek out like-minded types and join them in partnership. Some people may react to this with a tendency to self-isolate, which can be beneficial in appropriate doses, but detrimental if the person becomes over-sheltered. Bats also symbolize sexuality in some cultures and are said to evoke lust. People with bat medicine may be quite sexual or fascinated by acts of love and pleasure.

Bats are highly perceptive animals, and thus, people with bat medicine may hear, see, and feel things, both physically and psychically, that most others wouldn't notice in a million years. Their ability to navigate the darkness allows the person working with bat medicine to gain greater insight into the mysteries of life.

CAT

All feline species symbolize grace, freedom, and luck, although we are most familiar with the housecats we keep as pets. Cats' eyes reflect the full moon's radiance, and those with feline guides are therefore attuned to the lunar cycles. Cats' eyes also represent psychic ability, so a person working with cat medicine will certainly develop in that area.

In many cultures' mythological systems, cats are emanations of the divine. Early Egyptians kept domesticated cats as pets and held the species in high regard. The goddess Bast (Bastet), the daughter of Ra, was much revered in ancient Egypt.[1] She assumes the shape of a cat, or a woman with a cat's head, and is the protector of felines as well as humans. In Hinduism, the childbirth goddess Shasthi is depicted riding a cat. Greek mythological literature occasionally mentions the goddess Artemis/Diana shapeshifting into the form of a cat. The Teutonic goddess Freyja's chariot is drawn by two black cats.

The cat may very well be one of the most evolved animals on earth. Its pristine grace, along with its obvious ability to perceive spirits, faeries, and other ethereal beings point to the fact that there's more going on than meets the eye. Likewise, people with cat medicine have both grace and a natural leaning to clairvoyance. Just as cats have night vision, people with cat medicine can "see in the dark," perceiving what is unseen to others. They have natural visionary powers and an uncanny ability to astrally project and shift between planes, skills they can hone with rigorous practice and dedicated work with the astral guide.

Those with cat medicine are also observers who are aware of the happenings around them. They can be kind and compassionate, but may just as easily be angry and defensive if they feel threatened. They are, however, predisposed to acting arrogantly, a tendency anyone with cat medicine ought to keep in check!

If you are pretty sure you have a cat spirit guide, research the various species of cats, their behavior and metaphysical associations, and try to specify which type is your own. Is it a housecat, a cougar, lion, panther, lynx, bobcat, or something else?

CHAMELEON

These animals are known for changing their skin color at will. When chameleons are born in the wild, they do take on the colors of their natural environment. But, contrary to popular belief, their colors don't change drastically from moment to moment. If you place one on green, yellow, or polka-dotted fabric, it won't up and change to match the pattern. Their appearance doesn't actually shift with the look of their surroundings—though it would be wonderful to have pinstripe-patterned pets! Instead, temperature, light, and mood determine the change, which is achieved by the contraction and retraction of the animal's colored pigment cells. It is also interesting to note that true chameleons have a third "eye" on the back of the head, which is used to sense changes in light. Because of this, the chameleon's medicine is powerful in the realm of psychic awareness.

Just as the animal changes appearance based on a set of determining factors, people with chameleon medicine do the same. They have the unique ability to alter their appearance, be it immediate or long-term. In an immediate social situation, they can identify with the topic being discussed and easily communicate their thoughts. In the greater scheme of things, they empathize with the interests of others and often determine much of their personality based on the people they surround themselves with regularly.

Magickally speaking, reality works in spirals and cycles, and those with chameleon medicine are able to "hop vibrations." They can be immersed in one thing and embrace the next right away.

People with chameleon medicine have a tendency to change and adapt *too* frequently at times. What may seem interesting one day may not be the next, depending on the exposure to new things the person receives. Not to mention, emotions can be overly extreme if there is not a firm base in the self, as they have a natural empathic ability that can easily get damaged. It's up to people working with chameleon energy to understand what truly interests them as an individual rather than morphing too frequently. Because of constant shifting, the chameleon spirit must be worked with regularly to harness its power and unique ability. Most importantly, people with chameleon medicine can hop planes and access veiled layers of consciousness quicker than most; this skill is invaluable in spiritual and magickal practice.

CROW

Slightly smaller than its cousin raven, the crow is associated with both light and darkness. It is diurnal (active during the day) rather than nocturnal, and its shiny black feathers remind us of the polarity of darkness in the light. The crow is a scavenger and aids in the end-of-life cycle of decomposition, speaking of the necessity of death to sustain life. After all, a flock of crows is called a *murder*! The Navajo viewed this bird as the psychopomp, or transporter of dead souls. People with crow medicine have a greater perspective on the cycle of life and death, and have an innate ability to voyage the planes and communicate with departed souls.

Crows are avian watchdogs. They warn other animals of the intrusion of hunters and predatory animals. For this reason, they are associated with awareness and message-bringing, and their dark color reinforces this link with prophecy. They communicate with acute awareness, and each bird is closely tied to the others. I have noticed many a crow communicate telepathically (usually when I'm throwing them crackers) to call others to accompany them at the feast. Likewise, people with crow medicine are naturally connected to one another and can intelligently adapt to a given situation. Crows also keep a safe, protective, and neurotically clean nest. So those with crow medicine find themselves doing the same, putting much stock in the wellness of health and home.

Though the crow and raven are similar in many ways, they have different cawing voices. Surprisingly, the crow is a member of the songbird family, though it is one of the few songbirds that doesn't have a steady song. Their caws can be likened to a summoning from the divine: haunting and intense, permeating and constant, the crow is there to remind us that Spirit is always present.

People with crow medicine may tend to be misunderstood, often finding themselves torn between extremes. They are naturally psychic to some degree but may have a difficult time coping with that fact. They are also master illusionists, able to skew and manipulate situations to their liking: a talent that can be used for both positive and negative ends. They are stubborn in their own way and will fight for what they believe to be right, again a double-edged tendency.

Like all scavengers, crows may snoop where they shouldn't, and they sometimes overstep unknown boundaries. This is an annoyance to many people, as is the person's naturally flighty or spacey nature. If awareness is given to these predispositions, the crow can be an extremely powerful animal with which to work.

FOX

This is another animal associated with mystery. The fox's ability to camouflage and remain hidden to even the sharpest eyes speaks of its powerful medicine: that of invisibility, analysis, and shapeshifting. Foxes are ideal to call on when one needs protection from outside influences and possible danger, including the need for immediate invisibility from creepy folk in public. Preferring nighttime, they use darkness as a shroud. The fox is elusive, thus dawn and dusk are its prime times. Both times of day are associated with Otherworld liness: times when the veils shift from light to dark; dark to light. This is a reason the fox is associated with magick and the realm of the fae. Seeing a fox at random is said to be an omen that very soon the faerie realm will open before us.

Worldwide, mythologies speak of shapeshifting between foxes and humans. This came about from the fox's association with nighttime: the time of transformation and change. Most shapeshifting tales speak of the fox transforming into a woman or magician, and thus the fox has gained association with femininity and magick. As a member of the canine family, the fox has a masculine vibration. Still, it exhibits feline characteristics, which are associated with femininity. For this reason, the fox is a profound symbol of balance in both gender and energy.

In Japan, foxes have a great deal of mythology built around them. Japanese culture recognizes Inari, the Lord of Rice who takes the form of a fox. He is praised in numerous forms with different attributes: spirit foxes are called Kitsune, and those sworn to Inari's service are called Myobu. Inari is the healer, the guardian against illness, and the bringer of wealth. He is also a powerful shapeshifter and master of disguise.

A sly creature who hides in the woods, the fox is known as a covert watcher of others' lives. People working with fox medicine have the ability to see patterns in events unfolding around them and come to conclusions based on evidence at hand. They generally remain silent, but will come out into the open and speak when need be, usually not concerned with small talk. They have extrasensory powers in a multitude of ways and see things others neglect to notice.

Both actual foxes and people working with their medicine are solitary and monogamous in nature and are comfortable sticking to their own company more often than not. Foxes are associated with cunning; people working with their medicine have the ability to be sly or manipulative in order to get what they want, so these people must remember to keep their behavior standards high.

OWL

The owl has long been associated with Witchcraft. Its nocturnal nature points to its kinship with those attracted to the energy of nighttime. Owls can see in the dark, just as magickal folk have the ability to scry, seeing into the past, present, and future. Owl medicine helps the user develop psychic prowess and learn the mysteries of the moon. The word *owl* in Latin is *strix*; the same word from which the Italian *Strega* comes about, which is synonymous with the English word *Witch*.

Because of its all-seeing eyes and general body structure, the owl has been called the "cat with wings." Both the owl and cat are associated with nighttime, the moon, and nocturnal esoterica. One should pay strict attention to the silent flight and echoing hoot to decode omens the bird is trying to communicate. The owl is a channel of the divine, whose presence can be perceived as good, bad, or anything in between. They are the silent seers of the nighttime, whose penetrating eyes tell the observer, "Wake up from the dream." The owl's moon-like eyes and seemingly expressionless face have earned the animal associations with both profound wisdom and fear.

The Native American Mescalero nation has long believed that the hoot of an owl foretells death and that owls are inhabited by supernatural, usually evil, forces. The Ojibwa nation has similar associations for the bird, but in the Pawnee and some other Native American traditions the owl is seen as a protective being: an emanation of the Great Spirit.

For many years, Christian belief held that the owl was a messenger of the devil because of its ability to turn its head nearly 360 degrees around. (And yes, *The Exorcist* was created well after this myth came about!) The "blink of an owl" was an old term for a Witch's curse. This paranoia, combined with some native views of owls as prophets of death, gave the owl a bad rap and strengthened its association with Witchcraft and magick (which had already been maligned for years prior).

Owls are great astral guides for peering into past lives and getting to the root of present circumstance. People with owl medicine are watchers … observers of the natural world. They are also quite solitary by nature.

Even owl pellets have their message. These are the regurgitated remains of rodents and other small animals the owl has consumed: bits of fur, bone, and any other substance not digestible by the bird. Owl pellets teach those working with owl medicine to reject that which is not beneficial to their path, to absorb only what provides spiritual sustenance—a lesson in spiritual discernment essential for seekers to learn.

People who work with the owl can develop the ability to detect falsehood and discover hidden secrets, swiftly getting to the facts of the matter in a given situation. Like the owls themselves, they notice sudden movements and thus can see when someone is lying and judge their character based on subtle cues in body language. This discernment feels invasive to some people who hide great portions of themselves from the rest of the world— even themselves. The owl is not fooled by the external and easily perceives the subtlety of things. A person working with owl medicine must consider when to speak and when to hold silent. A feeling of social alienation is a frequent reaction to having such psychic ability, and it's easy to think that no one else shares the gift. People with owl medicine must be aware of their powers, but not let them push them too far away from life.

RAVEN

A larger version of its crow cousin, the raven is known for its wide wingspan and haunting, guttural caw. The raven's caw is the dark voice of Spirit, calling and summoning others to hear the cries, reminding the world that the ancient mysteries are always present and should be sought. Those with raven medicine do the same, which is reflected in their interests, speech, and behavior. Also, a flock of ravens is, interestingly, called an *unkindness* or a *conspiracy* ... but I promise we're not all rudely scheming!

The raven is undoubtedly a most mysterious and enigmatic avian creature. It is the largest of the songbird family, and is akin to the crow but larger in nature. Similar traits apply for both ravens and crows. The raven has clear associations with rebirth and bringing the light from the darkness, as does the crow. The raven has long been seen as a messenger of the gods (primarily due to Norse mythology), and raven medicine can be used in magick to "send" a spell long distances through the night undetected, assuming the animal spirit is willing. The raven is also associated with shapeshifting, due to its dark and mysterious presence. In the darkness, all things can shapeshift and change. The raven is also associated with transformation and rebirth for this reason. Raven medicine is extremely helpful in magick dealing with change and adaptation. Ravens have long been associated with magick and are excellent mystical allies in the magickal arts. They are the keepers of secrets and bringers of knowledge.

In the Christian tradition, the raven is a bird of ill-omen, foretelling plague, death, and warfare. These associations were given due to the bird's scavenger nature in feeding on animal corpses. The bird's black feathers speak of its dark nature, and we all know Christianity was anxious to turn anything black into "evil." The Bible actually forbids the eating of ravens due to their dark associations. In Greek mythology, the raven was once white but was turned black as a punishment from the sun god Apollo. Similarly, in both Tlingit and Miwok Native American mythologies, the originally white raven was turned black from the sun. The Norse god Odin (Woden) is mythologized as having two ravens as his messengers; he could also shapeshift into raven form at will.

The Celtic goddess called the Morrigan was able to shapeshift into the form of a raven. She is the Queen of the dark fae and is the overseeing war goddess who swoops over the battleground to acknowledge death. The caw of a raven has been, since the superstitious Middle Ages, a foretelling of death and/or war.

One particular Buddhist community in a Himalayan region of the South Asian nation of Bhutan believes the raven to be a highly spiritual creature, each one being an emanation of the Bhutanese guardian deity Gonpo Jarodonchen. In fact, killing a raven is seen as a sin so serious that it is comparable to killing a hundred monks.

People with raven guides tend to be prophetic and observant. They have skills in divination and cyclical healing and are experts at magick and spellcrafting if practiced to perfection. They may also be able to predict someone's physical death or know when the "death" of a negative pattern must occur in a person. They prefer simplicity and solve problems by looking for the easiest and most practical answers in given situations. People with raven medicine are also awesome writers. (Okay, so I made that one up.)

Like the crow, people with scavenger medicine have the potential to overly involve themselves in the affairs of others, sometimes unaware of boundaries. This translates as a nuisance to many people and, as with many bird spirits, their flighty or spacey nature can translate as naïvety. Thus, the messages they are trying to convey can get convoluted or misunderstood, and those with raven medicine must always be aware of people's boundaries. Kept in check and given proper mindfulness, the raven's medicine is powerful and beneficial to work with.

SNAKE

Serpentine medicine is extremely intense and powerful. Many Native American nations associate the snake with healing and endurance. Hermetic magicians associate it not only with healing but sexuality. The Greek messianic figure Hermes Trismegistus is depicted carrying a caduceus wand with two snakes spiraling around it, meeting at the top face to face. Still used as a healing symbol in Western medicine, the wand signifies the raising of consciousness in the form of kundalini, especially through the acts of sex or transcendental yoga.

In ancient Egypt, a metal crown called the uræus was worn, usually by those in royalty. Showing a snake protruding from the center at the third eye chakra, the uræus was an initiatory symbol, signifying the wearer's entrance into realms of higher knowledge. The Egyptian Funerary Texts also discuss the snake as an ultimate creature of protection and defense.

The snake is an earthen creature that is associated with the Underworld. This association came about in ancient religions because of the snake's ability to travel stealthily through the grass, water, and sand, positioned lower and closer to the metaphorical Underworld than most other creatures. The cunning nachash, the Bible's mythical snake, carries Underworldly connotations as Adam and Eve's temptation to disobey God in the Garden of Eden.

In the tale of the Buddha Siddhartha Gautama, he is protected by Muchalinda, the King of the Nagas, preceding his enlightenment. Muchalinda takes the form of a cobra that coils around the Buddha, protecting him from rain and any possible attack. This story symbolizes snakes' protective qualities and their associations with intelligence.

Those with the serpent's medicine can be fierce and predatory, vengeful, and motivated. They can also be contemplative and dedicated, prophetic and wise. People working with snake medicine must monitor their actions and see where their energy is best placed. They must prioritize, knowing when to lend their encouragement to others and when to move on, when to attack and when to remain in the shadows.

Snakes have the ability to coil into a spiral: a sign of the everlasting and infinite cycles of life, reassuring us that nothing really ever begins or ends, only changes. The serpent also sheds its skin, a sign of growth and transformation. Anyone with snake medicine should work with it regularly to shed the old in order to embrace the new. When those with snake medicine neglect their spirit animal work, they often find themselves caught up in the tides of life and unable to move past a point in the natural cycle. When properly worked with, snake medicine is intense and highly spiritual.

SPIDER

Arachnids are interesting creatures that have long been maligned and misunderstood. Some esoteric theorists believe that all the animals on earth, including humans, were taken from different planets by our extraterrestrial creators and put in a single space to coexist. If this is true, the spider must come from a distant alien galaxy, as arachnid traits and behavior are like no other creatures'.

The spider's venom is associated with death and poisoning. Spiders capture their victims and cocoon them in a suffocating death before finally injecting them with venom. They are sneaky "creepy crawlies" who show up in the most unlikely of places. People with spider medicine must be very discerning, must be able to tell fiction from reality and know when an attack is justified, as they also have the inherent ability of psychic vampyrism,[2] which can be used for both good or ill.

The nervous system is the "web" inside the human body. Information flows along the web of nerves to the brain and throughout every bit of the body. Spiders are shaped something like nerve cells. This parallel, and the web correlation, make this unique spirit animal attuned to the sending of information, magick, and energy, showing that the spider is a communicative and influential creature indeed. Spider's magick is like none other.

But as well as symbolizing death, the web-weaving spider is more appropriately a symbol of creation. The web is the symbol of life and the interconnectedness of all things: physical and Otherworldly. The web is the crystallized spindle of the spider's magick, showing its ability as a builder and artist of nature. The spider is both the creator and taker of life. The bodies captured in the web are drained of life and fed upon to encourage the cycle of death and rebirth. The spider teaches these mysteries.

In many Native American traditions, the spider is the Great Grandmother, the weaver linking the past to the future, all aligning in the present. She teaches that all behavior, activity, and thought in the present intricately forms the future. She reminds us that we are the creators of our own experience, that it is we who weave our own webs.

Spiders are teachers of balance, understanding that any extreme is unhealthy. Their many eyes teach the student to see all aspects of a situation on *all* levels and planes. They also teach the necessity of studying the past, including ancient and historical research and past-life regression, and other space-time mysteries. If you come across a dead spider (do *not* kill one for this purpose), the shriveled body may be used in magick aimed at binding and capturing energy, even poisoning an aggressor. The body is also a channel of the energy of rebirth. If working with a spider corpse, call forth Grandmother Spider to invite her ageless wisdom.

People working with spider medicine are natural artists and writers, bringing ideas in the mind to physical form. They are independent, creative, and natural daydreamers. With focus, they can develop acute self-awareness and knowledge of the workings of the universe. They are excellent weavers of energy, projecting magick through multiple planes. Spider medicine is extremely powerful magickally and must be approached with reverence and respect.

In any sort of relationship, people with spider medicine must remain conscious of how they feel about the other person, as they tend to become overly attached and consuming, just like the spider who captures its victim in the web. Although they might initially have difficulty forming an emotional attachment, once they do, a strong sense of trust is instilled that has the potential to last a lifetime. Some female spiders perform sexual cannibalism, killing and devouring the males after mating. This indicates the dangers one must consider when working with spider medicine, especially insofar as relationships are concerned. Let's not have any cannibalism, actual or metaphoric.

People with spider medicine should work with their animal guide regularly to develop a clear and balanced relationship. This will ensure connectedness between the guide and its student so that no negative cycles can develop unexpectedly.

VULTURE

Worldwide, vultures (also called buzzards) are aligned with death energy and the afterlife. Numerous creation myths incorporate the vulture, a member of the raptor family, as a supremely powerful animal. In addition to deathly alignments, vultures have been associated with purification and transformation, and are widely seen as birds who are in touch with both the mundane realm and the spirit world. Vultures do not tend to be feared by societies who observe the animal regularly. Instead, they are seen as transcendent creatures whose role in the life cycle is worthy of veneration. Contrary to popular belief, vultures do not kill their own prey; they feast only on bodies whose lives have already been taken.

People with vulture medicine should pay particular attention to their actions, minding that others judge and view them by their deeds. Vultures have very keen eyesight. Those with vulture medicine likewise have the ability to hone astral sight and physically see things that others tend not to perceive, such as subtle energy patterns. And because of the bird's ability to fly effortlessly for miles upon miles, those who work with the vulture can similarly glide through life and gain an acute sense of their life's direction.

Like people with other scavenging animals' medicine, those who work with the vulture should keep in mind that they have natural inclinations to "scavenge" and energetically feed on others. Any relationship can be dangerous if appropriate boundaries are not secured.

WOLF

The wolf is a very strong animal spirit to have in your life. Wolves are known as wild and free, and will invoke similar characteristics into those working with their medicine. Wild wolves have a strong family bond, especially to their children and social groups; those working with wolf medicine will undoubtedly seek their kin and remain close to them once found. They are protectors of themselves and their kind. They will metaphysically assist those who petition their help who are in need of protection and building strength.

Wolves communicate in extensive body language as well as growls, whines, and whimpers, and also have highly sensitive sight, smell, and instinctual perceptions. Strongly bonded to one another in wild packs, they get along with each other for the most part and are generally more peaceful than is commonly believed. They are a disciplined species, having a very precise social structure wherein each member understands its place and responsibilities, each animal adding to the greater success of the pack.

In the Roman pantheon, the twins Romulus and Remus were the sons of the god Mars and Priestess Rhea Silvia. In the ancient story, they were abandoned and later found by a she-wolf who took care of them, suckling and nurturing them back to health. Later, a shepherd found the boys and adopted them as his own. In a fight over power, Remus was killed by his brother, who declared political dominance. Rome is said to have been named after Romulus.

Even to this day, elements of the ancient Lupercalia festival, possibly an early St. Valentine's holiday, still live on in Rome. The word *Lupercalia* has the same Latin roots as *lupus* and *lupine*, meaning "of or related to wolves." In the festival, Roman Priests called Luperci gathered at the cave where Romulus and Remus were allegedly suckled. After reenacting sympathetic magick to draw on the mythological event, the Priests ran through the town wearing only goatskin loincloths, striking townsfolk with ropes of goatskin, which was thought to make them fertile. This was also a purification rite: all touched by the ritually charged whips were cleansed, purified, and imbued with the venerated powers of wolf medicine.

The mouth is a prominent canine feature. In the wolf it represents death and the Underworldly Abyss. People with wolf guides can thus be outspoken, charismatic, and influential. They must remain aware of both the cycles they create and those they place their trust in. They naturally intensify any situation and always look out for their own best interests, as well as those of their loved ones.

In the wild, wolves make the most of their environment, respecting territory and sticking close to their own. When hunting, they devour every bit of the hunted animal, signifying their influence on making the most of every situation, respectfully taking advantage of opportunity. Those with wolf medicine can learn these necessary characteristics when working with their guide. These people are also naturally quite determined. When a task is at hand, they will work on it until they are satisfied with every detail.

One problematic issue for people with wolf medicine is that they are predisposed to arguing for the sake of claiming "top dog" position. This is generally a subconscious instinct and occurs mostly between people of the same gender (remember that wild wolf packs have both an alpha male and an alpha female). There is also the "lone wolf" disposition: if someone with wolf medicine feels wronged, that person may end up angrily disassociating from the "pack" and becoming isolated, often for unhealthy periods of time. This usually occurs because the person has put such stock in the individuals or circumstances at hand that the separation seems all the more betraying and harmful. If it is a real betrayal, the disassociation may be rightful, but perhaps there are misunderstandings or misinterpretations. For this reason, discernment is the wolf's key to success.

The wolf is ferocious and bloodthirsty, yet at the same time compassionate and protective. These traits also apply to people working with their medicine. People with wolf guides have strong emotions and can be vicious as well as loyal. They have a very strong sense of kinship, be it to family, friends, or to certain ideas and perceptions. If one idea makes sense, they are likely to latch onto it, hanging on to its energy for a long period of time. This is another reason why a person working with a wolf guide must carefully consider what is healthy and real, and what is idealistic or fantastic. Again, discernment is the key to utilizing this powerful animal's medicine for the greater good.

Discovering Your Spirit Animal: A Ritual Meditation

Do you know your spirit animal? Not every Pagan does. Discovering these animals takes much time and reflection, and the answer may not come about as quickly as one would wish. Sometimes the animal chooses to remain in the shadows and does not reveal itself until the appropriate time. But if the seeker has enough motivation and perseverance, they can be discovered and worked with for many years.

This meditation is useful in discovering your animal guide. If you already know your primary animal, or have an inkling as to what it may be, it's still beneficial to attempt this working as a form of reconnection and acknowledgment. It aids in discovering the spirit animal based on which elemental kingdom it belongs to. Keep in mind that just because an animal lives in a particular environment, that doesn't always mean you'll be drawn there in the meditation. For example, the lion may represent Fire to some people, though it lives on land and may thus be seen as Earthen. The jellyfish may also represent Fire, though it's a Water creature. For both of these examples, the seeker could be drawn to the Southern terrain of Fire just as easily as to the element of the animal's physical environment. Stay flexible; the meditation is not set in stone and the seeker should be open to accepting the unexpected!

When contact is made with the animal spirit, a metaphorical bridge is made between the individual human consciousness and the collective animal unconscious. The animal whose energy is most closely aligned to the seeker's own vibrations finds the seeker and makes its presence known. You must clear the mind of unnecessary thoughts first and foremost, going into the meditation without any preconceived notions about the animal. There should also be no immediate judgment placed on any animal that presents itself. Believe it or not, even the hippopotamus, mosquito, and earthworm have essential things to teach any partner.

Your animal guide may also give you a part of your magickal name during this meditation or introduce you to other spirit guides (who may or may not assume human form). These events come with time, as a person's astral senses are fine-tuned. Feel free to ask its name and it will reveal it to you if the time is right. Discovering the name is not necessary but will assist in calling the spirits forth in the future.

This meditation may be performed outside in a natural environment or at your altar. Cast a circle beforehand as you normally would; it's not good to risk the possibility of intruding energies that could throw you off guard or convey inaccurate information. I highly recommend burning sage in the area and around your aura both before and after the meditation to ensure that all unneeded energies are neutralized.

Finally, don't be disappointed if an animal doesn't make itself known to you the first time. Keep trying, and project your will to the universe to manifest the attraction. It will happen when it is supposed to. And keep in mind that this meditation may spark visions of your animal in your waking life or in a dream, not necessarily within the meditation itself. The results vary for each person. This working opens the doors of invitation for the animal to make itself known.

1. After constructing sacred space around you by casting a circle and calling the quarters as you normally would, sit comfortably to start the journey. Begin by clearing your mind. Take three deep breaths in through the nose and out through the mouth. Let the thoughts of the day drift away like moving clouds. This is not the time to focus on what happened today or what you need to do tomorrow ... allow the common world to dissipate as you enter the sacred terrain of the mind. For several minutes, sense the oxygen entering your nostrils and exiting your lips. Bring absolute focus to your breath.

2. When you feel appropriately grounded and centered, it is time to begin the journey. Visualize yourself standing nude in your human form with only blackness around you. There is no gravity and your weight is supported; you are free to do as you please. Now that blackness surrounds you, it's time to feel your way around. You are naked before the gods and the spirits.

3. In your mind, call forth the elements associated with the cardinal directions. North and the essence of Earth ... East and the essence of Air ... South and the essence of

Fire … West and the essence of Water.[3] See the elements around your visualized or astral body … Become aware of their presence and know that they are ready to assist you on your journey. See browns and greens in the area of Earth. See whites and soft yellows in the area of Air. See orange and red in the area of Fire. See blues and deep greens in the area of Water. You are surrounded by their subtle energies and are aware that each element is a part of you.

4. You stand in the middle of the four elemental energies. It matters not which direction you are facing, and you are free to move as you please. You are balanced and you are calm. This is a place of peace where nothing can cause harm. See a white cord connecting you to each direction, entering into the center of your body around the heart chakra. You have four soft, white cords of energy coming into the center of your body which extend to the elemental kingdoms around you. Look around your astral body, seeing and sensing these cords.

5. Feel a magnetic connection between yourself and the elemental kingdoms; each one is of a different vibration and pulls you at a different rate. Allow plenty of time to feel out these connecting cords and perceive which one pulls you the strongest to its area. At this point, call out to your spirit animal in your mind, asking it to present itself to you this evening. Pay attention to the omens and see if any images flash before you. If you do get visions, determine which elemental kingdom they belong to. You are in the process of discovering which element your spirit animal belongs to.

6. Once you have determined which cord pulls you the strongest, begin to follow it into its territory. Brush off the other cords and journey to the kingdom that calls. Move closer and closer to that area, and feel surrounded by their inviting energies. So which one is it … Earth, Air, Fire or Water?

7. **Earth:** If you feel yourself drawn to the element Earth, enter into its kingdom by moving forward to its terrain. You are now walking barefoot on soft, moist soil. Trees are on either side of you and the air smells of musk. You feel grounded and secure. Take a few steps forward and notice the movement ahead in the distance.

You can see a shadow rustling ahead, making its way toward you. You feel a rush of pleasant excitement as this animal comes closer. Now in front of you, notice the animal's characteristics. Begin to perceive the shape of its body and get to know it however it allows you to. Take your time. Once experienced, bow to the animal and make your way back from whence you came.

Air: If you feel yourself drawn to the element Air, enter into its kingdom by moving forward to its terrain. You are walking on air; white clouds are on either side of you. You now begin flying, slowly at first, moving faster. Your arms are outstretched like wings and you're welcome to travel anywhere you wish. You begin to notice a speck straight ahead, making its way toward you. You feel relaxed and inquisitive in this weightless environment. The animal ahead may be large or small. You come to a stop and let it approach you. Now in front of you, the animal allows you to make out its shape. Take your time. Once experienced, bow to the animal and make your way back from whence you came.

Fire: If you feel yourself drawn to the element Fire, enter into its kingdom by moving forward to its terrain. You are walking on burning embers and flat volcanic rocks, yet feel no heat or pain. You are surrounded by unthreatening, flickering walls of flame. You feel happy and invigorated. You notice a spot ahead in the distance. Something is making its way toward you; you invite its presence. Now in front of you, the animal allows itself to be seen. You are permitted to perceive it as it wishes. Take your time. Once experienced, bow to the animal and make your way back from whence you came.

Water: If you feel yourself drawn to the element Water, enter into its kingdom by moving forward to its terrain. You are immersed in water but can breathe just fine. Move forward by swimming. Clear blue water is around you on every side. You feel peaceful and at ease. You see soft movements in the distance and an oceanic figure making its way toward you. You are at peace while this animal begins to make itself

known. Now in front of you, the animal allows you to make out its shape and get to know it. Take your time. Once experienced, bow to the animal and make your way back from whence you came.

8. After you have experienced an element, go back the way you entered and allow yourself to stand in the middle of the elemental kingdoms once again, all four white cords once again attached to your heart chakra. If, for some reason, you feel another kingdom pulling you in, follow the cord and enter the element. When you have experienced all that you were meant to, slowly begin to come back.

9. Allow the surrounding elemental kingdoms around you to spin deosil (clockwise), faster and faster until they merge into pure white light surrounding your astral body. Allow this sphere around you to grow larger and larger, spanning into infinity. Now in empty space, you wish to reenter your physical body.

10. Take deep breaths in through your nose and out through your mouth. Wiggle your fingers and toes, slowly beginning to sense your body. Make slight movements and very slowly open your eyes when the time is right. Remember where you are on the earth plane and allow awareness of the environment around you to come into vision. Ground and center yourself however you do best and take the rest of the day easy, knowing that you've just made connection with the elements, having come back with knowledge gained.

Spirit Guides: Summoning Our Allies
An essay by Estha McNevin

My Priestess, Estha McNevin, is gifted in the psychic realm of spirit-sight and guide connection. Because she is especially talented in these areas, I have asked her to explain the concept of spiritual guides and guardians here. — R. D.

For many Pagans, spiritual guides (or "spirit guides") act as protective and inspirational beings, those who aid us in times of need, trial, or doubt. In many cultural traditions, people believe that each of us is assigned a guardian spirit of one kind or another. Spirit guides operate in our lives to motivate us toward a genuine development of our vast potential. They often emerge in our esoteric rituals or in our dreams and meditations. While this can result from our seeking them out, most people, including myself, have found that spirit guides often act in tune with synchronicity and have a way of manifesting their consciousness precisely when it is needed.

While spirit guides are a part of our own psyche, they are not bound by our ideas of earthly reality or obligation. In this way, our guides can act as a limitless projection of our own higher potential. Through their influence, they offer us a moral compass with which to gauge life and its occurrences as we experience them.

But our own capacity to receive and conduct this influence can, in fact, breed issues of doubt and separation. It can be difficult to accept truths of the higher self. These perceptions can make our guides seem to have a will of their own. In this way, guides are both a part of us and separate from us; they introduce into our conscious thought stream ideas that we might not normally consider or take seriously.

As a result, our minds manifest the illusion of separation so that we may more readily consider the information being offered as separate from our own interpretation. Guides are objective observers of our potential; they are unfettered by the mundane conflicts that can complicate our own observations. In this way, guides are a projection of the raw, objective soul-self. Our need to see them as distinct from ourselves is what gives them the power to reveal that unlimited potential in innumerable ways.

The effect that guides have on the conscious observation of the material world leads many spiritual seekers to believe in a higher connection. Our guides help us see the divine nature of life, and they facilitate the pursuit of our greatest potential within that reality. When we meet our guides, the event is often laid out in the synchronicity of the universe;

it all comes down to timing. The higher consciousness of each person is influenced by this synchronicity as the energies of the universe direct each life-form toward its own greater potential. As we receive this information, it becomes our job to observe, with greater clarity, the realities of earth. Once we make contact with our guides, we strive to receive that insight and use it within our daily lives by exercising our own free will.

In this way, spirit guides can help us cope with the lessons of life, with trauma, and with our own quest for fruition. Once this trust in the self is cultivated, our guides offer us priceless clarity even in the most oblique situations. Most often, these Old Ones, these archetypal projections of the greater universal consciousness who have walked the earth long before us, emerge to teach us to trust our own psychic instincts.

Carl Jung was the first psychologist to propose that our guides and protective spirits are mental projections that we channel from the greater source of the collective human unconscious. In modern psychology, the concept of spiritual guides takes the form of archetypes such as those of Mother, Father, Son, Daughter, Hero, Villain, Martyr, and so on. These function as the prototypical characters and mythic principles of human experience that mirror our moral or ethical themes of good and evil. Spirit guides provide us a way of drawing hope and inspiration out of the endless images and stories that we have been exposed to in our lives. They anchor us to our true potential and serve our absolute spiritual aspirations. Similarly, religion is designed to be that platform from which we embark upon our individual journeys of self-realization. As we make the trek through reality, we evolve from helpless infants to complex beings endlessly processing our experiences. As such, we have a largely subjective understanding of the world and the effects of our actions within it. The structures of society may offer us the terrestrial lessons of worth, consequence, and reward, but often, it is our emotional wealth that determines our true happiness in life.

As spiritual seekers, we may be slow in learning to trust ourselves enough to pursue what makes us happy. It is easy to fall prey to our faults or insecurities, which leave us convinced that to succeed in society we must censor our feelings and thoughts. For the sake of wealth and security, many of us compromise, giving up what we enjoy doing for the sake of what we must do to survive; our fear of failure can greatly limit our reality. Our internal desires can even seem dangerous; we may believe we must suppress or snuff them out in order to carry on. The result is that we fall into the habit of second-guessing, or altogether disregarding, our true perceptions. It can seem easier to hide our own true needs, wants, and desires—both from ourselves and from others— than to face our faults and progress beyond them.

This inner conflict is often the catalyst for self-discovery because it is the very discomfort of the experience that leaves us so desperate for change and growth. When we feel disillusioned enough, we open ourselves to the idea of something better than what we've settled for. It becomes natural to examine the new things that we may feel genuinely drawn to discover or master. In such moments of divine creative potential, we come to know those spirits and energies that are meant to guide us ever toward our true happiness.

Spiritual guides operate on the astral or mental planes of consciousness. They do not have physical bodies; they are mental projections of archetypal personalities. Like the Celtic Old Ones, or what some cultures call angels, they are seen as beings who are both within us and all around us. They represent what Jung termed the collective unconscious. Psychologically speaking, guides represent cultural and esoteric archetypes that we have accepted unconsciously as projections of our higher potential. These primordial images correspond to our life experiences, our shared memories, ideas, and modes of thought.

Archetypes, according to Jung, manifest symbolically in religion, myth, faerie tales, and fantasies. Throughout the world, people are raised and educated within the mythic symbolism of various diverse cultures. As we seek to survive and grow, our habitual thoughts and feelings tend to hone our character into evident personality types. But at the same time, we can also draw on the collective unconscious, where the creative associations of myth and religion are not limited by our character.

We instinctively assign symbols and pictures to the greater themes of our lives, to our often unexpressed ideas, morals, or ethics. Spirit guides are invaluable to our spiritual progress because they use the collective unconscious to help the conscious mind cope with repressed feelings and thoughts. The empowerment we receive from the higher aspect of the self taps into our unrealized potential, invigorating us to grow beyond our preconceived boundaries. Spirit guides can appear to us as our familial ancestors, heroes, mentors, angels, mythic creatures, and even as our very own self-created strangers.

No matter where they originate or how they discover our need, the simple truth is that spirit guides help us hone and trust our own intuition and abilities. They comfort us and protect us from avoidable danger or trauma. By teaching each of us our true role within the natural and spiritual cycles of life, they show us our profound connection with the symbiotic life of earth. Spirit guides verify our objective understanding of reality, enabling us to achieve goals that, at one time, might have seemed impossible to us.

Calling on Your Spirit Guides

The most effective method of spiritual guide contact is through creative or physical endeavor. When we express ourselves physically, mentally, and emotionally, we are open to all consciousness and can better cope with our own experiences throughout life. As a result, we create much less drama and find it easier to perceive and respect boundaries. Guides help us to connect with our internal self, and as that relationship evolves, a trust in the abilities of the self emerges.

Learning to accept what we see and feel is not an easy task. Sometimes our thoughts and emotions are not kind or considerate, even if we would like them to be. Learning to respect others' boundaries and to know humbly our own limitations is something that our spiritual guides specialize in. To open the door for your spiritual guides, try calling on them during a meditation.

For best results, perform this call in a quiet space that has special meaning to you. Ground and center yourself before beginning. You may fortify the space in whatever way you are accustomed to, but as you announce the call, funnel all of your need into the words as you speak them. Allow your mind to enter an altered state of consciousness.

I call out to the Old Ones,
To all those souls who have come before me,
Open your wisdom unto me.
Great ancestors,
Keepers of the Gates of Passage,
Place your loving hand upon my shoulder and lead me on.

I call out to all of the energies of humanity,
Let my life be full of your guidance.
Supreme souls who draw close to the breath of life,
Teach and inspire me in the laws of golden intuition.

May all those who tenderly awaken and motivate
Hear my prayers.

I call out to my personal guardians and protectors,
Arise fresh and active to counsel and aid me;
In your astral perfection I summon thee.

Come Unto Me,
Come Unto Me,
Come Unto Me,

So Mote It Be.

After repeating the call three times during your meditation, stay as still as possible and return your focus to the space that you are in. Try to perceive the space in your mind and discern the boundaries of the area. Are you still alone? Does it seem as if someone is standing next to you, in front of you, or behind you? If you ask a question in your mind, does it seem that an echo of an answer filters back to you? The time you spend in this space is your own. Once initial contact has been made, a variety of endeavors can act as a platform of manifestation for your guide: esoteric studies, art, or any creative pursuit.

Once you are done, give thanks and offerings to your guide or guides, even if they did not noticeably appear. Either way, you may find that when you have done this exercise once, your guide (or guides) may appear later in a dream, or may otherwise make themselves known when your awareness is altered. The object of this call is to awaken the guide within you. Remember that this does not happen overnight. As you strive to align with the desired experience, perseverance is the best path to success.

Estha McNevin is the founding Priestess of the Opus Aima Obscuræ tradition. She is passionate about ancient history and art, is an avid bookworm, campus lecturer, writer, psychic intuitive, and metaphysical teacher, and is co-owner of the metaphysical business Twigs & Brews, specializing in magickal bath salts, herbal blends, essential oils, and incenses. In addition to hosting public rituals for the Sabbats, Estha hosts personal women's divination rituals each Dark Moon and holds private spiritual consultations and Tarot readings for the community. She can be reached at www.myspace.com/twigsandbrews.

---

1. Some mythological accounts depict Bast as the sister of Ra.

2. For more information on psychic vampyrism, please reference books by Michelle Belanger.

3. If you belong to a tradition that uses different cardinal associations, feel free to use them, modifying accordingly.

IV
The Shadow of Nature

Fully accepting our dark side might lead to nonconformity, however, it can also inspire sensitivity and creativity. The majority of those who understand these nuances of life consider themselves free. They understand that darkness is not simply the absence of light, but is an integral part of it; just as one side of the earth feels the sun's rays, so the other half dwells in shadow.

—Corvis Nocturnum
Embracing the Darkness

Romancing the Moon

In the daytime, the sun reigns bright in the sky, showering the world with light and making visible the physical plane. But as the sun descends beneath the horizon, other energies begin to stir. A certain calm and stillness takes over, and the gathering sense of mystery makes onlookers curious. The rustle of the former day begins to wane and another force begins to take shape. There is a unique comfort in the night. When the physical plane is shrouded with shadow, other planes become revealed. Deep night sets in and, at this time, the majority of the world is asleep, at least on your end of the globe. Energies are at a lull; everything moves a bit slower at nighttime and the world isn't quite so chaotic.

Nighttime is the subconscious. Nature is a direct reflection of our minds—our internal reality—which is why Pagan spirituality is so sacred. Whereas daytime is aligned to our extroverted, conscious selves, nighttime reflects our deeper aspects. For the deep-thinking introvert, a love for the safe, unthreatening darkness of night is particularly holy. Because the night is the time of internal reality, it is the center of shamanic work. Because the essence of Witchcraft is based in shamanism, the nighttime can be considered the territory of the Witch. All magick is woven from the subconscious.

The night appeals to shadow magicians for obvious reasons. This is the best time to utilize magickal energies! Spells weave into the universe with less interference, while the calm of night allows for reflection and contemplation. Magick is easier to send and project when the rest of the world is asleep. The invisible information superhighways, that is, the threads in the fabric of reality, are much clearer of mental traffic while the majority of the land is asleep and dreaming.

When the sun has descended, shadow magick reigns. Communication becomes much clearer—not only between individuals but between the self and Spirit. Many artists reserve their endeavors for nightfall, finding the energy much more conducive to the creative process. Communication between the worlds also becomes stronger, the hidden areas more accessible. Ancestral and spirit contacts are strengthened while darkness enshrouds the land. Ancient Pagans of all types associated nighttime and the moon with hidden realms, often including the worlds of the ancestors and the fae. They saw these realms as far more accessible at nighttime when the veil was thin as tissue.

In the glow of night, the moon is queen.

Regenerative Introspection: The Dark Moon

As the moon rises, Witches are invited to dance in the splendor of night. In the Craft, the Goddess is represented by the moon. The moon stands for the feminine aspects of existence. Whether full or dark or in between, the limitless energy of the moon is there every night.

During the lunar cycle, the term *dark moon* refers to the three-day period when the moon is invisible: its illuminated half is facing the sun, and the dark half faces the earth. In some ancient cultures, this time was called the *dead moon*; in others, the *mystic moon*. The term *new moon* refers to the middle of that three-day period: the day when, astronomically, the cycle is at its pivot point, poised between waning and waxing again. As with the full moon, the new moon happens thirteen times a year. But because the Gregorian calendar has only twelve months, there is always a month with a second full moon (a *blue moon*) and a month with a second new moon (a *black moon*).

The shadow-shrouded moon represents the Crone aspect of the Goddess. In Celtic lore, the Crone is the wise old woman who sees all and knows the mysteries of magick. She is the most knowledgeable of all Goddess aspects and will lend a sliver of her wisdom before the moon rebirths and begins to wax in its youthful phase. Witchcraft also recognizes three nights for the full moon—the astrological apex date, the date before it, and the date after.

For those who work with the shadow, the dark moon is a time of great mystery, perfect for castings of growth and regeneration. Some Witches, however, choose not to perform any castings at this time, reserving the days for personal reflection and meditation. This is understandable, as the darkened moon draws energy inward to be finally sorted with the waxing cycle.

The dark moon is the time of new beginnings. It is the time to plant the seed you wish to have permanently bloom in your life. It is the time of introspection and a healthy dose of withdrawal. The dark moon allows us time to analyze our lives, our security, and our happiness, and to plan for what's ahead. Dark Witches revel in this time because of the power of creation the moment holds. This is a great time to empower magickal tools and jewelry by drawing shadow energy into them, ushering metaphysical darkness (or "newness") into working tools. It's also perfect for divination, especially when looking at issues of a darker nature. The deepest of questions and issues can begin to come to light if the dark moon's energy is utilized.

Celestial Shadows: Lunar & Solar Eclipses

One special and highly noticeable instance of natural shadow is the eclipse. Both solar and lunar eclipses have a certain "time out of time" feel to them, and their eerie presence speaks of something magickal afoot. For the metaphysically aware, eclipses can be harnessed for far-reaching personal transformation.

An eclipse takes place when the sun, moon, and earth are aligned. In a lunar eclipse, the earth passes directly between the sun and moon, shrouding the moon briefly in shadow. Sun and moon appear in direct opposition to each other in the zodiac; a lunar eclipse occurs only when the moon is full. Conditions are right for a lunar eclipse about once every six months.

Solar eclipses are more rare. Here, the moon passes directly between the earth and the sun—blocking our view of the sun, since both bodies appear to be about the same size in our sky. A solar eclipse occurs only at the new moon, with the sun and the moon in the same sign. When this rare event takes place, we have a direct and accessible magickal doorway in the center of a planetary alignment. (Partial eclipses carry the same influences as full eclipses, but to a lesser degree. They are not as visually or energetically intense, but they have their own powers to be utilized.)

Because of their surreal qualities, eclipses of both types were at one time associated with fear and dread, seen as bad omens or warnings from the gods. With the development of astronomy, eclipses came to be seen as natural, rather than supernatural, occurrences.

According to modern astrology, eclipses of any type represent extreme transformation. During an eclipse, energy is both totally vacant and immensely heightened at the same time. It is the ultimate paradox. The occurrence acts as a blank slate waiting to be carved; an empty canvas waiting to be painted upon.

This profound, enigmatic state should be used for magickal workings with deep personal balance in mind. Any magick performed during an eclipse should address great issues, not superficial concerns. For example, a spell to make someone fall in love with you could have extreme repercussions (this is always true, but especially during an eclipse), whereas a spell to improve health could have positive long-term benefits. Pathworking, meditation, and divination during an eclipse can also be very powerful and lucid.

Keep in mind that the moon represents the internal, covert landscape while the sun represents the external, the overt. Solar eclipses influence events on a more visible level and their effects are more noticeable. Because solar eclipses can only occur during a new moon, they lend intense energies of rebirth and newness in an external sense.

Lunar eclipses are more emotionally and intuitively based; they provide an immaculate setting for personal workings. Because they occur only during a full moon, they are ideal times to release old habits or cycles. Eclipses of both types present an extreme opportunity to realign with their illuminated zodiacal energies (see the following list).

When the moon or sun is eclipsing, call out to the gods; chant your spell and take advantage of the tremendous boost of power this blink of time has to offer. All spells, rituals, meditations, sacred baths, and such should be determined and planned out beforehand, taking into consideration what is most beneficial at this moment. The astrological signs that the moon and sun are in should be known previously, and the ceremony mapped out in accordance with its influence. The following list gives a good idea of the various astrological signs and their general metaphysical influences in the event of an eclipse.

- **Aries** (Mars) – Physical energy, motivation, leadership, exercise, anger, personality, new beginnings

- **Taurus** (Venus) – Physical issues, money, possessions, values, self-esteem, practicality, sexuality

- **Gemini** (Mercury) – Dichotomy, balance, communication, community, study, mental states, versatility, rationalization

- **Cancer** (Moon) – Compassion, nurturing, intuition, emotions, habits, property, consuming, home life, family

- **Leo** (Sun) – Art, self-expression, hobbies, self-esteem, ego, pride, entertainment, fashion, pleasures, interests

- **Virgo** (Mercury) – Judgment, analysis, opinions, diet, health, habits, skills, employment, routines

- **Libra** (Venus) – Relationships, partnerships, friends, social issues, love, sexuality, balance, legal partnerships, harmony

- **Scorpio** (Pluto) – Reactions, control issues, secrets, attachments, ambitions, goals, debt, resources, organization, self-worth issues, death and dying

- **Sagittarius** (Jupiter) – Religion, philosophies, beliefs, opinions, travel, independence, opportunity, finances

- **Capricorn** (Saturn) – Leadership, career, public image, reputation, structure, creation, materialism, discipline, life and death

- **Aquarius** (Uranus) – Goals, friendships, kinships, group structure, expectations, career, research, individuality

- **Pisces** (Neptune) – Healing, emotions, empathy, psychic development, independence, discretion, art, reflection, imagination

Eclipses truly are profound instances of nature's splendid darkness, and should be utilized by shadow-working magicians, Witches, and spiritualists of all types.

Many people believe that all eclipses have lasting influence over human affairs. Some astrologers say that the number of hours a *solar* eclipse lasts, from start to finish, translates into *years* of its enduring influence, and that the number of hours that a *lunar* eclipse lasts translates into *months* of influence. This view gives significance to the astrological sign that the moon or sun is in at the time of the eclipse: that sign will run its course for the period of time indicated. Other astrologers feel the influence of an eclipse lasts until the next one. Either way, the eclipse's power mustn't be brushed aside.

As noted earlier, lunar and solar eclipses amplify the energy of the sign they are in at the time. They reveal to us things that are hidden and open gates of consciousness in accordance with the astrological influence. This is the time to reevaluate everything in terms of the issues represented by the sign; it's time to make adjustments, come back into balance, and plan for the future. The sign that the moon or sun fall under at any given eclipse has much effect on the energies it exudes. In solar eclipses, the sun's sign is the most significant. In lunar eclipses, it's the moon's sign.

Connecting to the Eclipse: A Ritual Meditation

The following ritual, or a variation thereof, can be performed to connect with a solar or lunar eclipse. Included are calls to Sol (sun) and Luna (moon), depending on the type of eclipse, as well as a place for any desired self-crafted spellwork to be performed. Rituals like the one below can certainly be performed at times of partial eclipses, though, needless to say, full eclipses are the most powerful. Similarly, visible eclipses contain the most potency for the practitioner, but eclipse magick can be performed even if it is nonvisible—that is, a solar eclipse on the other side of the globe, or a lunar eclipse during daylight hours, for example.

Humans cannot look safely at the sun with the naked eye—don't try to do so during a solar eclipse. You can consider a viewing device or special sunglasses, or simply decide to observe the eclipse's effects on the surroundings.

When an eclipse is over, energies are born anew. This is the ideal time to create change in your life. I would compare the process of an eclipse to the energy of an entire moon cycle compressed into a few hours, if that. The sun or moon appears full one moment, wanes to dark, and waxes back to full. *Theurgia potentissima!*

1. This ritual should take place outside, beneath the light of the eclipse. The working should begin about a half hour before its apex (the precise time of the eclipse's climax, as typically shown on an ephemeris or calendar). After constructing sacred space around you, sit comfortably to start the journey. Begin by clearing your mind. Take three deep breaths in through the nose and out through the mouth. Let the thoughts of the day drift away like moving clouds. This is not the time to focus on what happened today or what you need to do tomorrow ... allow the common world to dissipate as you enter the sacred terrain of the mind. For several minutes, sense the oxygen entering your nostrils and exiting your lips. Bring absolute focus to your breath.

2. In the case of a **solar** eclipse, look at the sun *only* if you have special shades or a viewing box designed for observing the eclipse. If you don't have a viewing device,

observe the changing light's effects on the environment, wherever you are. Reflect on your wishes until the apex, noting the astronomical changes.

In the case of a **lunar** eclipse, gaze at the moon until the apex arrives. Because of the lunar—and thus psychic—implications, this is a great time for divination with an oracular tool of your choice. Consider divining on issues pertaining to the sign in which the moon is eclipsing.

3. When the peak of the eclipse occurs, stand tall and breathe deep, filling yourself with the rare energy of the occurrence. Raise your arms to form a half-circle, inviting the energy into your person. Do the same with your hands, pretending to cradle the object in the sky. Form a triangle with your hands by touching your thumbs and pointer fingers together, and continue to draw the energy from the celestial body into your own.

4. In the case of a **solar** eclipse, declare something like this: "Great Father Sun, he who rules the reality external, fill my spirit with your divinity as I honor this spiritual transformation. Hear my prayers, mighty King; he who has been known as Sol, Helios, Ra, and a hundred thousand other names. Hail unto thee, Father Sun!"

In the case of a **lunar** eclipse, declare something like this: "Great Mother Moon; she who rules the reality internal, fill my spirit with your divinity as I honor this spiritual transformation. Hear my prayers, mighty Queen; she who has been known as Luna, Seline, Diana, and a hundred thousand other names. Hail unto thee, Mother Moon!"

5. At this point, perform any and all spellwork having to do with the eclipse, be it lunar or solar, and the zodiacal sign it is eclipsing in. There is no better time for weaving pointed magick than right now. Take as much time as needed. Mediate and soak up the energies.

6. When finished with your astrologically aligned spellwork, say your own prayer of thanks to the celestial body, meditate for a while longer, and perform any other work your intuition guides you to do. Afterward, take down the circle and depart the quarters as you normally would.

Black Sun: The Dark Part of the Solar Year

Naturally, the moon is the illuminator of the path of the shadow magician, especially those with Pagan tendencies. Keep in mind, however, that although we may prefer and feel more affinity with moonlight, we still honor the sun and acknowledge it as the central force of creation.

In common folklore, when the sun rises, the vampyre turns to dust: the light vanquishing the creature of the night. The ascending sun can be used in magick similarly, to shine off negative darkness, casting it away and back into the Abyss at sunrise. Why not utilize both and stay awake for both sundown and sunrise if time permits? Both times of day are very auspicious for magickal use.

In the sun's daily cycle, the shadow magician prefers dusk for obvious reasons. We revel in the beauty of the sunset, knowing that we are preparing to embrace the grand darkness to follow. Old Pagan beliefs say the souls of the dead who have passed that day descend to the afterlife with the sacred sun, escorted by the psychopomp, or transporter of the dead. In accordance with this belief, you can cast away unwanted energies at the end of the day, asking the sun to let them die alongside the sun's descent. As the sun dips beyond the horizon, you can send your own wishes along with it. Thank the sun, the divine representation of the God and the masculine current, for illuminating the day and for providing much-needed energy to all of the land.

Unlike the moon's monthly cycle, the cycle of the sun lasts the whole year round, determining the seasons and "tides" of nature. The sun's influence is much more noticeable than the moon's, and the long solar cycle is marked by the Sabbats of the Witches' path. This is the Wheel of the Year, and these are the darker sides of the cycle of the sun.

Autumnal Glory

Autumn … truly the season of the dark Witch! Just ask any Pagan Priest or Priestess; this is the busiest time of the year as far as community outreach, ritualism, and magickal workings are concerned. At this time in the sun's yearly cycle, the lush season of summer begins to die. The harvest is coming to a close and we are given time to reflect on the abundance of the year. The once-green turns yellow to orange, deep red to brown. Leaves fall and disintegrate, smelling of earthen decay. The world truly looks aflame, and anyone whose spirit is attuned to the glory of nature is naturally taken aback and overwhelmed by the splendor of the dying year.

The darkwave band Faith and the Muse created an album with these themes in mind: *The Burning Season*, the title representing both internal and external changes as reflected in the autumnal shift. In the song "Sredni Vashtar," vocalist Monica Richards whispers lyrics that speak of the turning Wheel of the Year and the darkness it carries. William Faith accompanies her vocals with driving electric guitar, adding to the message: No matter how dark or chaotic life seems, it is but a natural and necessary turning of the tide. This holds true for the dying season as well as for the personal cycles that sometimes reveal our darkest sides, for these internal cycles often naturally mirror the seasonal ones.

The dying season has a special place in the heart of the shadow magician, particularly those who walk an earth-based spiritual path. We magickal folk feel the season much more intensely than the average person; seasonal shifts alter emotions and affect the mind. For many spiritualists, the autumnal tide is just as depressing as it is enchanting. Seasonal affective disorder is a very real thing. Scientists describe SAD as a mental disorder occurring in some people during the dark months when the days are shorter and light is limited. With this shift in light, a person's circadian rhythm changes, affecting the mood. Levels of serotonin in the brain decrease with less exposure to sunlight. This neurochemical balance modulates emotions, mood, and sleep, and lower serotonin levels can easily make a person depressed and lethargic. For people with SAD, going to bed and snuggling up in the blankets for days may feel like a better option than going about the daily routine … autumn and winter lethargy is just part of our biological structure! Our ancestors understood the seasonal shift; they slowed their metabolism and body processes in autumn and winter to function more efficiently and expend less energy. Even if modern indoor heating provides comfort from the cool, our bodies still respond to the season in ancient ways.

Witches understand that science and magick are interlinked and that the scientific explanation of SAD is certainly valid. One modern treatment for the so-called disorder is spectrum light therapy, whereby the person sits under a light box to absorb the mock "sunlight" it generates. Many portable commercial lamps are also available on the market. With increased therapies, the person often begins to feel more active, rejuvenated, and less depressed. Another way to treat SAD is to take kava-kava root or the legendary St. John's wort (*Hypericum perforatum*), which can be taken in pill, tincture, or tea form. With continued use, St. John's wort works on a physical and metaphysical level to help alleviate minor depression and clear the mind. Many people have found it effective medicinally in battling mild to moderate depression, though the reason why it works is not fully understood; modern medicine has only theorized about it.[1] Magickally, the herb has been worn or carried in the pocket to ease sadness. It only makes sense that its metaphysical influences are aligned with its physical effects. Our ancestors knew the physical and metaphysical benefits of St. John's wort, and it has thus assumed associations with light energy and the sun.

Highly sensitive people also empathize with the death energy of the season. The Oak King—the force of growth in the Celtic pantheon—begins to metaphorically die at Midsummer and isn't fully laid to rest until Lughnassadh. Death energy is all around, reflected externally in nature and internally through shifts in mood. For Witches, the dying tide of nature is metaphorically enacted in ritual with the Oak and Holly Kings. These two gods exchange the throne at the two major seasonal shifts, summer and winter, and each is an archetype for its seasonal polarity. (Of course, these seasons refer to the Northern Hemisphere; the Sabbats and seasonal observations are reversed for Pagans in Australia and other places in the Southern Hemisphere.)

The Holly King is the embodiment of winter and the cold months, reigning from Midsummer to Midwinter. Santa Claus, the bearded sage reminding us of winter's joy, is the modern archetype of the Holly King. His brother the Oak King represents the sun and the warm months. He reigns from Midwinter (Yule) to Midsummer, bathing the earth with the light needed for sustenance. The Oak King's descent is metaphorically reenacted in Wiccan ritual that is designed not only to honor nature, but also to hone the magick of the seasonal shift within ourselves. When the Oak King dies, something dies within each and every one of us. If enough mind is given to this change, we can appropriately banish that which is unwanted and unneeded in our lives through ritual.

Corn dollies can be burnt as they were in old Europe (and elsewhere), honoring the dying Horned One making his way into a place of slumber beneath the earth's crust. Memoirs, written petitions, and other effigies can also be set aflame alongside the dolls to aid in the banishing magick. Create your own spell or ritual for the Fall Equinox or Samhain that draws on your own observations of the season.

In autumn, Pagans can take advantage of the changing greenery. If a tree's leaf catches your attention, use it in your autumnal magick. I've found it extremely powerful to pick a tree's leaf (with the dryad's permission, of course) that's half green and half yellow, red, or orange. This catches the leaf in suspended transformation and is ideal to use in a spell aimed at personal change in attunement with the autumnal tide. And if you see a single leaf fall from a tree, make a wish! It's a nod from the universe.

Halloween: Honoring the Other Side

Hail be to Hallows'! Samhain (meaning "summer's end") begins at nightfall on October 31: the verge of November 1, and thus directly opposite Beltane (May 1) in the solar year. The energies of Samhain balance those of Beltane, as each Sabbat would not exist without the other acting as a polarity. November 1 marks the beginning of the Celtic year. Therefore, all past karma and sorrow is left behind on Samhain, and the turning of the day to November represents a divine shift from the yearly cycle of the past to that of the future.

Samhain itself can be equated to the solar year's new moon. Energies similar to that of the new moon prevail during Samhain, though obviously drawn out for a longer period, and much more externalized. New moons around Samhain become all the more powerful as a result. Both Samhain and new moons represent rebirth, new beginnings, and an opportunity to lay the past to rest, moving to a brighter future. The full moon closest to Samhain is known as the blood moon or harvest moon, depending on tradition. Alongside the moon's "bleeding," the Witch has a perfect opportunity to purge his or her spirit and face subconscious issues and life patterns that may have been veiled for the past year. This happens to some degree naturally, as the seasonal cycles have very strong influences over humans, plants, and animals.

Just as Beltane celebrates the experience of life, Samhain celebrates the inevitability of death as a necessary and beautiful part of the infinite cycle. It is the peak of the dark season and helps connect us to the depths of our spiritual experience on Mother Earth. According to Wiccan tradition, the seasonal Goddess is in her Crone aspect at this time. She is the Elder sorceress and bestower of the wisdom of the ages. To some, she is the Bone Woman or Lady of Truth. By her side is the Lord of Death; the empowered Reaper or Holly King in his dying aspect. The greenery of the earth is now laid to rest; now begins the slumber of the year to rejuvenate for spring's rebirth.

The early Christian church didn't approve of honoring *all* dead souls at this time; only those who were *hallowed*, or "blessed by God." Thus, Samhain became known Hallowmas or All Hallows' Day, and later All Saints' or All Souls' Day.

In pre-industrial times, livestock were gathered at this holiday to either be ushered into the barn for safekeeping, or slaughtered and salted to preserve their meat for sustenance through the cold months. This is another reason the Sabbat is associated with death.

In those times, people also left plentiful offerings of food and alcohol for spirits passing by. It was believed that if these offerings were not given, the spirits would be left unsatisfied and play malicious pranks and practical jokes on the household. This, along with the tradition of dressing up to blend in with the spirit world, is the origin of today's trick-or-treating.

Old Celtic customs and activities associated with Halloween are still practiced by the masses, albeit diluted now. Jack-o'-lanterns used to serve as devices to scare away evil spirits. Apple bobbing was a form of divination, and costumes were worn both to frighten away malicious spirits and to blend in them. Many ancient Hallows' traditions are carried over to our own time, and many non-Pagans adore this holiday, spending countless hours decorating, planning, getting made up, and preparing for the trick-or-treatin' children! On an unconscious level, they are resurrecting ancient folk customs in order to integrate the energy of earth- and ancestor-based spirituality with modern life, even if for just one day in the year.

Ancient Celts saw Samhain as a day out of the boundaries of time, the one day of the year when norms fell and chaos ran rampant. The astral and the terrestrial planes intersected, time periods overlapped, spirits came forth, and lucid reality became much more unstable than any other time of the year. The dead were believed to come back and walk the earth on the first of November. The fae, too, came out and danced, capturing mortals and bringing them into their realm.

Witches always say that "the veil between the worlds is at its thinnest on Halloween." This veil is not only the dimensional separation between the living and the dead; it also separates ourselves and our ancestors, the conscious and the unconscious, the physical and unseen planes, the idealized and the actualized. This veil separates polar aspects of our existence during Samhain, letting us access the formerly hidden portions of our mind that need contemplation and healing. At this time, mourning and its rituals are common because the season acknowledges those who have crossed the veil into the world of the dead. Pains of the past tend to surface, and learning to accept our circumstance becomes our guiding light. Experienced astral travelers journey to the Otherworld to guide souls to the light, and modern necromancers work magick to release earthbound disincarnates— ghosts.

Samhain is traditionally the final day to collect plants, herbs, vegetables, and fruits of the earth before winter. It's not only a time of mourning, but one of celebration. The celebratory aspects of this High Holiday are to welcome forthcoming change and cultivate an understanding of the tides of life. Fires are often lit to remind practitioners of the light within the darkness. All Hallows' is considered the darkest holiday due to its associations with death. But technically, the Winter Solstice (the Sabbat after Samhain) is the darkest day of the year, with the shortest period of sunlight. The Solstice solidifies the energies raised at Hallows' and welcomes the beginning of the tide of rebirth.

As practitioners of shadow magick, we must remind ourselves not to get too swept up in all that is the HallowsTide. It is easy for us to immerse ourselves in this season for too long, profound as it is. We may hold on to the comfortably depressive energy of Samhain and carry it through the rest of the seasons. If we do this, we're not fully embracing the beauty found in each turning tide. Naturally, many of us are attuned to this season and it's always tugging at our heart, the time of year mattering not. Still, the seasons turn and a plethora of energies cycle around us waiting to be celebrated. Samhain prepares for the rebirth of the world. Let us revel in Halloween but not drown in its depths afterward.

Herbcraft and Wortcunning

In Latin, the word for Witch is *venefica*—a word associated with the ability to heal magickally and medicinally, suggesting knowledge of the poisonous properties of herbs and how to use them. The earliest word for Witch in Western literature is *pharmakis*, meaning one who has knowledge of healing and the use of herbs, and we can see this root in our words *pharmacy* and *pharmacist*.

The Old English word for *herb* was "wort." *Wortcunning* means herbal wisdom. Witches work with herbs magickally and medicinally. All herbs and plants have both physical and magickal properties, and these are the very essences that Witches and natural magicians utilize in spellcraft. Witches make use of the earth's medicinal and magickal gifts, knowing that every natural substance can be utilized both physically and esoterically. And in fact, herbs have been used for magickal purposes throughout the ages, and by countless religious traditions and cultures.

Witches have a special connection with nature. We hear Gaia's voice regularly, and we pay attention to the symbolic patterns of the natural realm. The earth has created a cure for everything, on every level imaginable. It's just a matter of knowing how to use the gifts surrounding us, including those that sprout from the land.

Each herb (and plant, tree, animal, mineral, and so on) has its own spirit, its own individual vibration. Each carries its own associations with metaphysical properties such as healing, love, luck, protection, peace, binding, cursing, and so forth. Herbs can be cultivated

The Day of the Dead

Native Mexicans traditionally celebrate the Day of the Dead (*Dia de los Muertos*) on November 2, and many additionally celebrate the day before it, too, which is also the official date of Samhain. Originally, the festival was held for the duration of a month in the Aztec calendar, falling around our current August. But upon the Christianization of Mexico, it was shifted to All Saints' Day, thus aligning it to the Celtic Samhain.

For this annual celebration, friends and families gather to adorn their houses, neighborhoods, and themselves with décor representing death and dying. Arts and crafts made throughout the year are paraded on this day and many people dress like corpses or invoke a certain attitude to lend in performance art. Traditional Mexican practices celebrate not only the dead, but small children as well, so that death can be recognized alongside the continuity of life.

On this day, people picnic beside the graves of departed family and friends, including them in a meal (as with the Witch's Dumb Supper, in which a silent Samhain meal is eaten, with a plate set aside for a deceased relative, friend, or pet). Altars are erected and candles lit to pay homage to the dead. Homes are spiritually cleansed of vibrations that have gathered over the past year. Parades, entertainment, and festivities aplenty are held at this time, alongside tears and ancestral remembrance. The holiday reminds people who have recently lost a loved one that they are not alone and that working toward acceptance is the key to understanding death.

Many cities worldwide observe the Day of the Dead on or around November 2. My hometown of Missoula ("Twin Peaks"), Montana, is one of them. The celebration welcomes everyone and encourages people to be free of pain, accepting the cycle of life and death as a natural part of human existence.

according to particular lunar and solar phases to further imbue them with specific properties. Those who don't have garden access can hop on down to a reputable local herb or magick shop to secure their supplies.

When an herb is used in spellcraft, the practitioner must *connect* with its energy to bring out its magickal properties. It must be analyzed and meditated upon. The practitioner can focus intent into the herb through the projecting hand until it feels "full" of the intention, as matched with the vibrational properties of the herb. From there, the herb can be used in a spell or magickal working. Beforehand, it's best to meditate with the herb— while picking it live, or while grinding it with a mortar and pestle—to get to know its spirit, gaining a direct rapport with the magickal helper.

The magick-worker should also take some time to visualize the herbs radiating with specific energies attuned to the spell. When the enchantment is complete, the herbs will seem to "glow" with an ethereal vibration tailored to the working. There are a number of things one can do to acutely awaken the metaphysical properties in plants, minerals, and other substances.

Keep in mind that a small piece of an herb can be used just as effectively as an enormous amount. For example, say you wish to add a boost of luck to a spell and are drawn to Lucky Hand Root for this purpose. If you find in your herb cabinet that you only have a grain of the root left, use it in the spell just the same. As long as what you add carries the genetic imprint of the plant (or stone, feather, shell, or whatever), it still constitutes a speckle of the substance, and its energy is added. At the same time, with such a small amount of a spell component, I advise taking more time to "awaken" that specific property in the working.

The longer an herb dries, the less available its magick becomes. Still, magick can be brought out of the herb at any time regardless of its age. It just takes a little more work to fully charge and enchant older herbs than it does fresh.

Herbs can be sprinkled in the ritual space, added to incense, boiled in the cauldron for potions, placed in a medicine bag, and so forth. If the spell or working is designed to banish forces, the spell's remains, including the herbs, are generally cast to moving waters or winds. If the spell is to manifest, the herbs can be buried or sprinkled about the property, or kept nearby in a spell bag or bottle to continue weaving their magick. Only herbs documented to have positive health benefits are taken internally in the form of teas, tinctures, and gelcaps (or vegicaps).

The Weird Sisters of Shakespeare's *Macbeth*

The magickal uses of herbs are famously chanted in William Shakespeare's *Macbeth* (Act IV, Scene I). In this scene, three Witches have gathered 'round a cauldron during a thunderstorm to create a brew of mischief and mayhem. Before crafting the spell, the sisters make mention of their animal familiars who were referenced in Act I. They include Graymalkin (a cat), Paddock (a hedgehog), and Harpier (an owl). Upon Harpier's cries ("'Tis time, 'tis time"), the Witches begin:

> Double, double toil and trouble;
> Fire burn and cauldron bubble.
> Fillet of a fenny snake,
> In the cauldron boil and bake;
> Eye of newt and toe of frog,
> Wool of bat and tongue of dog,
> Adder's fork and blind-worm's sting,
> Lizard's leg and owlet's wing,
> For a charm of powerful trouble,
> Like a hell-broth boil and bubble.

The spell continues, ending with an encounter with the goddess Hecate, their patron deity and overseer of their deeds. The Witches then go on to empower their brew in Hecate's presence. Upon Hecate's departure, the second Witch seals the spell with blood: "By the pricking of my thumbs, something wicked this way comes!" (Some believe that Hecate's scenes were added at a later date by another playwright, while others believe that the part originated entirely with Shakespeare.)

So what does this scene have to do with wortcunning? Most of the ingredients used in this spell are actually the folk names of various herbs and plants. Others, like "liver of a blaspheming Jew" and "baboon's blood," which are used in the second portion of the spell, may have been either associated with other natural ingredients or added for theatrical value. Some obvious herbs were also included in the mix, like hemlock and rue.

In pre-modern times, many herbs were named for their physical characteristics. This simple form of classification allowed for easy identification of local plants. In a literary sense, mentions of obscure and bizarre ingredients maintained the mystique of Witches as being extra-special, having access to all sorts of unfathomable goodies. We still see the practice of naming herbs after body parts carried over today with some common flora having names like cat's claw (a bark) and dragon's blood (a resin).

I suspect Shakespeare had a fair amount of information about early European Pagan practices, or at least common charmery, making the task of devising this spell that much easier. Some theorists believe he gathered information, realistic and fantastical, from the numerous people he interacted with, later incorporating portions into his plays. In his life, Shakespeare interacted with a wide array of individuals with radical and blasphemous ideologies for the time, many of which most certainly influenced his writing.

It is also worth noting that the Witches of *Macbeth* are called the Weird Sisters. The word *weird* is rooted in the word *wyrd*, meaning "fate" or "destiny." The ancient Greeks personified fate and the cycles of life in the form of three sister goddesses called the Fates or the Moirae, who were daughters of Zeus. In the mythology, the Fates oversee and control the lives of both gods and mortals, weaving their destiny moment to moment. Clotho spins the threads of the web of life, beginning its course; Lachesis weaves the threads, deciding the duration of life; finally, Atropos cuts the threads, ending life.

In Ásatrú and Norse religion, three sisters are also recognized in a nearly identical tale. Called the "Sisters of Wyrd" or the "Sisters of Fate," they are the presumed basis of Shakespeare's tale. The first sister is named Wyrd (or Urd), the second is Verdandi, and the third is Skuld. They have virtually the same life-directing roles as the Greek Fates and are seen as the guardians of Yggdrasil, the Norse Tree of Life. They represent the past, present, and future as well as the stages of existence.

Modern Wicca also recognizes the triple goddess: the Maiden, Mother, and Crone. Each represents a phase of life and is further associated with the stages of the lunar and solar cycle, probably having direct links with the Greek idea of the three sisters.

"Fire burn and cauldron bubble"

I invite readers to similarly experiment with herbal name associations for personal use. Giving alternate names to plants used in magick can both fancify a spell and codify the ingredients. It can also be a fun way to add theatrics to a ritual, which can in fact lend power to a working through an added air of mystery.

Of the folkloric herbal associations made in *Macbeth*, a number have been either identified or speculated about, as shown here.[2]

Fillet of a fenny snake: Probably chickweed, though some believe it to be bistort.

Eye of newt: Refers to the "eye" or central part of flowers, probably either of daisy or horehound. Others believe it to be a form of yellow mustard seed resembling a small eye, formerly used in medicinal blends.

Toe of frog: Bulbous buttercup.

Wool of bat: Holly leaves or moss.

Tongue of dog: Houndstongue (a European leafy, toxic plant also called gypsy flower).

Adder's fork: Dog's tooth (a type of violet), or plantain.

Blind worm's sting: Possibly wormwood, poppy, or a twisty twig.

Lizard's leg: Lizard's tail, a swamp-dwelling plant characterized by its long, drooping flower clusters. Some believe "lizard's leg" to actually refer to a sort of common creeping plant instead.

Owlet's wing: Probably holly leaves or a similar leaf.

A Darkly Herbal

Through the ages, various herbs have become known for their dark qualities. Most magickal books don't speak fondly of them, if they mention them at all—so some of the most common, and useful, are listed here.

Although most of these herbs are insidiously poisonous, they have strong magickal associations nonetheless. Shamans have long understood that, physically, herbs with toxic properties could also be used in moderation for healing or psychedelic journeying. The same concept holds true in metaphysics: these dark herbs can be used for spiritual ends but mustn't be approached nonchalantly. The outcome of a spell could be quite different than intended if the practitioner doesn't give careful attention to the plant's correspondences, which, in many cases, are indeed sinister.

Many of these infernal plants are part of the Solanaceæ family, whose broad range of flowering species includes our everyday tomato, potato, eggplant, and petunia. The dark side of the Solanaceæ family is its group of toxic plants often called the *nightshades*. These include belladonna, henbane, datura, mandrake, and tobacco—herbs long used in medicine and magick, but ones that aren't exactly comparable to your ordinary chamomile or peppermint tea. Because of their poisonous properties, these dark herbs became known as *Witches' herbs* in the Middle Ages because, obviously, Witches were doers of evil.

Two of the items in this Darkly Herbal are known as a *signature plants*. Signature plants are those whose medicinal traits can be seen symbolically in their own anatomy. For example, creases in certain types of beans resemble the vulva, and beans can be used medicinally for vaginal problems. Surprisingly, in some indigenous cultures people refrain from eating beans entirely, and in others beans are eaten only for purposes of fertility and reproductive health. Even Pythagoras and his followers refused to eat beans, seeing them as germinal souls.

Along the same lines, the small Amazonian plant called *eh-ru-ku-ku* that grows in the shape of a snake can be used to withdraw venom from a snake bite wound. Mandrake roots are shaped like little humans, and the root has been used to aid in childbirth through the ages. One can also apply this in a magickal context: the mandrake root has also long been used for working any sort of magick having to do with a person, be it yourself or someone else.

Beyond any literal resemblances, signature plants can also hint at their metaphysical uses—predominantly through personal identification, as herbs and plants can represent different things for different people. Perhaps you associate certain bell-shaped flowers with music, and would thus choose to use them in magick aimed at honing your musical or artistic skills. Perhaps you associate weeds of any type with mental poisons or negative external influences, and thus choose to make weeding your garden a psycho-magickal act, or to use weeds in banishing spells. There are many ways to utilize and personalize items drawn from the natural world in the magickal arts. Magick is driven by intention, and intention can be channeled in limitless forms.

This Herbal also includes a few *roots* that have been used in Hoodoo (rootworking), Vodou, Witchcraft, and other magickal traditions for centuries. The root of a plant sustains its life force and therefore contains the most powerful essence of the plant itself. It is for this reason that only a tiny amount of a root is needed in magickal work. Roots can also be seen as a plant's darker half. Most roots are entirely immersed in soil, never seeing sunlight until they are pulled. Therefore, they are connected to darkness. I would imagine that magicians of old recognized this, perhaps seeing roots as linked to the chthonic (the Underworld). This seems likely, considering the ancient belief that the dead were connected to the Underworld when buried.

Some Cautions and Recommendations

Please don't use any of these herbs internally, and handle them carefully (wash yer hands after touching them!). Most of them are toxic and can kill you deader than a doornail if used improperly. Witches who use these herbs are careful to attune each plant with its intended magickal purpose when using them in spellcraft. Due to the laws of metaphysics, the properties of herbs can be brought forth when used both internally and externally. **Please don't brew these herbs as teas;** their effects won't be pleasant! **And please don't burn these herbs** unless it is outdoors and no smoke is inhaled; these herbs are poisonous even in a combusted form. (Exception: it's okay to burn dragon's blood resin, as it is nontoxic.)

Ideal ways to utilize these so-called "dark herbs" are to incorporate them in medicine bags or sachets, put them at the base of candles, bury small bits on the outside of a property, or bubble 'em in an outdoor cauldron to release their properties. (After boiling, discard the mixture in the trash or bury it deep in the earth, depending on your intention.) One can also engage in a shamanic-style meditative journey wherein the practitioner's consciousness voyages into that of a plant. Keep the plant nearby during the meditation, and it will communicate its essence—its spirit—to you, helping you form a closer relationship with both the herb and the earth.

Another warning: if you use any of these herbs in spellcraft, please balance them with the use of "lighter" herbs, so that any dark energy raised will not overwhelm the spell or ritual. Balance is essential; all of these herbs should be used alongside others that will not restrict the workings at hand. This goes especially for any type of cursing or crossing.

And now, a tour of some of these darkly herbs.

ACONITE (*Aconite napellus*)

Gender: Feminine
Planetary rulership: Saturn
Elemental rulership: Water

Aconite is also known as wolfbane or monkshood. Believed to be sacred to the goddess Hecate, it was actually known as *hecateis* at one time. True aconite is probably the deadliest plant associated with Witchcraft. The name wolfbane or "wolf's bane" comes from the ancient Greek practice of dipping arrows in the poisonous extract of aconite for the purpose of hunting wolves.

Aconite and its botanical relatives are used in shapeshifting magick and for connecting with the animal realm. It's also used for astral flight, invisibility ("cloaking") magicks, and general protection. Infusions of aconite have been used in the past to cleanse and consecrate magickal blades such as that of an athamé, sword, or boline. Aconite is an ideal herb to use in spells for voyaging the Underworld or communicating with chthonic deities.

A *great* substitute I have found for aconite is the nontoxic herb arnica, which, like aconite, has been known to some traditions as wolfbane. In magick, arnica can be used for the same purposes as aconite. It is relatively inexpensive, and its flowers are usually sold in herbal shops.

BELLADONNA (*Atropa belladonna*)

Gender: Feminine
Planetary rulership: Saturn
Elemental rulership: Water

The word *belladonna* means "beautiful lady" and is associated with improving one's beauty and self image. Some say the plant's name is derived from the Roman death-bringing goddess of war Bellona. Some Renaissance-era women used extracts of the herb's poison to di-late their pupils for a more "innocent" look. Belladonna is a strain of nightshade; it's called *deadly nightshade* for a reason. Its alkaloids are extremely toxic, and many people have skin reactions by merely touching the plant. Its black berries are the most poisonous parts of the plant and have long been called "devil's apples."

Belladonna is a strong feminine herb and can be associated with the sphere Binah on the Qabalistic Tree of Life. It can be used to access the divine feminine—the Goddess Mysteries, especially that which is aligned to the energy of the Crone. It is also associated with astral projection and vision-seeking. Though the latter most likely came about due to its physical toxicity, belladonna does not have to be used internally to access its potency. It is best used in medicine bags or in potions or brews that are not to be used internally. Any part of the plant can be utilized.

Belladonna is associated with darkness and illusion. It appears very beautiful but is deadly in reality. Thus, the herb can be used in magick to uncover disturbing secrets about a situation—something very pertinent to shadow magick. Belladonna can best be utilized when working with any dark, painful occurrences the mind is holding on to. Its energy brings the Witch to face his or her darkest fears, even if emotional pain may result. Consider using or meditating on belladonna, or any of the nightshades, in the "Internal Shadow" magick examined in this book's first chapter.

BLOODROOT (*Sanguinaria canadensis*)
Gender: Masculine
Planetary rulership: Mars
Elemental rulership: Fire

Bloodroot can be used for any issues regarding the blood, or what is represented by blood: from physical blood (and thus DNA) to love and other workings of the heart. In some Native American tribes people decorated themselves ceremonially with the root's red extract, and also smeared it on their hand before shaking the hand of the person they wished to marry, in a sort of magickal effort to win favor. This shows its longtime metaphysical associations and it's believed that the darker the root, the greater the potency.

Bloodroot can be substituted for iron (associated with blood) in a magickal working and is best associated with the protection of a household. It may also be worn in a medicine bag to avert harmful vibrations sent by others. In my own practices, I like to incorporate bloodroot, bloodstone, and a couple of drops of my own blood, when performing magick aimed at the "heart" of any personal issue or dilemma.

CLOVE (*Caryophyllus aromaticus*, ETC.)
Gender: Masculine
Planetary rulership: Jupiter
Elemental rulership: Fire

Cloves have long been used in Witchcraft for various purposes. Whole cloves are often substituted for nails in cursing spells to "drive" the lesson home, or in protection charms such as a Witches' bottle or sachet. The sweet smoke is highly protective and clears a space of harmful vibrations, also aiding in memory. It's also reputed to stop gossip and attract money and lovers. Perhaps, for those readers who are into dark subculture, clove cigarettes *do* have benefits at the nightclub!

Though clove cigarettes are a nice treat (especially the black ones), use the herb with caution! In this form, "clove" is actually tobacco with bits of ground clove. Usually imported from Indonesia, the tobacco is typically of a finer grade than in typical American cigarettes, but the clove actually makes it more unhealthy than most. Ironically, clove cigarettes were originally invented for medicinal purposes, in the 1800s by Haji Jamahri of Java. An asthmatic, Jamahri used to rub clove oil on his chest to ease difficult breathing. He also rolled ground cloves into cigarettes and smoked them for what he erroneously thought were healthy benefits. Later they became popular for recreational smoking.

DATURA (*Datura* SPP.)
Gender: Feminine
Planetary rulership: Saturn & Venus
Elemental rulership: Water

Datura, also known as thornapple, Jimson's weed, or Angel's Trumpet, contains tropane alkaloids, and is thus a close relative of belladonna. When thrill-seekers attempt to get high off datura root or belladonna foliage, more often than not, they report horrifically unpleasant and terrifying experiences both mentally and physically. The internal effects of tropane alkaloid-containing plants are nothing to fool around with. Even the tiniest of doses can lead to permanent injury or death.

When used purely energetically, it works similarly to its cousin belladonna: it helps us handle the mind's darkest places. If there is an experience you wish to come to terms with or a dark aspect of yourself you wish to understand, datura can assist. The herb also carries associations with astral projection, dream magick (such as dreamwalking, encouraging prophetic dreams, or remembering one's dreams), and protection from harmful vibrations. It's also used for breaking hexes another person may have sent your way, and can be used for hexing and cursing itself, if the need is dire. Bits of datura can be used for banishing; it seems to be one of the best herbs available for this. I've found that it makes an excellent addition to a sealed sachet or medicine bag designed for the aforementioned purposes, particularly protection and magick dealing with the darker emotional realms.

DRAGON'S BLOOD (*Dæmonorops draco*)

Gender: Masculine
Planetary rulership: Mars & Pluto
Elemental rulership: Fire

Dragon's blood is a deep-red resin which, in liquid form, looks as if could have been drawn from draconian veins. The resin actually gets its name from the tree whose fruit it's extracted from: a palmlike Indonesian tree covered in dragonlike scales. Dragon's blood has long been used as an astringent; that is, it restricts the flow of blood from a wound by constricting body tissues. This is an example of a signature plant, one that mirrors physically its effects medicinally. In this case, the bloody appearance speaks of its ability to help in ailments of the blood. Like bloodroot, dragon's blood can also be a sympathetic link for actual blood in a magickal working, and also targets issues of the heart. It is associated with love and lust because of its color, and has long been used in spells of that sort.

For use in ritual, dragon's blood resin is awesome. It is used to strengthen any spell; just add a pinch of it in your concoction to amplify its power. The resin is *incredibly* aromatic and enchanting, adding an "air" of mystic ambience to any magickal working. It's also used for cleansing an area of negative vibrations in rites of purification and exorcism. Not only does it drive away unwanted forces, but it also invites strong energetic protection to any area where it's burned. The smell is divine and the resin is nontoxic, so burn away!

FOXGLOVE (*Digitalis* SPP.)

Gender: Feminine
Planetary rulership: Venus & Pluto
Elemental rulership: Water

This gorgeous but deadly plant has long been associated with Witchery. Of foxglove's alternate names, the terms "Witches' bells" and "faerie thimbles" point not only to the structure of the flower but to the plant's mystical associations.

Though foxglove is used in spells of protection, its most potent use is that of communication with the Otherworlds, particularly the realm of the fae and the realm of the dead. Like most of the herbs listed here, foxglove is aligned to the Underworld because of its poisonous associations and can thus be used in necromantic rites. (The modern use of the broad term *necromancy* can include anything from summoning the dead to simply meditating and speaking aloud to the dearly departed.)

Foxglove is one of the plants most associated with the faerie realm. It has been said that faeries favor the thimbles (flowers), whose variety of vibrant colors (varying with the species) give it associations with the world of fae. The plant can be carried, planted, or left as an offering when performing any sort of communal work with the faerie realm. It is said that such work should be pure of heart and never deceptive, lest ye shall become an enemy of the wee folk!

Appropriate to the name, and to its faerie alignments, foxglove has associations with invisibility. While physical invisibility may not be an option, carrying the herb when you wish to remain incognito, or in the background of a scene, can serve to deflect attention, thus rendering you invisible in a sense. Additionally, when performing "covert" magick—that is, any type of spell wherein you wish to cloak or mask your energy pattern—use a bit of foxglove in the working.

The medication Digoxin or Digitek, also known as Digitalis (the Latin genus name), is a digitalin: a medicine containing foxglove extract. These drugs are used to treat a variety of heart conditions. Magickally speaking, then, foxglove could be applied to magick dealing with metaphysical issues of the heart. Obviously, it should not be taken internally.

Foxglove can be dried for use in medicine bags, sachets, and the like, or can be planted and grown in an area undisturbed by animals (as with most of these herbs, it is toxic to them as well).

HEMLOCK (*Conium maculatum*)
Gender: Feminine
Planetary rulership: Saturn
Elemental rulership: Water

Hemlock has a pretty bad reputation in Witchcraft. It is said to have been used to cause quarrels between lovers, destroy sexual drive, summon evil spirits, and leave both crops and animals barren. Jeez! Whether or not this was a Christian fabrication to further persecute supposed heretical magick-workers, hemlock is in fact a dark herb that can be used for both beneficial and harmful purposes.

Hemlock is actually a member of the carrot family. It's a sedative when used in small quantities and a poison in larger doses, if taken internally. In ancient Greece, an extract of hemlock was used to put convicted criminals to death. The philosopher Socrates killed himself by drinking an extract of hemlock. For this reason the plant is associated with death and the depths of sorrow. Thus, the herb's energy aids a person in coming to terms with the shadow self, inducing sadness to be faced and recognized. Curiously, some ancients believed it could counter insanity and give balance to a person. It's good to use in magick for this purpose: bringing balance to the off-centered, especially if the imbalance came as a result of emotional pain.

Beware if looking for wild yarrow: hemlock looks very similar! Hemlock tea will have quite the opposite effects of yarrow tea, so don't ingest anything unless you're absolutely certain what it is.

HENBANE (*Hyoscyamus niger*)
Gender: Feminine
Planetary rulership: Saturn
Elemental rulership: Water

A member of the nightshade family, henbane is also known as black nightshade. The ancient Greeks associated it with the sun god Apollo and with divination. In Greek mythology, the dead receive a crown of henbane leaves upon entering the Underworld.

Magickally, the herb allows the caster to summon demons, dark forces, and both evoke and perceive spirits, especially through burning. Though only a handful of Witches actually practice this style of magick, it does have its time and place. The herb is also associated with barren wastelands and is said to have the power to render an area of land (or a person) infertile.

On a lighter note, henbane is said to aid in matters of psychic perception and in the concoction of love spells. It can also help induce prophetic dreams if kept in a sachet close to the bed. Henbane's greatest magickal property is in helping a magician see through the veil to perform great acts of divination, astral projection, and spirit communication.

MANDRAKE (*Mandragora officinarum*)
Gender: Masculine
Planetary rulership: Mercury, Uranus & Pluto
Elemental rulership: Fire

Mandrake is one of the most popular roots used in Witchcraft, and is certainly the most widely used root in shadow magick. In ancient Germany, it was called *Hexenkraut* ("Witches' plant"). Ancient Greeks referred to it as Circe's plant because of the mythological Witch's use of the root in her potions. It has been used since ancient times to induce states of trance. Be extremely careful if ingesting it; numerous people have overdosed and there is a good chance it could kill an inexperienced user, as has been documented. Some herbal and magick shops have actually stopped carrying the plant because of teenage misuse. Many shops carry American mandrake (mayapple), a plant unrelated to true mandrake but sold under the same name because of its nearly identical magickal associations and visible similarities.

Mandrake is also called sorcerer's root because of its vast magickal powers and its metaphysical effectiveness. The root is a signature plant, growing in a roughly human shape with a head, arms, and legs. It can thus be used for magickal workings on oneself or another person. If a person's energy pattern is locked into an effigy of the root, it is said to have power over that person: a belief that has long been used for everything from healing to cursing. A whole root does not have to be used, as a simple pinch contains its imprint.

Mandrake is much more widely available than most (semi)toxic herbs and is a *perfect* substitute for any of the nightshades. It has aphrodisiac qualities and is ideal in spells for spiritual love and communion. It's also said to ward off disease and misfortune, and may be hung in the home to invite protection. Mandrake is also associated with spells of binding, health, money, love, and fertility. It is ideal to use in spells requiring banishment of harmful people, ideas, or energies. Its energy vibration is intense and should only be used in the most meaningful of workings. Maybe the old folktale of mandrake roots shrieking and screaming when pulled from the earth is indicative of their esoteric power! I've always felt that mandrake is one of the most powerful plants in the book, and its accessibility (even if it's mayapple) makes it tempting to use in any deep magickal working.

POPPY (*Papaver* SPP.)

Gender: Feminine
Planetary rulership: Saturn, Moon & Neptune
Elemental rulership: Water

Who can forget the infamous scene in *The Wizard of Oz* wherein Dorothy, Toto, and the Cowardly Lion fall under the lulling spell of the poppy field? Indeed, the flowers were the creation of the Wicked Witch of the West in the film, a spell woven to divert the group from their destination, the Emerald City. Though it is theorized that the film was making a deliberate reference to the influence of opium in the nineteenth century, I find it more interesting that the plants are associated with the Witch. In a sense, it speaks of their power.

Others have written extensively on opium's historical influence on trade, politics, government, and economics, but I'm more interested in its magickal use—or more accurately, the magickal use of the flower from which it is extracted.

Opium is the resinous extract of the ripening poppy pod. It is from this resin that we get morphine, which can be processed into heroin. Opium also contains the opiate alkaloid codeine, which, for medical use, is either isolated chemically or synthesized from morphine. It has also long been used for the relief of pain, as well as to inspire restful sleep, and it was used as an aphrodisiac for centuries in China. This factor, in addition to the romantic appeal of the flower, make the plant one associated with love and lust. Because of its associations with both dreaming and the numbing of pain, poppy is also linked with death: the release of the physical body.

Poppy has been used in folk magick for a variety of purposes. It has been said that carrying the seeds can attract vibrations of wealth and financial luck. Poppy, like foxglove, is also reputed to render a magician "invisible," and can thus be used similarly to foxglove in that regard.

In magickal terms, the energy of all the properties of *opium* can be accessed by simply planting or placing the flower or dried pods in the home. To inspire creativity, opium poppies—which are legal when sold for decorative purposes—can be placed in the area where one creates art. To intensify sensuality and sexuality, or to combat insomnia, poppies can be placed by at the bedside. If making a sachet to aid in physical healing and pain relief, either for oneself or another, why not add some poppy seeds to the mix? The ethereal nature of *Papaver* allows the magician much creativity in his or her endeavors.

PSILOCYBIN (MAGICK) MUSHROOMS (*Psilocybe* SPP.)
Gender: Feminine
Planetary rulership: Neptune
Elemental rulership: Earth & Water

Also known as magick mushrooms, and not to be confused with the dangerous red-and-white-capped *Amanita muscaria* (fly agaric or "Alice in Wonderland") mushroom, psilocybin—which is scientifically recognized as virtually nontoxic—has long been ingested for shamanic and ritualistic purposes in various cultures. Perhaps most notable are the Mazatec Indians of southern Mexico, who ingest psilocybin for purposes of vision quests, shamanic healing, and experiencing community and kinship. The Aztecs referred to mushrooms as *teonanácatl:* "the flesh of the gods."

In addition to marijuana, psilocybin is considered a holy sacrament by many Witches, Pagans, shamans, magicians, mystics, and psychonauts. Psilocybin is an entheogen: a mind-altering substance taken for ritualistic and spiritual purposes. Worldwide, shamanic traditions include entheogens in ritualistic practices aimed at healing, spirit communication, ancestral magick, divination, and communal experience. Mushrooms in particular are said to be connected with the energies of death and rebirth, and many users report experiences of this nature. Above all, mushrooms are linked with vision quests and visionary experiences, which comes about from the perceived rending of the "veil of reality" between this world and that. I personally know magicians who gained visions of their life's destiny whilst dancing with the psychedelic spirits, others who have accurately perceived the faerie realm and Otherworlds, and others still who have reported life-changing psychological, emotional, and spiritual rebirths. Of course, such rebirths are only possible by facing our inner demons and past darkness, coming to terms with them, and releasing them.

Because many of us are heavily haunted by past experiences and their imprints, it can be difficult to undertake a mushroom trip in a purely social setting, rather than a more deliberate, spiritual one. The equal-opposite paradoxes of extreme sorrow and extreme joy can become blurred (and even experienced *simultaneously*) when the veil of reality is lifted. If the mushrooms are ingested in the wrong setting, or in the wrong frame of mind, a "bad trip" can ensue. The results of any drug are relatively unpredictable and depend largely on the surroundings, including other people, as well as the user's mental, physical, and emotional health. Mushrooms can also force-release much of the ego and catapult seekers into deeper—and yes, "shadowed"—aspects of the mind. So users should be balanced and comfortable with themselves before navigating the planes. Psychedelics and psychological imbalance (or even a history thereof) are rarely a good combination.

The effects are wide-ranging. Experienced 'shroomers report a direct connection to the spirit of Gaia, a perception of the fabric of reality, a realization of synchronicity and the immaculate construction of the universe, a profound dimensional shifting, intense psychic development, spirit-guide contact, astral travel, the honing of shamanic and magickal abilities, past-life regression, bilocation, mystical connections to oneness and God-consciousness, temporary enlightenment, and a vibrational awareness of our era's shift in consciousness (often said to be marked by the year 2012).

Some Witches and Pagans enjoy "taking a trip" once or twice a year—often at Samhain or Beltane—to reconnect to their spiritual path and gain visions for the year. Psilocybic medicine is said to be closely linked with the vibrations of the faerie realm (both benevolent and cunning), spiritual purity/innocence, the astral planes, euphoria, and spiritual joy—usually in the form of belly laughter, exaggerated humor, lots of yawning, and creating trippy art.

Of course, I know none of this from personal experience: remember my caution against ingesting any substance on this list. Hey, just covering my bases.

RUE (*Ruta graveolens*)
Gender: Masculine
Planetary rulership: Mars
Elemental rulership: Fire

Rue has long been used for its hex-breaking and counter-magickal properties, and is said to be particularly effective when added to bathwater. Its use is prevalent in African diaspora religions such as Vodou, Ifa, and Santeria (Lucumi), as well as in Hoodoo. Its energetic feel is simultaneously light and dark; honest and vengeful. It can be used for many purposes, especially those of deep-seated spiritual transformation or much-needed protection.

Its most widely recognized and utilized property is exorcism and the banishment of harmful forces. Rue is a great herb for protection and has been used as such since Etruscan times. It has also long been associated with purification—the smoke or a watered infusion of rue can purify an area—and protection against malicious sorcery. It can enhance psychic or clairvoyant powers, expose the truth about a situation, and help unlock hidden realms and clarify chaotic thoughts, bringing balance to those who use it.

The herb is associated with depression and sorrow, and can help one emerge from these mental states. It's also linked with death and necromancy, and is used in ancestral communication: in ancient Greece, necromancers used a rue ointment for communication with departed souls. In Italian Witchcraft, it is called the "bitter essence of the God" and is associated with the Lord of the Harvest. The plant's name comes from the Greek *reuo*, meaning "to set free."

SOLOMON'S SEAL (*Polygonatum officinale*, ETC.)
Gender: Feminine
Planetary rulership: Saturn
Elemental rulership: Water

This herb's root is associated with high magick, and its mysteries are both accessible and limitless. Pieces of the Solomon's seal root can be tailored into talismanic amulets or inscribed with sigils to use in a spell. It is said that all the herb touches becomes enchanted.

The root lends protection and security to any environment. Its feel is very dense and powerful. It stores a profound wallop of energy just waiting to be tapped! It is also said to be useful in rituals involving disciplined or intense forms of magick such as exorcism or the controlling of spirits. Its other uses include increasing wisdom, gaining luck, guidance, success, personal growth, and sustenance. It's best used as an incense for this purpose. Sealing a spell with an emphatic "So Mote It Be" or "Abracadabra" whilst using a bit of Solomon's seal can close a working like none other! [3]

King Solomon, the (debatably fictional) last king of Israel and son of King David, as according to the Koran, was said to be a practicing magician. He wore a ring known as Solomon's Seal, which was said to bless him with the ability to accomplish any task and, through a stone set in the ring, to scry thoroughly on any situation, no matter how fantastical. When the plant named for Solomon's ring dies in autumn, hexagram-shaped markings are left on the root. Folklore says that Solomon left his mark on the plant to point toward its magickal worth.

Regardless of origin, the hexagram images on the root signify the herb's magickal potential. In early Hermeticism, the hexagram represented the alchemical combination of the four elements and seven recognized planets, so Solomon's seal root carries similar properties. The herb is fairly rare but can be found through some occult supply shops.

TOBACCO (*Nicotiana* SPP.)
Gender: Masculine
Planetary rulership: Mars
Elemental rulership: Fire

The tobacco plant is associated with wisdom. In the Native American Yokut nation's creation myth, the hawk spirit chewed tobacco to become wise before creating the mountains. The Absarokee believe that tobacco is a star that descended to earth, implying that the plant may be extraterrestrial. The Kickapoo and the Cahuilla both say that the Creator took tobacco from his own heart and gave it to the peoples of the earth. In some native cosmology, it is believed that the gods themselves smoke sacred tobacco.

Many native people perceive tobacco as a female energy, though some nations such as the Cherokee see it as a masculine force and refer to it as Father or Grandfather, believing the plant to be an incarnation of celestial bodies. In general, the tobacco plant is seen as an intermediary between the physical world and the astral world. It is smoked, often in a shared ceremonial pipe, to send prayers to spirits, the directions, ancestors, and the gods: the smoke carries intention and can be blown to the winds to project prayers. The leaf is also smoked to induce mental calm and expanded awareness. A shaman or healer can blow pure tobacco smoke on a patient to strengthen the healing process, to spiritually see the cause of the ailment, and to chase off harm. Tobacco is also one of the best offerings one can give to the spirits, and has been widely used by Native Americans and other indigenous cultures for this reason.

According to some native traditions, tobacco is protected by ethereal beings—beings who seem to be similar to the gnomes in most Pagan and Wiccan traditions. Following this belief further, *every* herb may have its own set of personal guardians, just as trees have their dryads.

Because tobacco smoke is an intermediary between the worlds, it is plausible that the addictive act of tobacco smoking is a person's subconscious attempt to reconnect with the spiritual world. It is for this reason that spiritual "voids" may be temporarily filled by the act of smoking, much as with other drugs.

People who use the herb very sparingly don't tend to develop nicotine addiction, but still can be prone to it if they don't monitor their use properly. Many people like to use tobacco in combination with alcohol in social settings, but at no other time. Some Pagans restrict the use of tobacco to ritual circumstances only.

Certainly, not inhaling smoke at all is the healthier choice. But if one chooses to smoke tobacco, the kind that is not "chemically enhanced" is preferable from a health point of view. Not only that, but any magick sent with tobacco smoke is much more effective when the tobacco is in a purer, less diluted state.

VALERIAN (*Valeriana officinalis*)
Gender: Feminine
Planetary rulership: Venus & Jupiter
Elemental rulership: Water

The only root that officially smells like dirty socks, valerian has a long history of both medicinal and magickal use. Valerian is first and foremost associated with protection because its strong smell creates an "astral bug repellent." The cut, ground, and sifted root can be sprinkled around a property to help form a protective barrier, and hanging it in the house ensures that harmful energies will be kept at bay.

Valerian is also said to bring peace and harmony to a situation, useful for soothing quarrels between lovers. It is also used for magick working to physically manifest what one desires, such as money or even a sex partner. Physically and metaphysically, valerian root is used to promote deep, sound sleep. It can also help manifest self-acceptance and ease the mind of sorrow. The root may also be used in some manner whilst doing magick to contact one's spirit animal. Like catnip, it also drives cats bonkers. Lols für teh kittehs!

On a darker level, valerian is associated with the energies of the Underworld. African-based tribal practices such as Hoodoo, Vodou, and Santeria include the use of "graveyard dirt" or "graveyard dust." Valerian, alongside mullein and sage, is said to be a substitute for this kooky ingredient. Because of its power as a pungent root, its vibrations are inherently connected to the lower astral levels. For this reason, the herb can be used in death magick, cursing, and necromancy as well.

VENUS FLYTRAP (*Dionaea muscipula*)

Gender: Feminine
Planetary rulership: Venus, Mars & Saturn
Elemental rulership: Fire

Few plants are as mysterious as the carnivorous varieties. These plants grow in areas low in nitrate ions, the form of nitrogen easiest for plants to assimilate. As a result, they are forced to capture their own meals as a living supplement.

Ruled in part by the planet Venus, the flytrap is a very curious plant indeed. The double leaves of this insectivore are hinged like a clamshell, each half with a row of soft but spike-shaped "teeth" on the outer edge. When a bug walks on the inner surface of the leaves, small hairs are triggered and the trap closes shut. Soon thereafter, the leaf releases acidic fluids to dissolve and absorb the insect's body in a slow and agonizing process of digestion.

The association with Venus, the Roman goddess of love, came about because of the double leaves' resemblance to the vulva, the "mouth" of the vagina. Therefore, its metaphysical uses include alignments with both love magick and lust magick as well as any sort of capturing, especially capturing a lover. But ethical issues accompany any sort of manipulative love or lust magick, especially if it's performed on a specific person; I don't recommend it whatsoever. (The plant's acidic digesting fluids suggest just how "consuming" and destructive the possibilities are.) In keeping with its double-edged properties, the flytrap is also said to be able to both enhance and destroy feminine sex drives. The results of sexually-centered magick with this plant could be quite adverse.

The flytrap can also represent confinement and isolation. Thus, it may be used in workings centering on this energy, as well as in binding magick. If performing binding magick of any type, be sure to intend it for the goodwill of all involved and add a hefty dose of "light" for balance and potential progression.

While so many animals eat plants for sustenance, it's only proper that some retaliate and eat animals in return. A few carnivorous plants are actually capable of devouring small rodents and lizards, though most are simply insectivores. Sorry, no real-life *Little Shop of Horrors*!

Some varieties of pitcher plants—a certain type of carnivorous plant—undeniably resemble snakes and fangs in their physical appearance, telltale signs of their lethal prowess. At a glance, it would almost seem that insectivores represent a *merging* of the plant and animal kingdoms. This and countless other wonders of these kingdoms are, for me, undeniable evidence of a metaphysically interconnected world.

WORMWOOD (*Artemisia absinthium*)

Gender: Masculine
Planetary rulership: Mars & Chiron
Elemental rulership: Fire

Wormwood was held sacred by the Greeks, most notably in Græco-Roman Egypt, and was said to be an herb venerated by the gods. In some ancient spells, it was also called the "blood of Hephaistos," Greek god of smith crafts and son of Hera.

Wormwood is a member of the Artemisia family. Its Old English root word, *wermod*, means "spirit mother." Its Greek name, *apsinthios*, means "absent of sweetness," as it's a very bitter herb. It is poisonous in large doses and its green oil extract is particularly toxic in large quantities. Wormwood is the primary ingredient in the legendary liquor absinthe (the name derived from the Greek). Both absinthe and wormwood were and still are associated with artistic creativity, love, and lust. In antiquity, wormwood was also used for summoning spirits in necromantic rites, and it can still be used for those purposes in shadow magick.

Because absinthe that includes wormwood is addictive, the herb can be used in magick for breaking addictions. Wormwood is externally used for sleeping and dream magick. It can also be used to target issues of anger and ego, and is said to have the power to remove curses as well as create them, which makes sense considering its Mars energy. Like its cousin mugwort (which it's often mistaken for in the wild), wormwood is excellent to use in divination. I like to keep a small bag of mugwort and wormwood with my Tarot decks and seal bits of it to candles specifically designed for divination.

Appropriate to artist-types, wormwood is associated with improving creative ability. It's not a bad idea to keep a bottled or bagged herbal charm in an area where artistic endeavors are undertaken. It's also a good herb to use as an incense in meditation, especially for reflecting on a loss of any type. It helps one come to terms with the reality of losses that accompany life changes.

Ye Olde Flying Ointment

I simply can't forego mentioning the Witches' flying ointment, also called "Færies' Oynt-ment," "Witches' salve," and *sabbati unguenti* in days long past. Everyone knows the image of Witches flying across the moon on their broomsticks (called *transvection*), sweeping the stars and cackling through the night. This seems like a far-fetched fantasy but in truth, it's not entirely fictional. A mix of fact, fiction, and metaphor may say it best.

In pre-industrial times, many peoples enacted rituals to foster the fertility of the land. European Pagans ran through their crop fields, jumping up and down to encourage its pro-ductivity—magick for survival's sake. Women did indeed straddle broomsticks, while men typically did the same with pitchforks or shovels. In addition to this suggestive magick, a homemade hallucinogenic herbal concoction, now known as a flying ointment, is said to have been smeared on the practitioners' often naked bodies to induce astral projection and amplify the magick—rubbed on the areas that would quickly absorb it, such as the neck, wrists, underarms, genitals, and feet. These ointments may have sometimes been used along with the aforesaid broomstick fertility rites, but they were generally reserved for astral projection rituals.

The broom-jumping activity, along with a heavy dose of herbal drugs, could well have produced the illusion of flight. Reportedly, the person fell into a nearly comatose slum-ber for anywhere between four hours and four days and, during that "trip" (especially the early part of it), the person shapeshifted astrally into animals—wolves, birds, fish—and mimicked those animals whilst under the trance. Upon awakening, the person reported fantastical experiences and information about the planes they had visited.

Modern scholars have considered this herbal drug magick akin to hallucinogenic sha-manic practices outside of Europe, noting such similarities in virtually all forms of ancient magick. Narcotic potions have been used in varied forms by Witches,[4] shamans, and re-ligious peoples of many cultures worldwide, each culture using locally available ingredi-ents. But some Craft scholars debate whether "flying ointments" were really used by early Pagans. Was the practice a modern-day fabrication to explain the origins of the broomstick flight myth? I agree that it is questionable, and that fiction may have been blended with fact—with such known rites as jumping through the fields to encourage crop growth. This need not negate the flying ointment's validity, but it's good to question all the "facts" of al-legedly ancient Witchcraft, regardless of the source.

I have no doubt that any users of the ointment were flying on the astral, as physical flight is obviously impossible. Witch hunters knew of the Pagans' belief in the Otherworlds (astral planes) and translated associated activities like hallucinogenic "flying" into myths of actual flight by means of sorcery with the devil. It is up for question whether these practitioners *believed* they were physically flying or not, as the advent of common science (and *common sense*) hadn't occurred until the Renaissance, when it was disproved they were actually flying. Science accompanied religion during the period of the 1400s to 1600s, and the Church's concept of Heaven, Earth, and Hell being the whole of reality necessarily excluded shamanic-based understandings of the multi-faceted layers of existence.

The oldest documented mention of flying ointment in one of its forms seems to be a classical text dated 1458, translated around 1900 by modern occultist Samuel Liddell MacGregor Mathers. In *The Book of the Sacred Magic of Abramelin the Mage*, book 1, chapter 6, an Austrian Witch presents Abraham with a hallucinogenic unguent that induces the experience of astral projection for hours on end. While this account isn't necessarily concrete evidence, it presents the idea that flying ointments were known and most likely utilized to some degree in the fifteenth century.

Many of the ingredients in the varied forms of ointments are either obscure or illegal in this day and age. Today, some magickal practitioners use "modern flying ointments" made of less harmful blends, often legal herbs only. Rather than having major psychoactive effects, the herbal ingredients are used magickally to help with trance meditation, psychic awareness, visionary powers, and astral projection.

Included here strictly for historical interest—not for use at home—is a flying ointment recipe said to be a traditional English one from a Gardnerian grimoire; the resulting mix was blended with oil or lard. A number of these plant species belong to the order Solanaceæ and contain atropine as well as other hallucinogenic alkaloids such as hyoscyamine and scopolamine. Just finding all the ingredients and researching their risks for a blend could take at least a life or two! Not to mention, if the brew was not administered safely by someone well-versed in the effects of rare and toxic herbs, the result could be lethal.

In other words, *don't don't don't try this at home*, for the gods' sake! (Many Neopagans feel they do not require herbal blends and potions to induce astral projection; they have learned to draw upon inherent abilities for such endeavors.)

WITCHES' FLYING OINTMENT

Traditional recipe: for historical interest only!

- 250 grams Indian hemp (a white-flowering plant related to the poisonous herb dogbane—not actually marijuana)
- 50 grams extract of opium (poppy resin)
- 30 grams betel (a Southeast Asian climbing plant)
- 15 grams belladonna (deadly nightshade)
- 15 grams hemlock (water parsnip)
- 15 grams henbane (black nightshade)
- 6 grams cinquefoil (a powerful herb bearing the properties of the pentagram, whose yellow flowers have five petals and whose leaves grow in sets of five)
- 5 grams cantharidin (a chemical compound from the bright green European medicine beetle *cantharis*)
- 3 grams annamthol (possibly referring to *anethol*, a substance derived from parts of anise, fennel, and other herbs)

Other ingredients used in flying unguents around the world include these herbs: Aconite (monkshood, wolfbane), mandragora (mandrake), foxglove, climbing nightshade, sweet flag (calamus), datura (thornapple), smallage (wild celery), saffron, poplar, marijuana/hashish, tobacco, hellebore, briony, mugwort, thistle, skullcap, gum tragacanth (astragalus), asarabacca (hazelwort), toadflax, benzoin, vervain, sandalwood, morning glory, sunflower, and basil.

---

1. Recent studies suggest that St. John's wort can negatively interact with some antidepressants, birth control pills, and other medications. As with all treatments, research the product thoroughly before taking it. Everybody's constitution is different, so reactions to any medicine vary from person to person.

2. Some of these terms are common folk names for herbs; others are based on my own informal research.

3. A Græco-Roman magickal term, recognized as part of the classical *voces magicæ*, or Words of Power, used in ancient spells both to bless and to curse. A Thelemic variation proposed by Aleister Crowley was "Abrahadabra," which has specific numerological alignments.

4. Or, rather, those whom we would now refer to as Witches.

V

The Shadow of Society

The shadow and its projections not only affect us individually, but also collectively. Every society—every nation—has an identity of its own to which we relate. This group mentality creates its own shadow whereby people identify with an ideology or leader that gives expression to their fears and inferiorities as a whole, giving rise to religious or racial persecution, Witch hunting, scapegoating, and genocide. The collective shadow is the root of social, racial, and national bias and discrimination; every minority and dissenting group carries the shadow projections of the majority.

— JOHN J. COUGHLIN
Out of the Shadows

A Tainted World

Throughout human history, violence, iniquity, and social injustice have been widespread and constant. Today, our problems are myriad: severe poverty, torture, deceptive governments, overpopulation, pollution, rapid global warming, political and religious violence, manipulation, genocide, animal abuse, and the rape of the earth for her resources—these are but drops in the bucket of the world's suffering, and all filter into the everyday lives of everyone on this planet. If these issues keep escalating as they are now, our species is absolutely doomed. *Massive* changes in the earth's atmosphere and global consciousness are inevitably and irreversibly upon us as a species, but the degree and intensity of the impacts are yet to be determined.

In many ways, the tainted quality of the world is more visible now than it ever has been. Along with this fact comes the necessity of self-responsibility. Are we doing our part to positively change the world, or are we enabling its decay? How do we *really* treat other people? What corporations, products, and industries do we support or boycott? How do we individually make use of what we are given, including natural resources, human-made materials, and our own emotions and bodies? To what extent are we functioning as cogs in the human machine, and in what ways are we reclaiming our freedom and lessening the suffering of others? Do we *really, truly* care about where the world is going, or do we apathetically and conveniently ignore our own impact? Do we care about global consciousness or just our own? Do we honestly help other people, including those who live far from us, or do we just think about doing it, focusing instead solely on our *own* survival? Do we just send energies of love and light to beings who are suffering, or do we actually act on those energies in the *physical* world as well? These are key questions to ask as we examine society and our place in it.

Our society is a strange beast, yet this animal *can* and *must* be tamed, one person at a time. As magickal, spiritual individuals, we must do all we can to attune ourselves to the welfare of the earth and its beings. We must change our ways accordingly and dare to conquer apathy with action. We are here for many reasons, not least to help the planet; now more that ever, it is imperative that we awaken to our ways and attune our lifestyles to the beauty and peace we wish to see overtake this plane. At this moment in human development, we must turn our focus away from the trivial and toward the world at large.

Scrying the Telly: A Ritual Meditation

This meditation offers insight into how the media—television in particular—shapes our culture and our own psyches. It's vital to look in depth at how our Western society operates, where we stand within it, and how our contributions affect the greater whole.

Initially, the thought of performing a meditation in front of the TV might seem a bit odd. Well, it is. But there's good reason for it! Along with the Internet, television is the most highly influential medium in the Western world. Any idea, suggestion, or social issue can be conveyed and amplified on the screen. There are programs and channels devoted to almost everything under the sun. By analyzing and deconstructing this magickal tool of communication, we can get a better sense of the society in which we live, and the dread shadow that dwells beneath the plastic masks.

Like any other medium, TV can convey supremely spiritual messages, destructive messages, and absolutely anything in between. For this exercise, I invite readers to sit in front of their television set (or someone else's if you have chosen against owning one—a wise choice indeed) and look at this catalyst of our culture in a different light.

1. Begin by sitting in front of a turned-off cable television. That's right, just sit there with the remote control in hand. Today it will serve as a makeshift anti-brainwashing magick wand (hence the sacred "mute" and "off" buttons, which shall luckily be utilized). Get comfortable and begin by clearing your mind. Take three deep breaths in through the nose and out through the mouth. Let the thoughts of the day drift away like moving clouds. This is not the time to focus on what happened today or what you need to do tomorrow … allow the common world to dissipate as you enter the sacred terrain of the mind. For several minutes, sense the oxygen entering your nostrils and exiting your lips. Bring absolute focus to your breath.

2. Having entered a slightly altered state of consciousness, declare your intent, saying something like this: "Great Spirit of Truth and Wisdom, I ask you now to part the veil of illusion, illuminating for me both the sacred and the profane of the society in which I find myself. As I sit now before this Pandora's Box of pixels and satellite signals, I ask that my mind become expanded rather than numbed. I ask that I may clearly see reality through this machine of illusion."

3. Close your eyes and envision an orange tentacle of energy between your *ajna* chakra—your third eye—and the center of the TV screen. Then see this tentacle breaking off from the TV and retracting about halfway toward you. Envision the tentacle growing an eye; it is now becoming an extension of your third eye.

4. Now that your perception is somewhat separated from the influence of the television, take a deep breath and click it on with the remote, opening your eyes. Visualize the third-eye tentacle watching the screen as your physical eyes do the same.

5. The TV is now tuned to a commercial, an infomercial, a sitcom, a drama, a movie, the news, a documentary, or something else. If it's static, click to the nearest channel. Turn off the closed captioning (unless you are hearing impaired) and set the volume low. Regardless of the program, view it for a couple minutes: not "watching TV," but rather "monitoring the programming." Do not laugh at the jokes, wince at the violence, or absorb any of the conveyed emotions: remain neutral and expressionless. See beyond the façade presented. Note how your psyche becomes transfixed and even hypnotized by the screen. Observe the actors: to what extent are they acting, and what might they *really* be thinking? What messages are the writer, producer, and director of programming trying to convey? Get inside their heads. Are they trying to charm you into buying a product (and if so, why do they *personally* want your money)? Does the program emphasize sexuality or certain body types (and if so, for what purpose)? Are they simply trying to entertain the audience (and if so, might there be something deeper … a hidden agenda)? Ask yourself questions upon questions. See "behind the scenes" and psychoanalyze the image in front of you. Try to be as realistic as possible; that is, not overly paranoid nor overly trusting.

6. Now hit the "mute" button and analyze the programming in that manner for two more minutes. Again, visualize the orange tentacle *not* linking you to the TV set, but remaining independent. This time, pay particular attention to people's expressions, the images shown, the colors used. How calculated are these details? Why are they displayed in these manners, sequences, speeds, and patterns?

7. Close your eyes and reflect on what you just witnessed. What energy, emotion, or *influence* is being conveyed to the viewer? What do the programmers *want* you to think? What social norms, ideas, taboos, expectations, fears, or glorifications does the programming seem to reinforce? What details do you observe that might usually go unnoticed or unseen? Deconstruct what you just viewed; "deprogram" the programming. Contemplate how many people might be under the spell of the programming at *this very moment*. Reflect on how this may influence our society.

8. Unmute the TV and continue the exercise for another thirty to forty minutes, moving to eight or nine other channels. Use your intuition to decide where to stop channel surfing, or, if you are familiar with the stations, flip to one that might be of particular interest for this exercise, such as an infomercial, a fundamentalist preacher, or youth culture program. Cover a wide variety of material but, for purposes of this exercise, shy away from *intelligent* programming.

9. Click the "off" button. Close your eyes and ground your energy. Visualize the tentacle receding into your third eye, blessing you with psychic sight and discernment.

10. Take time to write down your observations and insights, and keep this list for comparison when you do the exercise again in the future. (What are the similarities between the lists, and what does this suggest about our greater society?)

11. When finished, thank the Spirit of Truth and Wisdom in your own words. Give homage to the energies summoned forth, stating that you are gaining more knowledge into the "programming" of society, and that you will actively strive to align your behavior to spiritual ideals over social falsity.

12. Close the circle and dismiss the quadrants as you normally would. At this point, I wouldn't blame you if you wanted to kill your TV!

Fantasy Magick: A Shadow Side of the Occult Scene

In a chapter focused on the shadow of society, I cannot fail to discuss a "shadowed" aspect of the modern magickal scene that far too often goes overlooked, yet poses a serious problem to the legitimacy and balance of our chosen lifestyle. I term this syndrome "fantasy magick."

Many of this book's readers have probably encountered this all-too-common form of manipulation in the Pagan and magick communities. Fantasy magick takes hold when a person's mental line between fantasy and reality blurs or is or erased altogether, thus intermingling those worlds to an unhealthy degree in the person's life. This dishonest negation of the perimeters of reality is often displayed by a person's vehement proclamations of supernatural powers, superhuman abilities, and nonhuman status. Personally, I have encountered self-proclaimed kings and queens of the faerie realms, descendants of the Nephilim and the Anunnaki, interdimensional warriors and voyageurs, time travelers, and people with "98 percent faerie blood" or "40 percent dragon DNA." I have also met a number of "incarnate" deities, archangels, and role-playing game characters, and at least a good handful of Crowleys, Merlins, and Cleopatras. Still, some practitioners wonder why Pagan spirituality isn't always taken seriously.

Sadly, it is begging to be said: it is highly unlikely that we are reincarnations of ancient gurus, gods, or gremlins. We are *not* fallen angels, archangels, demons, dragons, faeries, elves, mermaids, sirens, griffins, sídhe, unicorns, Wookies, Gelflings, or Ewoks. We are human. We are *all* human. As magicians, it is our responsibility not only to seek to recognize when we are being lied to, but to assist others who may, themselves, be victim to any sort of magickal manipulation.

Often, a fixation on fantasy magick is simply rooted in escapism. When a person feels dissatisfied with life, and is also aware of magick and the existence of other planes of reality, an easy-seeming remedy for the emotional pain is to over-embrace, exaggerate, and otherwise take overboard one's participation in these magickal spheres. Blending reality with fantasy can make life seem less dull. Merging the worlds of fantasy and mythology into ordinary existence can make everything seem more attractive. If our magickal lives really were like they are in *Charmed*, *The Craft*, or role-playing games, it would make things more exciting and dramatic—most definitely! However, the worlds of fantasy and mythology should be recognized and enjoyed for what they are; they only lose their artistic value if they are fancied as "alive" beyond a mythical or psychologically archetypal sense.

Escapism often grows out of a desperate need for a sense of self-worth. Believing oneself to be a creature of fantasy, for example, can add to one's sense of importance and also justify feelings of loneliness and isolation. An ego-inflated person who presents this illusion to others can psychologically trick himself or herself into actually believing the fantasy, beginning a downward spiral of lies, manipulation, and possible psychosis.

More often than not, these beliefs are formed as a result of others' attempts at manipulation. When a person is awakening to the magickal world and is coming to realize that reality is much more intricate than it seems, new doors of perception are opening. It is while a person is in this state that manipulation from others can be most effective. A metaphysical teacher or initiator is likely to realize this spot of vulnerability, which is why the student has the responsibility to question and analyze everything that is taught, regardless of the source, and step back to consider the direction in which they are being taken.

To comment specifically on nonhuman identification, I will say that though our physical bodies are very much human, our astral bodies can vary from that form. This is where the difference lies: a part of us may vibrate and resonate with these nonhuman things on a spiritual level. For example, I "am" a raven and I "am" Water. I have friends who "are" faeries or elves in the sense that they feel a kinship with the archetypes of these forces. We may feel a strong, and perhaps past-life, connection to Avalon or Egypt, but that does not mean that we "were" Morgan la Fey, King Arthur, Isis, or Tutankhamen.

It is also worth saying that our *spirits* may not necessarily be "from here." Many discerning, reality-based members of Otherkin communities recognize that their bodies are 100 percent human, even if their souls feel predominantly nonhuman. There are plenty of people who feel as though their spirits are from elsewhere, and this is certainly a valid perception. Is it possible that some people's spirits are Pleiadian or Andromedian? Or that they existed in Atlantis or ancient Greece? Who knows? It sure is possible! These things cannot be proven; they can only be felt or experienced. Personally, I feel that beliefs such as these should not be instantly accepted when the idea arises, but should be explored with honesty, skepticism, and objectivity. Otherwise, it is too easy to blur the line between actual experience and mere flights of fancy.

Sometimes, as is the case with some Otherkin groups and individuals, a simple misunderstanding of terminology is where the problem lies. Take vampyrism, for example. Imagine a person—a woman, let's say—who honestly and objectively requires human *prana*—energy—to maintain her own energy levels, and thus recognizes herself as a vam-pyre. If she were to tell an ordinary person that she is a vampyre, she may be perceived as a crackpot who thinks she needs to bite people's necks and can turn into a bat. The same ap-plies with the therianthrope community, and particularly with the lycanthropic members. Imagine a man who frequently practices astral-body shapeshifting into the form of a wolf (which is also likely a spirit guide), performs magick and meditation using wolf medicine, and identifies as a werewolf for these reasons. But if he describes that to a person who doesn't understand the concept of astral shapeshifting, the person may assume that this man thinks he actually grows wolflike fur, claws, and fangs when the moon is full. This is, of course, just as silly as thinking that New Age lightworkers can ascend the physical plane at will, or that those who practice Goetic evocation have half-animal/half-demon fetches or familiars. Then again, I'm sure that there are still people out there who claim these things of themselves.

Some people don't *intentionally* twist facts and inject fiction into any given situation; they may simply have been misinformed. If a person has been told that dragons, demons, archons, specters, wraiths, wendigos, and hellhounds lurk behind every corner just wait-ing to be vanquished or ghostbusted, or has been taught to believe that a particular person *is* a supernatural being, that's manipulation. The person must unlearn these things to come to a greater understanding of these astral planes and mythologies. Reality is profound and mysterious enough as is; why must true magick be diluted with fiction?

When a person presents *known* fantasy as actual reality, it can give genuine practitio-ners a bad name. A few examples: For a person who really *does* work with Enochian or angelic forces, it is demeaning to be considered alongside others who claim they can grow wings and feathers if they focus hard enough (or who have been manipulated into be-lieving such things). For a real Druid Revivalist, it is insulting to be considered alongside those who boast of tracing an unbroken, thousand-some-year-old lineage to the original Druids (of whom we historically know next to nothing in the first place). For someone who was raised in traditional Wicca, it's degrading to be considered alongside those who claim to have a Book of Shadows from their great-great-great-great-great grandmother, or to belong to an ancient secret underground family tradition of Witchcraft (more on this in the next section of this chapter). Such tales are spread regularly in modern occult circles.

When a person's introduction to the magickal arts comes in the form of some other person's fantasies, that person is being misinformed, and may come to think that *all* Witches, Pagans, and magicians have such beliefs; it's a matter of guilt by association. Such pseudo-magickal spirituality also undoubtedly turns off potential practitioners who could have otherwise benefited from esoteric study. It's a bloody vicious cycle!

Fiction is metaphor; fiction is mythology. It is beautiful and powerful, but most of it is simply *representational*. Discerning this from our experience of reality is key in our search to know ourselves, and it is that very key that helps fuel our spiritual evolution and builds the strength of our community.

Deconstructing the Burning Times: The European Witch Hunts

In this book we are analyzing the shadow. While we have primarily examined philosophical spirituality and practical magick, an overview of the "dark times" of the Witchcraft persecutions will ground that understanding in history. Here this chapter shifts gears into a more socio-historical mode. As we review the European Witch hunt era, you will encounter more academic detail (straightforward and scholarly, but hopefully not *dry*) than in previous chapters. You have been forewarned!

I pursued this research both for the benefit of readers and for my own benefit. I wanted to convey an accurate history, and I enjoy academic work as a balance to metaphysics. My career at the University of Montana helped tremendously in encouraging me in these studies. Not to mention that the chaos magician in me wishes to ensure a balance of lighthearted and intellectual material within this book, just to keep myself and others on our toes. Additionally, huge thanks to John Michael Greer for his valuable edits and suggestions with the following material. You are a god among men.

✳   ✳   ✳

Long before the European Witch hunts (or "Witchcraze"), and most certainly to this day, what can be termed "black magick" has been viewed as a very real and powerful source of agony and human suffering. Whether this perception of magick-at-large stems from ideas of evil spirits, demons, Satan, earthbound disincarnate ghosts, sorcerers, or Witches, the concept of evil as a spiritually opposing force is a culturally necessary archetype. It has been and will continue to be a major player in religious and cultural developments across the globe. It seems as though people psychologically require an archetypal adversary to justify their own pursuits.

When Americans are asked to think about the Witchcraft persecutions, they tend to think of the Salem Witch Trial of 1692, in which twenty people were tried, convicted, and executed by hanging as a result of an eruption of hysteria in Salem Village (now Danvers), Massachusetts Bay Colony. Hundreds of townsfolk were imprisoned, at least five of whom perished in confinement.

Though the trial in Salem is significant, and is well documented, it is the tip of the iceberg that is Witchcraft's persecution. Or, more accurately, the persecution of that which is *deemed* Witchery. Because the Salem incident is relatively insignificant in the scope of the persecutions, as well as because it occurred in the Western hemisphere instead of Europe, it won't be discussed in detail herein. (For a parallel, think of the genocide of Native peoples in the Americas: truly the closest thing to this hemisphere's Witchcraze.)

Magick was originally used to describe the arts of the magi in classical antiquity, encompassing astrology, divination, ritual, and curative magick. The period of time now commonly known as classical antiquity began after the Bronze Age with the founding of Rome in 753 BCE, and ended when the last Roman emperor Romulus Augustus was forced to relinquish his throne in 476 CE.

Early Christian writers were quick to point out that the Pagan gods were in fact demons, demonstrating that they viewed Græco-Roman thaumaturgy as devilry.[1] Not until the thirteenth century did writers begin to differentiate between *natural* and *demonic* magick, the latter often termed *maleficia* or sorcery.

The image of the Witch began to form in classical antiquity, and can be seen in numerous liturgical representations of the time. Because females were viewed as inferior to men, a view held popular in ancient Judaism and which was certainly perpetuated with the rise of Christianity, Witches were originally portrayed as female. Certainly, male sorcerers existed in the ancient worldview, and men were condemned frequently. The belief in individuals being capable of having malefic magickal abilities was on the rise, and represented the gradual humanization of the demonic in common worldviews.

In the Græco-Roman world, a division between magick and religion gained prominence, with "magick" being seen as malicious, and not associated with the "natural" world, and thus the sphere of Witches. Originally the Pagans dominated religious thought and practice, often deeming early Christians as magicians, a view due especially to the control of demons they exhibited in exorcism rites, as well as their use of secret magickal names. Because the view was that magick relied on the help of the gods (Pagan *or* Christian), Græco-Roman Pagans opposed magick and its antisocial, maleficent implications. As

Christian thought grew, Christian writers spoke out against magick as a demonic activity and even turned the table on the Pagans, deeming their religion both inauthentic and inherently bound to magickal practice. These views of magick were strong in antiquity and saw a revival of sorts in the thirteenth century.

Magick in the Middle Ages

The era in Western European history now commonly known as the Middle Ages, or the mediæval period, began with the fragmentation of the Roman Empire's political power in the fifth century CE and lasted until the sixteenth century, spanning from the Migration Period to the Protestant Reformation. The Early Middle Ages are generally seen as the fifth to eleventh centuries, the High Middle Ages as the twelfth and thirteenth, and the Late Middle Ages as the fourteenth and fifteenth centuries.

THE ETYMOLOGY OF WITCHCRAFT

It is in Old English that the word *Witch* has its roots. Originally spelled *wicce* in the feminine and *wicca* in the masculine, the word referred to a diviner or fortuneteller. Many modern Witches, a large number of whom follow the twentieth-century syncretistic earth-based religion Wicca, mistakenly believe that the word originally meant "wise," thereby earning the modern Witch the title of "wise one," and their arts the "Craft of the Wise." This etymological misconception was pushed in the 1950s by Wicca's founder, Gerald Gardner, whose intent was to promote his new syncretistic religion as a positive and life-affirming path.

Linguistically, the Old English term for "wise one" is actually the root of the modern word *Wizard. Wicca* and *wicce*, however, come from a verb meaning "to bend or twist." This meaning has also been interpreted in a positive light by many practitioners of modern Witchcraft, who view it as implying a magick-worker's ability to bend, twist, and shape reality to their will. However, if we examine the Old English usage of the term, we find that "twist" was the antithesis of "straight" (meaning "proper"), revealing that the term was used to refer to someone who was *twisted, crooked,* or otherwise morally unacceptable.[2]

Modern practitioners of Witchcraft belong to both schools of thought: those who believe "Witch" to have been derogatory from the start, and those who believe the word was maligned only as a result of the Witch hunts. Neither uses the word to self-marginalize. Instead, Witches in general seek to reclaim a once-maligned term and alter the public perception of it, much as we see with terms such as "queer" and "nigger" in current times.

Additionally, despite common misconceptions, the word *warlock* was not originally gendered. Rooted in the Old English *wærloga*, the word means "oathbreaker" and was an Anglo-Saxon insult that was eventually used against those who practiced magick. It's likely that "warlock" as a term implying masculine sorcery was an eighteenth-century notion; at that time the words *warlock* and *Witch* were both being used as slanderous terms.

Though the term *warlock* was rarely used, *Witch* was recognized in antiquity and was referenced in literature at the time. The image of the malicious sorcerer gained momentum in the Late Middle Ages when Witchcraft was aligned with the gravest of all crimes: heresy.

THE PLACE OF MAGICK

For nearly the entire expanse of the Middle Ages, Christian tradition and Hermetic tradition (including its accompanying magickal practices) coexisted in Europe without issue. Many Christians also practiced magick, divination, and astrology. It was only near the end of the Middle Ages that a strict division between the *scientific* and *magickal* spheres was distinctly drawn. Before then, it was simply assumed, correctly, that an astronomer was an astrologer. It was likely that the classical notion of the philosopher-magician persisted to some degree at this time, though people practicing in these two fields were often separate, distinguishable by class and social status.

Mediæval European intellectuals recognized two forms of magick: the natural and the demonic. Natural magick concerned hidden powers within nature and was originally seen as a branch of science, including astrology and herbalism, for example. Demonic magick was seen, instead, as a perversion of religion that turned away from God.

THE HUNT BEGINS

In the Early Middle Ages, the church was not overtly concerned with issues of Witchcraft, although it had laws forbidding the very belief in the existence of Witches. In the High Middle Ages, especially in the 1200s with the rise of the Papal Inquisition, the Roman Catholic church sought to discover and punish heresy. Beliefs about Witchcraft were varied at this time. As many people began to view Witchcraft as less fictional and more legitimate, Witchcraft allegations started to rise, as people equated Witchery with heresy.

The Witch hunts began in what is now western Switzerland and the bordering areas of France. The "new heresy" of Witchcraft as a growing public threat was officially introduced to the church around 1375, only twenty-four years after the end of the bubonic plague pandemic. It was also only fifty-one years after the final eradication of the Knights

Templar, a step that had proved that the church was capable of wiping out entire groups of perceived heretics. And after the fact, it was easy to identify Witchcraft as a possible cause of the great bubonic plague—the Black Death—that had killed one-third of the population of Europe. According to this perceived threat, Witchcraft practitioners were working directly with the Devil himself, selling their souls and creating pacts to gain worldly wealth and self-serving magickal powers. Over time, the mythology of the Witches' Sabbath evolved to include fantastical accounts of demonic evocation, flight on broomsticks and pitchforks, human and animal sacrifice, cannibalistic infanticide, the use of black magick and cursing, demonic butt-licking, and all styles of fornication.

From modern-day Switzerland, Witch hunting and the resulting trials made their way up the Rhine River to areas of modern Germany and elsewhere. (For reasons unknown, the interest in hunting Witchcraft declined heavily for the first half of the sixteenth century.)

THE REVIVAL OF ROMAN LAW

In the 1200s, church scholars and civil governments revived ancient Roman legal doctrines. According to these laws, certain types of magick were deemed acceptable, such as those dealing with agricultural growth or medicinal healing. Any sort of magick aimed at empowering a person like a god, and thus having sway over the material world, was viewed as immoral and, according to the church, heretic. Magickal scholar and practitioner John Michael Greer characterizes the revival's effects this way:

> Roman law also brought a major change in the way criminal charges were handled. Most of Europe before the revival of Roman law followed a traditional "accusatorial" process—that is, charges had to be brought by a person who had been harmed by the alleged crime, and if the charges proved false the person bringing them faced severe penalties. Roman law, by contrast, made use of an "inquisitorial" process—that is, charges were brought by a public official, who was exempt from penalties in the case of false accusations. The study of Roman law in the universities led to the adoption of inquisitorial procedure over much of Europe. All these changes made heretics and magicians much easier to charge and convict.[3]

Indeed, at this time, the perception of Witchcraft was included in the persecution of magick. The revival of Roman law also influenced the legal use of torture, making it an acceptable method of extracting confessions. This methodology was on the rise and saw its greatest use as the early modern times began.

Witchcraft in Early Modern Times

What we call the early modern period began around the sixteenth century with the European Renaissance and spanned the Protestant Reformation, the Age of Discovery, the rise of the modern European state in the 1600s, and the beginning of the Age of Enlightenment. The Industrial Revolution of the late 1700s and early 1800s marks the beginning of late modernity. By this time, the social and religious mainstream concerned itself very little with seemingly obsolete notions of Witchery. In the late modern period, the question of the Christian church's position on Witchcraft has essentially lost its importance.

THE HEIGHT OF THE WITCH HUNTS

Contrary to the common perception that the mediæval period saw the height of Europe's Witchcraft persecutions, it actually began on a large scale only in the mid-1400s, the cusp of early modern times. From then until the late 1700s—virtually the whole of the early modern period—Witches were sought out, tortured, accused, and executed. This occurred all across Europe, with no area left untouched. Some areas had less activity (for example, fewer than one percent of all Witchcraft-related executions took place in all of England), but nobody escaped the fear and paranoia that gripped all Europeans socially and psychologically.

The belief in Witches was widespread and constantly reinforced socially. Even the most socially upstanding upper-class people were not exempt from the ideology and, in many cases, from its resulting persecutions. Virtually everyone believed, or feigned to believe, that Witches existed and that in fact anyone could be a Witch and could strike at any time. Anything that went wrong could be blamed on demons or the Devil, with whom Witches were obviously in league. During the craze, if something went wrong in the natural cycle, such as success in the harvest, the health of farm animals, or weather patterns, Witches were the prime suspect. Similarly, imbalances in a person's health, luck, mental state, or sexual performance was evidence enough to accuse Witches for the misfortunes. It didn't help that churchmen, upon realizing that Witchcraft and heresy were closely tied, frequently excommunicated or otherwise punished secular authorities who refused to confer the death penalty on the convicted.[5]

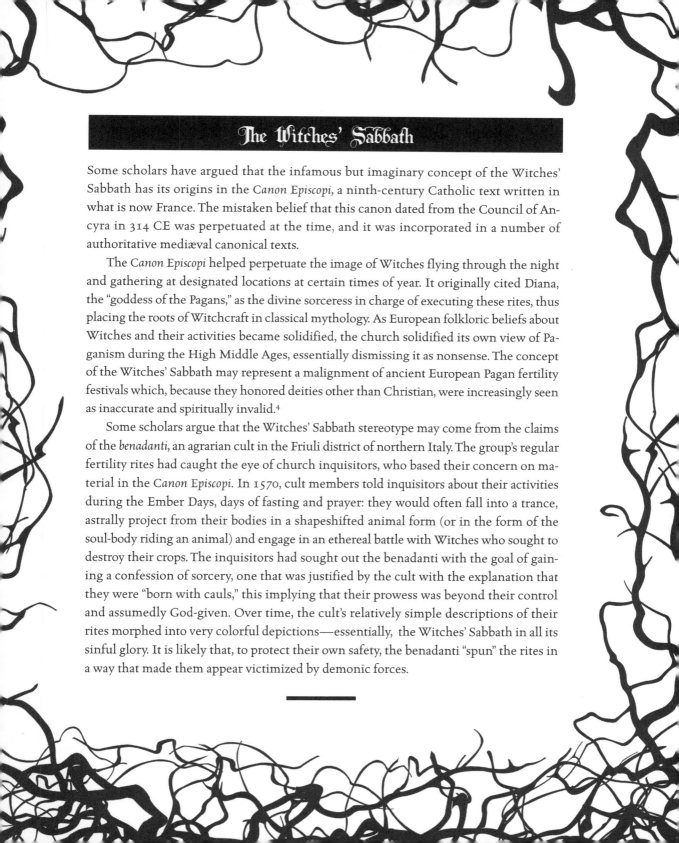

The Witches' Sabbath

Some scholars have argued that the infamous but imaginary concept of the Witches' Sabbath has its origins in the *Canon Episcopi*, a ninth-century Catholic text written in what is now France. The mistaken belief that this canon dated from the Council of Ancyra in 314 CE was perpetuated at the time, and it was incorporated in a number of authoritative mediæval canonical texts.

The *Canon Episcopi* helped perpetuate the image of Witches flying through the night and gathering at designated locations at certain times of year. It originally cited Diana, the "goddess of the Pagans," as the divine sorceress in charge of executing these rites, thus placing the roots of Witchcraft in classical mythology. As European folkloric beliefs about Witches and their activities became solidified, the church solidified its own view of Paganism during the High Middle Ages, essentially dismissing it as nonsense. The concept of the Witches' Sabbath may represent a malignment of ancient European Pagan fertility festivals which, because they honored deities other than Christian, were increasingly seen as inaccurate and spiritually invalid.[4]

Some scholars argue that the Witches' Sabbath stereotype may come from the claims of the *benadanti*, an agrarian cult in the Friuli district of northern Italy. The group's regular fertility rites had caught the eye of church inquisitors, who based their concern on material in the *Canon Episcopi*. In 1570, cult members told inquisitors about their activities during the Ember Days, days of fasting and prayer: they would often fall into a trance, astrally project from their bodies in a shapeshifted animal form (or in the form of the soul-body riding an animal) and engage in an ethereal battle with Witches who sought to destroy their crops. The inquisitors had sought out the benadanti with the goal of gaining a confession of sorcery, one that was justified by the cult with the explanation that they were "born with cauls," this implying that their prowess was beyond their control and assumedly God-given. Over time, the cult's relatively simple descriptions of their rites morphed into very colorful depictions—essentially, the Witches' Sabbath in all its sinful glory. It is likely that, to protect their own safety, the benadanti "spun" the rites in a way that made them appear victimized by demonic forces.

In the sixteenth century, fear heightened exponentially, and the Witch craze climaxed between 1560 and 1660. Mass Witch trials and executions were occurring in Switzerland and Belgium in the 1580s, and in France and Scotland a decade later. German Witch hunters, who fancied mass genocides, were burning people alive by the hundreds in some areas as early as the 1600s, including France, Germany, and Switzerland, and later in Sweden. It was popular to enforce a "catch-all" tactic of discovering, accusing, and punishing all people who even potentially had ties to Witchcraft.

The hunts continued during the 1600s across Europe. In England, they were ended in 1682. Over the next century, Scotland, France, and Germany followed by putting an end to legal Witchcraft executions, and Switzerland stopped a century after England, in 1782.

THOU SHALT NOT SUFFER A *what* TO LIVE?

During the early modern religious reformations, a strict and literal reading of certain or selected biblical passages was encouraged, namely Exodus 22:18, which was translated as "Thou shalt not suffer a Witch to live," even though neither the original Hebrew text nor the Greek Septuagint—the ancient Greek translation of the Jewish scriptures—used the term *Witch*.[6] The word *Witch* was used in the King James Version of the Bible, first printed in 1611. As accusations of Witchcraft grew, King James himself actually intervened on more than one occasion (even as early as 1616, just five years after the first printing), worried that innocent people were being convicted of things they had not done.[7] King James did not translate the Bible himself, but had sanctioned the legality of translations by dropping formerly enforced penalties for doing so. Douglas Linder, in his "Brief History of Witchcraft Persecutions before Salem," notes that "the word *Witch* in Exodus is a translation of the Hebrew word *kashaph*, which comes from the root meaning 'to whisper.' The word as used in Exodus probably thus meant 'one who whispers a spell.' In context, the Exodus passage probably was intended to urge Jews to adhere to their own religious practices and not those of surrounding tribes."[8]

Various other editions of the Bible translate the term as "sorceress," which does, in this case, imply *evil* magick performed by a *woman*, and is undoubtedly the most accurate translation in modern English. It makes sense historically, as early Judaic cultures generally held unfavorable views of women.

At the time Exodus was written (around 600 BCE), the word *kashaph* was meant to demonize more than just the Hebrews' surrounding tribes. It probably also referred to early Jewish mystical traditionalists such as the Ma'aseh Merkabah mystics and Kabbalists (who we do know were somewhat persecuted), Coptic Christians and other early Christians who used spells, charms, *voces magicæ* (Words of Power), and sympathetic or "imitative" magick—and, in particular, female practitioners. One could go as far as to say that early modern Witch hunters who backed their case with this Exodus passage were themselves unknowingly using charms and enchantments that would presently be considered Witchcraft—thus, that which they felt the passage itself forbade. Oh, irony!

THE *Malleus Maleficarum*

Secular courts and private groups—*not* the institution of the Catholic Church—were the source of the majority of Witch trials and executions. However, one publication helped not only to fuel the Witch hunts but to link them more closely to the church in readers' minds. Written by Heinrich Kramer and Jacob Sprenger, the *Malleus Maleficarum* was first printed in Germany in 1487. The cover of a 1520 Cologne seventh edition of the manual reads, "*Malleus Maleficarum*: Maleficas, & earum hæresim, ut phramea potentissima conterens," translating as "*The Hammer of Witches*: Smashing the Witches and their heresies with a mighty spear."

In 1484 Pope Innocent VIII had issued the papal bull *Summis Desiderantes*, which spoke against Witchcraft and sorcery in Germany and encouraged the extermination of Witches by any means necessary (how "Innocent" of him, eh?). This charter was included as the introductory portion of the *Malleus*, which gave readers the illusion that Rome fully backed the manual.[9]

The manual described pacts with the Devil (as a result of feminine lust), Witches' activities and evil abilities, how to discover a Witch, and how to properly prosecute and execute. The text assumed that Satan was quickening in strength, exceeding even God's influence on the earthly plane and its peoples. To back his publication, Sprenger promoted the idea that objecting to the manual, even questioning it, was an act of heresy in and of itself.[10] This branding of any sort of skepticism as heretical helped broaden the definition of what could be considered heresy.

The manual has strongly contributed to the perception of Witch hunting as woman-hunting, as it singled out women as Witches, never men. Women, according to the *Malleus*, were more inclined to devilry and heresy because of their inherently insatiable carnal desires. Similarly, the Devil was usually thought of as being male, and thus women were his obvious lusty disciples, an idea that is graphically described in the manual.

Still, the *Malleus* was not used by Witch hunters as widely as is often believed. The manual was viewed unfavorably by most secular courts and inquisitors, who saw it as paranoid and inaccurate at best. Its influence is thus still unclear. The few court cases that referenced the manual in their notes make it clear that its influence was relatively small in the larger scheme of things. Still, the ideas perpetuated by it may have fueled the hunts at least to some degree.

The Catholic Church officially condemned the manual in 1490, just three years after its printing, and actually encouraged people to *disbelieve* in the existence of Witchcraft as anything more than superstition. A number of Witch hunters and judges unrelated to the church continued to use the *Malleus* for their own hunts over the time of its multiple reprintings, and the manual influenced subsequent demonological literature.

TORTURE AND WITCH TESTING

The rise of Roman law in Europe aided in justifying torture as a legitimate method of discovering heresy. Demons, it was perceived, both possess people and fear pain, making torture and vicious violence against the accused entirely permissible. These were practiced both in the Middle Ages and the early modern times.

In France, for example, records have been discovered attesting to drawn-out treatments, such as imprisoning the accused in dungeons or tiny stone cells. The immured were given only bread and water and in many areas, such as in Spain, were brutally lashed every day to aid in the exorcism of demons. Many died of terror, being confined to darkness, in their own excrements and sometimes the bodily remains of others. A great number were also publicly humiliated, tormented, and jeered.

A number of sadistically brutal torture methods swept Europe. These included the limb-stretching rack; the strappado or pulley; thumbscrews and toescrews; red-hot irons; the submersion of hands and feet in boiling oil, water, or baths of scalding slaked lime (calcium oxide); leg vices; whipping stocks containing iron spikes; starvation; extreme beating, and other indescribably gruesome procedures. If the accused did not confess to the accusations, he or she was usually seen as being assisted by the Devil, and were thus as clearly guilty as if they had confessed.

Methods of "Witch testing," the practice of discovering if a person was indeed in league with Satan, included swimming, weighing, and pricking: all agonizing and often resulting in death before conviction. Swimming or dunking was the practice of submerging the accused in water: the person who floated was a Witch, while the person who sank was innocent (and usually drowned). Weighing was the practice of placing the accused on one side of a scale and a Bible on the other; a person who weighed more than the Bible was guilty. Pricking, by pins and needles, was used to discover a Devil's mark on the body of the accused; this was an area on the skin that seemed to be insensitive to pain. In most cases, the individuals were stripped naked and had all of their bodily hair shaved. Even a small mole, wart, or birthmark could suffice as enough evidence of guilt. Inquisitors would also look for a "Witch's mark," any sort of unusual protuberance on the body that could possibly be considered a teat from which demons would feed in the guise of familiars (pets).

It should be noted that in many countries, torture was not used as a confession device. And in those where torture was used, it was not the exclusive domain of Witch hunters, but was a general method of "discovering" heresy by forcing victims to confess to anything, true or not. Under agonizing torture, the accused would admit to virtually any theory or rumor the inquisitor or inquisitors proposed, and would accuse other people (often either projecting their own accusations onto another person or creating a new heretical story altogether) just to escape the pain. Of course, in most cases, the number of people blamed for *maleficia* increased with each session of torture. Harsher methods of torture were justified with each new conviction, and the torture resulted in a multitude of additional accusations. The question of whether the accused had actually *performed* the proposed acts of Witchcraft was almost never asked; the question was when, how, and with whose assistance was it done.

The definition of magick and its resulting persecutions changed with each generation, changed with the hype of the era (and area), and changed with the constantly altering view of moral versus immoral, sacred versus profane.

THE SPANISH INQUISITION

Although the Catholic Church's Spanish Inquisition is often associated with Witchcraft persecutions, the secular courts were actually far less lenient about these cases and far more responsible for the hysteria of the times. Self-styled independent Witch hunters, or groups thereof, were the prime movers, perfectly capable of sadistic methods of confessional torture.[11] Among these was the infamous bloodlusting Matthew Hopkins, "Witch-Finder General," who killed 230 accused Witches in England: more than half the total executed in England during the entire span of the Witch hunts.

Instead, the Spanish Inquisition focused on heretics of other types, as it had for centuries. This body was one of the Church's four commonly recognized inquisitorial systems, and it hardly played a role in the European Witch hunts at all. The Spanish inquisitors were highly organized, seeking out heretics, trying them, and punishing them in vicious ways. These included Jews, Muslims, and those deemed sorcerers (although they were much less frequently condemned). The organization was also skilled at discovering whether individuals *feigned* their conversions to Catholicism or were actually practicing.

When one particular Spanish Witchcraft panic broke out in the early 1600s as a result of the French Witch hunts, a Madrid-based inquisitor was sent to investigate the claims. Upon his return, he explained that his exhaustive research had found no evidence of any sort of anti-Christian organization involved in devilry, and further pursuit of the issue would be a waste of time.

Given the Inquisition's determination and its many prosecutions of heretics through the centuries, it's easy to see why it's often assumed that it administered the Witch hunts as well. In reality, the inquisitors were extremely skeptical about allegations of Witchcraft and sorcery. In 1526, the Suprema, the body's main council, made it known to its officials that bad weather or even the wrath of God were more likely culprits for crop failures than were Witches. The Inquisition was much more concerned with solid evidence, often viewing the Witch hunts with an eye of cynicism. Beyond a case in 1610 where a few accused Witches were burned at the stake in Logroño, Spain, and another comparatively small incident in the early 1500s, the Spanish Inquisition was little concerned with the realm of Witchcraft.[12]

THE BURNING TIMES

The phrase "The Burning Times" is used in Neopagan circles to refer to the European Witch hunts. It was coined by Gerald Gardner, the founder of the modern Wiccan religion, in the 1950s. In scholarly terms, the phrase itself can be misleading. In England, accused Witches were *hanged* rather than burned.[13] (Lynching was definitely faster than burning, and it preserved resources. It was also a far easier method of killing a number of people in a relatively short period of time.) Although accused Witches were not burned alive in England, they *were* burned at the stake in other areas, most notably Spain and Germany. In reality, the methods of torture, execution, and the levels of mass hysteria involving Witchery varied from region to region across Europe.

One of the most misconstrued points about the Witchcraft persecutions in Europe is the actual number of people put to death. One widely cited but erroneous figure is *nine million* people (or "women"), which nearly matches the number of people murdered in the Holocaust. According to the historical studies of Brian Levack, the most accurate estimate of the Witch hunts' death toll is 60,000, itself a very high estimate in the scholarly sphere, but it does include an approximation of unreported trials and trials for which logs are now lacking for whatever reason.[14] The difference between these figures should be noted: nine million is 150 times the more historically based estimate of 60,000. (Many current sources give estimates of only 40,000 to 50,000 victims executed on account of Witchcraft specifically.)

It seems that the figure of nine million was never a well-founded scholarly assertion. It was first proposed by an eighteenth-century historian, a miscalculation unrecognized at the time. But it was spread through publication, and Gerald Gardner used the figure in his work in the 1950s. It continued to be cited by feminists, notably in the 1970s, and again in the 1990 PBS documentary *The Burning Times* (part of a three-part series on Witchcraft), which put the statistic in the public eye. A number of modern Witchcraft traditions with ties to radical feminism also perpetuated erroneous ideas about the persecutions, including estimates of nine million and upwards in their accounts of *herstory*. So it remains a common misunderstanding in Neopagan and feminist spheres. Not only do countless books mention such a figure, but a couple of Pagan folk songs and a number of Craft teachers (who were themselves simply taught the misinformation) also cite the slaughter of nine million Goddess worshippers in the Burning Times. When they realize their error, many of them take no issue with correcting themselves, but others hold strong to the incorrect figures for reasons likely to do with pride or emotional attachment.

But even at the more realistic 60,000, the number of people tried and put to death for Witchery in Europe was both unprecedented and horrific. At the same time, the brutality is no surprise in the scope of history. According to historian Jeffrey Burton Russell:

> This mania, this eagerness to torture and kill human beings, persisted for centuries. Perhaps we put the wrong question when we ask how this could be. The past half-century has witnessed the Holocaust, the Gulag Archipelago, the Cambodian genocide, and secret tortures and executions beyond number. The real question is why periods of relative sanity, such as those from 700 to 1000 and from 1700 to 1900, occur.[15]

Considering the unfathomable cruelty rampant in Europe during the Witchcraze, I have no qualm with using subjective terms denoting the cruel nature of these practices, nor do I apologize for being an apologist for the accused.

THE ACCUSED: PAGANS, MIDWIVES, HERBALISTS, AND GODDESS WORSHIPPERS?

In her book *The Witch in History: Early Modern and Twentieth-Century Representations*, author Diane Purkiss notes that the Burning Times era "is often linked with another lapsarian myth, the myth of an originary matriarchy, through themes of mother-daughter learning and of matriarchal religions as sources of Witchcraft."[16]

Contrary to the belief of many in current Neopagan circles, absolutely no evidence exists to suggest that the Witch hunts were an attempt to annihilate a surviving organized or underground Pagan religion, much less an ancient Age of the Goddess that was driven underground by misogynistic men, nor that the people accused actually followed a religion of this sort.[17] In fact, by 1100 CE, there were essentially *no Pagans or Pagan fertility cults remaining in Europe.*

The idea that most Europeans were still Pagan in the Middle Ages and early modern times is a notion that now seems to have been fabricated by author Margaret Murray, or perhaps was an exaggeration based on others' previous assumptions. For example, her 1921 publication *The Witch-Cult in Western Europe* included an array of theses, partial case studies, and assumptions that are frequently perpetuated even to this day by some modern esoteric groups. Murray's hypotheses were, for the most part, accepted as factual history in scholarly circles through the 1960s. It was only upon renewed studies of Murray's source material that much of it was revealed as inaccurate.[18] Simultaneously, and paradoxically, many of these assumptions helped influence a great number of people to find their place in modern Wicca.

Additionally, no evidence exists to suggest that most accused village Witches were herbal healers or midwives.[19] Herbal healing, midwifery, and other "feminine" activities of the domestic sphere were not specifically targeted for persecution with the rise of modern Western medicine, though this idea was proposed in the 1970s. However, many of the accused, as has been recorded in numerous sources, were in fact elderly widows or people with unique personalities who could seem threatening, including those who were particularly eccentric or had mental disabilities. It was not the use of herbs or charms that perpetuated Witchcraft accusations, but people's perceptions of their neighbors, particularly those at whom fingers could easily be pointed in blame for local misfortunes of any sort. Many of the accused *did* practice herbalism or midwifery, but this was not the actual cause of the accusation. Common things such as herbs, charms, amulets, and potions could easily be construed as devices for heretical magick, which may be the area from which some of these misunderstandings arise.

Undoubtedly, folk remedies and healing techniques, both medicinal and magickal, were widely used in early modern Europe; these activities were not the exclusive domain of Witches or specialized healers and were not forbidden or otherwise controversial activities for anyone. Many midwives and herbalists are actually documented as *assisting* Witch hunters. Not all twentieth- and twenty-first-century political challenges in the West are the remnants of antiquated European political extremism. What is fringe or taboo now was not necessarily then, and vice versa.

THE BURNING TIMES AND FEMALE OPPRESSION

When considering the European Witch hunt era, many have viewed it as a form of female oppression resulting from patriarchal misogyny. This is an argument that has endured to a great extent in modern circles. In actuality, most accusations of Witchcraft at that time were from female, rather than male, "witnesses," whose hysterics were neither gendered nor an exclusive result of a patriarchal age. European society, for the most part, was just as oppressive of women before and after the period spanning 1400 to 1700; there was not a notable increase in misogyny during this time.[20]

It's easy for feminists and modern Witches—both of which I personally consider myself to be—to see Witchcraft persecutions as a feminine holocaust or even a *gynocide*,[21] and to fantasize about the nature of a glorious pre-Christian, Pagan age of matriarchy, magick, and Goddess worship. It simply *did not exist*.

Although I identify as male, I do not make this claim or cite other historical information with ulterior motives in mind. Being pro-feminist myself—one who strives for balance between all genders—the best I can do in this field (which, admittedly, is not my expertise) is to present the most accurate information I can. Unfortunately, some strains of radical feminism make claims that are based on only partially examined history. Because of increasing awareness of feminism and its implications in modern Witchcraft and Neopaganism, a number of emotionally loaded, exaggerated, and altogether erroneous notions have woven themselves into modern thought. Luckily, these notions seem to be losing power with time.

Still, the fact remains that women sadly were, and continue to be, more societally demeaned than men. It would be folly to think that gender played no role in the Witch hunts; it most certainly did. Though most of the accused were women—about three-quarters of them—plenty of men, children, and even animals were also murdered across Europe. (Yes, animals were actually tried as defendants in the eighteenth century, showing the enormous amount of insecurity and paranoia still present in the populace. And yes, the animals—alleged to be shapeshifting demons or familiars—were often represented by lawyers.)

The view of the Witch hunts as a specifically female genocide took hold in the feminist women's rights movement at around the time that its members were shifting their focus from public issues (such as social and political rights) to private issues. At this time, many proponents of radical feminism linked issues such as sexual abuse and domestic violence directly to the influence of a patriarchal society. Naturally, the image of the renowned evil female Witch came to be seen as an archetype of the victimized and helpless woman made inferior by male political domination. Of course, any stance challenging this view can easily be seen as anti-feminist by those who tend to view everything through the lens of historic female subordination.

It is sorrowing and likewise presently empowering for a modern Witch or feminist to contemplate the possibility of an enormous persecution of innocent herbal healers, midwives, benign spellcasters, and others who are virtually "free" and altogether naturalistic. Such activities are viewed as belonging to the domestic sphere, which is, more often than not, paralleled with privacy, femininity, and secrecy—things that both modern Witches and feminists are familiar with.

History's horrific events, including minority persecutions of all types, trigger highly emotional reactions in us. While this is quite understandable, especially for those whose biological or spiritual predecessors were oppressed, history mustn't be only partially examined. The validity of any claim, however emotionally charged, must be researched. This is not to downplay the seriousness of the European Witch hunts and their horrifying brutality, but only to say that discernment is crucial when seeking to understand the facts of any violent minority oppression (or any extreme issue for that matter), especially if the claims seem curiously grandiose. This is not to say that emotions must be nullified or done away with, but only that attachments to subjective viewpoints can easily skew or exaggerate events. This can actually weaken the legitimacy and credibility of one's viewpoints, which can in turn influence future events where a persecuted or once-persecuted group is concerned.

✳   ✳   ✳

With time, accusations of European women, men, children, and animals as being Witches and devils faded into history. New scientific and psychological advancements served to make this ephemeral hysteria obsolete.

When the last Witchcraft Act was repealed in England in 1951, only a glimmer of the fear present in the Witchcraft persecutions remained. But because many people seem to require a spiritual arch-nemesis to operate, it's doubtful that fears of Witchcraft or other forms of magick will disappear in the West. Indeed, it's apparent that these fears haven't dissipated in South Asia, Southeast Asia, areas of Africa, and other parts of the world, which makes a total disappearance questionable. However, we can at least hope that history has revealed itself to a large enough degree of comprehension and accuracy to, like the charm of an old Witch, ward against its repetition.

---

1. Thaumaturgy is magick (often healing magick) with the goal of producing effects in one's reality, as opposed to theurgy, the mystical practice of putting the practitioner closer to the divine through ritual or meditation. The notion of thaumaturgy is often restricted, in Classical Antiquity, to miracle-workers; those who were said to exhibit supernatural and divine abilities.

2. John Michael Greer, *The New Encyclopedia of the Occult*. St. Paul, MN: Llewellyn, 2003, 517.

3. Ibid., 291. Used with permission.

4. Jeffrey Burton Russell, *Witchcraft in the Middle Ages*. Ithaca, NY: Cornell University Press, 1972, 14.

5. Alan Charles Kors and Edward Peters (editors), *Witchcraft in Europe, 400–1700: A Documentary History*. Philadelphia: University of Pennsylvania Press, 2001, 73.

6. Ibid., 15.

7. Michael Streeter, *Witchcraft: A Secret History*. Hauppauge, NY: Barron's, 2002, 94.

8. Douglas Linder, "A Brief History of Witchcraft Persecutions before Salem," University of Missouri–Kansas City School of Law, 2005, www.law.umkc.edu/faculty/projects/ftrials/salem/Witchhistory.html, accessed May 2007.

9. Streeter, *Witchcraft*, 88.

10. Jules Michelet, *Satanism and Witchcraft: A Study in Medieval Superstition*. Secaucus, NJ: Citadel Press, 1939, 133–134.

11. Streeter, *Witchcraft*, 92–95.

12. Gustav Henningsen, "'The Ladies from Outside': An Archaic Pattern of the Witches' Sabbath," in Bengt Ankarloo and Gustav Henningsen (editors), *Early Modern European Witchcraft: Centres and Peripheries*. Oxford, UK: Oxford University Press, 1990, 193–194.

13. Diane Purkiss, *The Witch in History: Early Modern and Twentieth-Century Representations*. London: Routledge, 1996, 8.

14. Brian P. Levack, *The Witch-hunt in Early Modern Europe*. New York: Longman, 1987, 25.

15. Russell, *Witchcraft in the Middle Ages*, 84.

16. Purkiss, *The Witch in History*, 8.

17. Greer, *The New Encyclopedia of the Occult*, 77.

18. Ibid., 315–316.

19. Purkiss, *The Witch in History*, 8.

20. Streeter, *Witchcraft*, 100.

21. Mary Daly, *Gyn/Ecology: The Metaethics of Radical Feminism*. London: Women's Press, 1979, 208.

Conclusion

We live between two Pillars—that of Severity, and that of Mildness. If we err more to one side than the other, we will inevitably be called upon to rebalance our positions. Duality exists, it seems, in order to teach us to be skillful jugglers of light and darkness.

—Kala Trobe
The Witch's Guide to Life

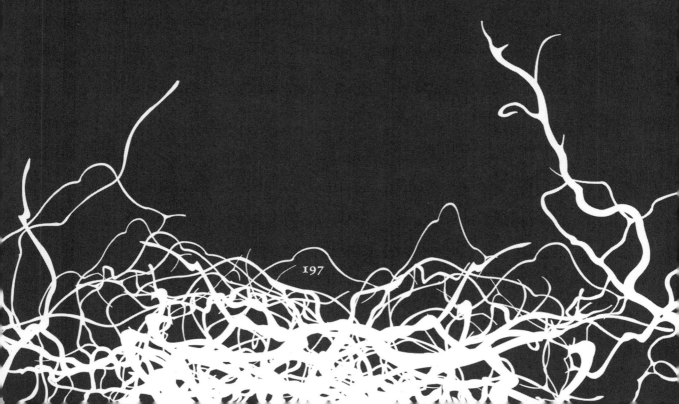

The Essence of Shadow Magick

The sun falls beyond the horizon at the close of the day … the Wheel annually turns to the bitter seasons … we sleep and we dream … we create art from the subconscious and work magick from the subtle planes … the shadow is never separated from our very existence, and demands that we give it attention. Whether it's the overwhelmingly vast blackened sky above us or the pitch blackness of the coffee we're drinking, darkness is all around us in one form or another—as well as in our minds.

Spiritually working with darkness—in whatever form it takes—is a technique of the shaman and the Witch, and is not something to be dismissed or disregarded. For those of us who walk a path that is more altruistic than self-serving, foreboding ideas of darkness can easily be replaced with ideas of wisdom and actual empowerment.

Far too often, people who have devoted themselves to magick and spirituality approach the shadow from an imbalanced perspective. For some, it seems comfortable and spiritually aligned to entirely avoid—and even repress—those aspects of the self and observations of the human experience that could be considered "dark." On the other hand, some individuals who are drawn to the power and ability of the magickal arts delve into the more negative, and seemingly more potent, dimensions of magickal work—often for the purpose of gaining control and justifying anger. Still, either approach is imbalanced: the shadow can be a scary and frightening place as well as a powerful and empowering platform, indeed, but in the end, it's just as important as the lighter side and can, ideally, be equally revered.

Nature makes no distinction between light and dark, life and death, day and night. The polarities of existence uphold the natural paradigm, including our own. Part of honing one's spiritual ability and aligning to the tides of the natural world necessarily includes an acknowledgment of all sides of the spectrum; nothing can be left out of focus. The infinite nature of darkness and spiritual subtlety is an indispensable aid in our search for clarity and balance.

As these pages have shown, shadow magick manifests within many religions, cultures, and creeds worldwide, having always been a necessary component of the human psyche. Shadow can be defined in countless ways, but the most significant is always one's own interpretation. The shadow is not to be feared, but rather embraced as a progressive contrast to the lighter aspects of spirituality. The shadow takes numerous forms, and part of its beauty is in its interpretation.

The modern practitioner is fortunate to be able to draw on many valuable components of a variety of beliefs, and to work idiosyncratically with these. When we examine the hidden or destructive aspects of our psyches, as well as those of the world around us, we are given the tools for limitless spiritual progression. Appreciating and aligning with the beautiful darkness of nature and the mystic planes of reality are also keys to our holistic development.

We are no longer required to fear and vilify the supposedly "dark" aspects of our religious and psychological constitutions. Instead, we may use these to elevate our consciousness and our spirit towards greater understanding and compassion both for self and for others. We can experience full integration with the cosmos in all of its glory, both light and dark. This is the essence of shadow magick.

Bless and Be Blessed,

~ O. R. D. N. ~

i20800rAdn4180

Au Lecteur (To the Reader)
by Charles Baudelaire
Translation by Kate La Trobe (Kala Trobe)

Folly and error, sin and avarice
Weigh on our spirits and our bodies outsource,
And we cradle and rock our cosy remorse
As mendicants nourish their lice.

Our sins are stubborn, so fearfully we repent,
Extorting high Heaven with confession and vow,
Then merrily back into the quagmire we plough,
Dreaming sin sloughed by tears, and blemish absent.

On the pillow of Evil, it's Satan Trismegist
Who perpetually lulls and bewitches our souls,
And the noble metal of our spiritual goals
Is all vapourised by this great alchemist.

The Devil holds the strings by which we are moved!
Glamoured by all that is filthy and wrong,
We descend towards Hell by a step – a furlong,
Into vile, reeking darkness we've guilelessly approved.

Just like some broke pervert who slobbers and bites
At the martyrised tits of a decrepit whore,
We swipe squalid pleasures from the lusts we deplore,
Stale oranges that in thirst we squeeze tight.

Seething, swarming in a maggoty mess,
An army of demons runs riot in our heads;
We inhale the pale river of Satan's undead,
Grievances muted and conscience suppressed.

If rape and poison, arson and knife
Have not yet embroidered their charming designs
On the pitiful canvas of our lives' confines,
It's only – alas! – that our souls flee from strife.

But amongst the jackals, panthers, monkeys, lice,
The vultures, snakes, the bugs and nits,
That screech and flit and howl and shit
In the tragic menagerie of our vice,

There is one even uglier, more inhumane!
Creeping and sliding and crawling so slow,
Devouring the world in a yawn as he goes,
Insidiously seeping into our brains…

It's *Ennui!*

His eye o'er-brimming with an opiate tear,
Dreaming of scaffolds, real consciousness ceased –
You know him, my reader, this delicate beast –
Hypocrite reader; *you*! Mine image: – Brother Dear!

Bibliography

Andrews, Ted. *Animal Speak: The Spiritual & Magical Powers of Creatures Great & Small.* St. Paul, MN: Llewellyn, 1993.

Ankarloo, Bengt and Gustav Henningsen (editors). *Early Modern European Witchcraft: Centres and Peripheries.* Oxford, UK: Oxford University Press, 1990.

Attar, Farid-Ud-Din and R.P. Masani (translator). *Conference of the Birds: A Seeker's Journey to God.* Boston: Weiser, 2001.

Baab, Lynne M. *Fasting: Spiritual Freedom Beyond Our Appetites.* Downers Grove, IL: IVP Books, 2006.

Bardon, Franz. *Initiation into Hermetics: The Path of the True Adept.* Salt Lake City, UT: Merkur Publishing, 2001.

Belanger, Michelle. *Vampires in Their Own Words: An Anthology of Vampire Voices.* Woodbury, MN: Llewellyn, 2007.

———. *Walking the Twilight Path: A Gothic Book of the Dead.* Woodbury, MN: Llewellyn, 2008.

Beyerl, Paul. *The Master Book of Herbalism.* Blaine, WA: Phoenix Publishing, 1984.

Blake, William. *The Marriage of Heaven and Hell.* Oxford, UK: Oxford University Press, 1975.

Blavatsky, Helena P. and Hillard, Katharine (editor). *Abridgment of H.P. Blavatsky's Secret Doctrine.* Whitefish, MT: Kessinger Publishing, 1996.

Bruce, Robert and Brian Mercer. *Mastering Astral Projection: 90-Day Guide to Out-of-Body Experience.* Woodbury, MN: Llewellyn, 2006.

Chopra, Deepak. *The Seven Spiritual Laws of Success: A Practical Guide to the Fulfillment of Your Dreams.* Hertfordshire, UK: Motilal Books (UK), 2003.

Cole, W. Owen and Hemant Kanitkar. *Teach Yourself Hinduism.* Chicago: McGraw-Hill, 1995.

Coughlin, John J. *Out of the Shadows: An Exploration of Dark Paganism and Magick.* Bloomington, IN: Waning Moon Publications/1stBooks Library, 2001.

Crowley, Aleister. *Magick, Book Four: Parts I–IV.* Boston: Weiser, 2004.

Cunningham, Scott. *Cunningham's Encyclopedia of Magical Herbs.* St. Paul, MN: Llewellyn, 1984.

Daly, Mary. *Gyn/Ecology: The Metaethics of Radical Feminism*. London: Women's Press, 1979.

Dass, Ram. *Remember; Be Here Now*. San Cristobal, NM: Hanuman Foundation, 1978.

Davida, Michael Alexandra. *Dominus Satánas, the Other Son of God: Rethinking the Bad Boy of the Cosmos*. Boulder, CO: CLSM Publishing, 2002.

del Campo, Gerald. *New Aeon Magick: Thelema Without Tears*. St. Paul, MN: Llewellyn, 1994.

Digitalis, Raven. *Goth Craft: The Magickal Side of Dark Culture*. Woodbury, MN: Llewellyn, 2007.

DuQuette, Lon Milo. *The Magick of Aleister Crowley: A Handbook of Rituals of Thelema*. Boston: Weiser, 2003.

Emboden, William A. *Bizarre Plants: Magical, Monstrous, Mythical*. New York: Macmillan, 1974.

Endredy, James. *Beyond 2012: A Shaman's Call to Personal Change and the Transformation of Global Consciousness*. Woodbury, MN: Llewellyn, 2007.

Farrar, Stewart, and Janet Farrar. *Spells and How They Work*. London: Robert Hale Ltd., 1992.

———. *A Witches' Bible: The Complete Witches' Handbook*. Custer, WA: Phoenix Publishing, 1981.

Filan, Kenaz. *The Haitian Vodou Handbook: Protocols for Riding with the Lwa*. Rochester, VT: Destiny Books/Inner Traditions, 2007.

Flint, Valerie I. J. *The Rise of Magic in Early Medieval Europe*. Princeton, NJ: Princeton University Press, 1991.

Graves, Robert. *The White Goddess: A Historical Grammar of Poetic Myth*. New York: Farrar, Straus & Giroux, 1999.

Greer, John Michael. *Atlantis: Ancient Legacy, Hidden Prophecy*. Woodbury, MN: Llewellyn, 2007.

———. *Secret Societies & Magical History*. San Jose, CA: Presentation at PantheaCon, 2007.

———. *The New Encyclopedia of the Occult*. St. Paul, MN: Llewellyn, 2003.

Gregory, Ruth W. *Anniversaries and Holidays*. Chicago: American Library Association, 1983.

Grimassi, Raven. *The Witch's Familiar: Spiritual Partnership for Successful Magic*. St. Paul, MN: Llewellyn, 2003.

Harris, Nathaniel J. *Witcha: A Book of Cunning.* Oxford, UK: Mandrake Press, 2004.

Harris, Stephen L. and Gloria Platzner. *Classical Mythology: Images & Insights.* Mountain View, CA: Mayfield Publishing, 1995.

Jung, Carl Gustav. *The Collected Works of C.G. Jung, vol. 9ii: Aion.* Princeton, NJ: Princeton University Press, 1959.

———. *Psychology and Religion.* London: Routledge, 1970.

Kaushik, Jai Narain. *Fasts of the Hindus Around the Year: Background Stories, Ways of Performance & Their Importance.* Delhi, India: Books For All, 1992.

Kieckhefer, Richard: *Magic in the Middle Ages.* Cambridge, UK: Cambridge University Press, 1989.

Kinney, Jay (editor). *The Inner West: An Introduction to the Hidden Wisdom of the West.* New York: Penguin, 2004.

Kors, Alan Charles and Edward Peters (editors). *Witchcraft in Europe, 400–1700: A Documentary History.* Philadelphia: University of Pennsylvania Press, 2001.

Larner, Christina. *Enemies of God: The Witch Hunt in Scotland.* London: John Donald Publishers, 1981.

Lehmann, Arthur C. and James E. Myers. *Magic, Witchcraft & Religion: An Anthropological Study of the Supernatural.* Mountain View, CA: Mayfield Publishing, 1985.

Levack, Brian P. *The Witch-hunt in Early Modern Europe.* New York: Longman, 1987.

Low, Clifford H. *Black Magic & Dark Paganism.* San Jose, CA: Presentation at *PantheaCon,* 2008.

Lupa. *A Field Guide to Otherkin.* Stafford, UK: Megalithica Books/Immanion Press, 2007.

Maslow, Abraham H. *Religions, Values, and Peak-Experiences.* Columbus, OH: Ohio State University Press, 1964.

Matt, Daniel Chanan (translator). *Zohar: The Book of Enlightenment.* Ramsey, NJ: Paulist Press, 1983.

McNevin, Estha. *Opus Aima Obscuræ.* Tradition materials and lesson notes. Missoula, MT, 2003–present.

Michelet, Jules. *Satanism and Witchcraft: A Study in Medieval Superstition.* Secaucus, NJ: Citadel Press, 1939

Nanamoli, Bhikkhu. *The Life of the Buddha: According to the Pali Canon*. Kandy, Sri Lanka: Buddhist Publication Society, 1972.

Nocturnum, Corvis: *Embracing the Darkness: Understanding Dark Subcultures*. Fort Wayne, IN: Dark Moon Press, 2005.

Penczak, Christopher. *Invocation, Channeling, & the Oracular Mysteries*. San Jose, CA: Presentation at *PantheaCon*, 2007.

———. *The Inner Temple of Witchcraft: Magick, Meditation & Psychic Development*. St. Paul, MN: Llewellyn, 2002.

———. *The Outer Temple of Witchcraft: Circles, Spells & Rituals*. Woodbury, MN: Llewellyn, 2004.

———. *The Temple of Shamanic Witchcraft: Shadows, Spirits, and the Healing Journey*. St. Paul, MN: Llewellyn, 2005.

Poe, Edgar Allan. *Poems*. Edison, NJ: Castle Books, 2000.

Pollack, Rachel. *The Kabbalah Tree: A Journey of Balance & Growth*. St. Paul, MN: Llewellyn, 2004.

Purkiss, Diane. *The Witch in History: Early Modern and Twentieth-Century Representations*. London: Routledge, 1996.

Roderick, Timothy. *Dark Moon Mysteries: Wisdom, Power and Magic of the Shadow World*. Aptos, CA: New Brighton Books, 2003.

———. *The Once Unknown Familiar: Shamanic Paths to Unleash Your Animal Powers*. St. Paul, MN: Llewellyn, 1994.

Russell, Jeffrey Burton. *Witchcraft in the Middle Ages*. Ithaca, NY: Cornell University Press, 1972.

Scholem, Gershom. *Major Trends in Jewish Mysticism*. New York: Schocken Books, 1946.

Shakespeare, William. *Four Tragedies: Romeo and Juliet, Macbeth, Julius Caesar, Hamlet*. New York: Washington Square Press, 1963.

Silverknife, Zanoni. *Lessons in Georgian Wicca, 101–104*. Class handouts and lecture notes. Missoula, MT, 1999.

Stace, W. T. *Mysticism and Philosophy*. London: MacMillan Press, 1961.

Streeter, Michael. *Witchcraft: A Secret History*. Hauppauge, NY: Barron's, 2002.

Thomas, Keith. *Religion and the Decline of Magic.* New York: Charles Scribner's Sons, 1971.

Too, Lillian. *Chinese Wisdom: Spiritual Magic for Everyday Living.* London: Cico Books, 2001.

Trobe, Kala. *Invoke the Gods: Exploring the Power of Male Archetypes.* St. Paul, MN: Llewellyn, 2001.

————. *Magic of Qabalah: Visions of the Tree of Life.* St. Paul, MN: Llewellyn, 2001.

————. *The Witch's Guide to Life.* St. Paul, MN: Llewellyn, 2003.

Tyson, Donald. *Soul Flight: Astral Projection and the Magical Universe.* Woodbury, MN: Llewellyn, 2007.

Wedeck, Harry E. *Dictionary of Magic.* Brooklyn, NY: Philosophical Library, Inc., 1956.

Wimbush, Vincent L. and Richard Valantasis (editors). *Asceticism.* New York: Oxford University Press, 1998.

Worms, Abraham Von, Georg Dehn, Steven Guth, and Lon Milo Duquette. *The Book of Abramelin: A New Translation.* Newburyport, MA: Weiser, 2006.

Zalewski, Pat. *Kabbalah of the Golden Dawn.* Edison, NJ: Castle Books, 2000.

Zell-Ravenheart, Oberon. *Grimoire for the Apprentice Wizard.* Franklin Lakes, NJ: New Page Books, 2004.

Index

To Write to the Author

If you wish to contact the author or would like more information about this book, please write to the author in care of Llewellyn Worldwide and we will forward your request. Both the author and publisher appreciate hearing from you and learning of your enjoyment of this book and how it has helped you. Llewellyn Worldwide cannot guarantee that every letter written to the author can be answered, but all will be forwarded. Please write to:

Raven Digitalis
⁒ Llewellyn Worldwide
2143 Wooddale Drive, Dept. 978-0-7387-1318-2
Woodbury, Minnesota 55125-2989, U.S.A.
Please enclose a self-addressed stamped envelope for reply,
or $1.00 to cover costs. If outside U.S.A., enclose
international postal reply coupon.

Many of Llewellyn's authors have websites with additional information and resources. For more information, please visit our website at http://www.llewellyn.com.